FROM BOX OFFICE TO BALLOT BOX

The American Political Film

M. Keith Booker

Westport, Connecticut
London

Library of Congress Cataloging-in-Publication Data

Booker, M. Keith.
  From box office to ballot box : the American political film / M. Keith Booker.
      p. cm.
  Includes bibliographical references and index.
  ISBN-10: 0–275–99122–9 (alk. paper)
  ISBN-13: 978–0–275–99122–7
  1. Motion pictures—Political aspects—United States. 2. Politics in motion pictures.
  I. Title.
  PN1995.9.P6B67   2007
  791.43'6580973—dc22   2006037773

British Library Cataloguing in Publication Data is available.

Library of Congress Catalog Card Number: 2006037773
ISBN-10: 0–275–99122–9
ISBN-13: 978–0–275–99122–7

First published in 2007

Praeger Publishers, 88 Post Road West, Westport, CT 06881
An imprint of Greenwood Publishing Group, Inc.
www.praeger.com

Printed in the United States of America

The paper used in this book complies with the
Permanent Paper Standard issued by the National
Information Standards Organization (Z39.48-1984).

10   9   8   7   6   5   4   3   2   1

For Adam Booker

Contents

Introduction:
The American Political Film

In an episode of the 1960s *Batman* television series, the nefarious villain Penguin (preparing for his own Gotham City mayoral campaign) gives advice to his minions that seems to have been followed by American political campaigns ever since. "Plenty of girls and bands and slogans and lots of hoopla," he says, "but remember, no politics. Issues confuse people." This highly popular program, one of the earmarks of American popular culture in the 1960s (it ran on ABC from 1966 to 1968), thus suggests an aversion to politics even in the midst of that highly political decade. This same aversion seems also to have been demonstrated by many other works of American film and television, which, all too often, have tended to avoid any real engagement with serious political issues.

Then again, all culture is political, in the sense that all cultural production is rooted in specific ideological contexts and all cultural artifacts carry the traces of these ideological origins. Film is political in a second sense as well, because the making (not to mention the subsequent marketing) of a theatrical film is a complex project that requires substantial financing, careful planning, and extensive negotiations among a variety of parties who are involved in the project either creatively, logistically, or financially. Yet, American films have a reputation for skirting difficult political issues and for treating such issues in superficial and simplistic ways, if at all. This book, a study of the fictional political film in America, verifies that reputation to some extent, but also argues that there may be more political commentary embedded in these films than is generally recognized.

There are many reasons for the limited political engagement of American fictional films. For example, there is no doubt that the special financial

1

considerations involved in the film industry contribute to the lack of genuine political inquiry in American film. After all, when products can be so expensive to make, the producers of those products do not want to alienate potential consumers. The film industry, with the traumatic historical memory of the anticommunist purges that swept Hollywood in the 1940s and 1950s still relatively fresh, is especially sensitive to the possibility that political controversy might damage the industry. Still, the very fact that many filmmakers might simply assume that political content might turn away potential audiences for their films also makes a broader statement about the impoverished state of political discourse in America.

Indeed, given the broader aversion to serious political discussion that seems to pervade modern American society, it is almost surprising that American films have engaged political issues to the extent that they have. Many films have, in fact, addressed important political issues, even if genuinely radical critique of America's ideology and institutions is essentially nonexistent. For example, many of the very early silent films (made at a time when film itself was widely regarded as a working-class entertainment) addressed working-class issues in decidedly political ways. These films were often made by working-class directors, often with the financial support of labor unions. Indeed, as Steven Ross has argued in his book *Working-Class Hollywood* (Princeton University Press, 1998), film became a crucial part of American working-class culture in the first decade of the century and continued so until the political repression associated with World War I put a virtual halt to the making of such films (and to radical organized labor activity in general). Even pioneer silent filmmaker D. W. Griffith, although often remembered for his racist politics in films such as *The Birth of a Nation*, had certain working-class loyalties and made numerous early films of protest against the exploitation of workers by emergent American capitalism.

The 1920s saw the beginnings of the reemergence of working-class film, though this phenomenon was quickly cut short by the rise to dominance of Hollywood studios and the Hollywood style in American film in the Depression decade of the 1930s. Hollywood films in that decade were largely escapist fare meant to provide some respite from the hardships of Depression-era life. Nevertheless, new forms with significant potential for political allegory appeared in the decade, including Universal monster films and Warner Brothers gangster films, while Warner also produced a number of "social problem" films that directly acknowledged the social and economic conditions brought about by the Depression. In addition, politically charged documentaries, such as Pare Lorentz's *The Plow that Broke the Plains* (1936) and *The River* (1937), were made under the sponsorship of the U.S. government as part of the New Deal. Independent leftist film companies, seeking alternatives to the Hollywood studio system, produced a number of films in the 1930s as well.

During World War II, numerous films were made directly in support of the American war effort, often with explicitly antifascist themes. After the war, congressional investigations and blacklisting in Hollywood brought a quick end to any genuinely radical critique in Hollywood films, though popular forms such as science fiction and film noir (flying under the anticommunist radar) continued to carry strong political implications. In addition, Herbert Biberman's *Salt of the Earth* (1954) was a notable attempt to make a pro-labor political film outside the Hollywood system. Political films from Hollywood studios also moved in new directions, with special emphasis on critiques of racism in films such as Mark Robson's *Home of the Brave* (1949) and Stanley Kramer's *The Defiant Ones* (1958).

In the 1960s, the blacklist was broken with films such as *Spartacus* (1960, written by Dalton Trumbo, blacklisted during the anticommunist purges of the 1950s), and a whole new kind of oppositional political films, in tune with the political movements of the time, began to be made, even by mainstream Hollywood studios. These films included further explorations of American racism and began to examine women's issues as well, while also representing the contemporary counterculture, as in Dennis Hopper's *Easy Rider* (1969). Formerly blacklisted director Martin Ritt made a particularly large number of working-class films in the 1960s and subsequent decades, while emergent directors such as Stanley Kubrick, John Sayles, and Oliver Stone treated numerous political themes in these decades, including labor activism, Vietnam, American imperialism, racism, and the role of the media in American society and politics.

Emphasizing films made since World War II, this book seeks to provide an overview of the issues central to the genre of American political film— that is, to that species of film which is directly concerned with the workings of politics and the role of politics in our lives. It is also intended as a guide to the various approaches that filmmakers have developed in order to confront these issues onscreen. This focus places some necessary limitations on the discussion of what might otherwise be considered "political" films. This work, for example, does not include coverage of films related primarily to race or gender. Nor does it include a discussion of the family of films devoted to the corrupting influence of the capitalist system—films such as David Fincher's *Fight Club* (1999) that deals with the dehumanizing and emasculating effects of consumer capitalism; and Sam Mendes's *American Beauty* (1998), which exposes the vacuity of suburban life in its contemporary America. Finally, this book (with the notable exception of the science fiction films discussed in Chapter 4, as well as a few other isolated examples) does not in general discuss the various genre films (science fiction, horror, Western, crime) that have commented on political issues in indirect or allegorical ways.

The discussion in this book concentrates on films that deal more directly with the political process. It is arranged thematically, though always with an eye toward the historical development of the American political film. It begins with a chapter on political films in the most literal sense: films about politicians, elections, and the electoral process. Such films, especially after the revelations about American politics associated with the Watergate scandal (which peaked in 1974), tend to be remarkably cynical about the political process. Interestingly, though, some of this same skepticism about the merits of electoral politics can be found even before Watergate, in films ranging from *Meet John Doe* (1941)—which worries about the possibility of the manipulation of the electoral process by a corrupt candidate—to *The Candidate* (1972), which worries about the manipulation of its candidate by a corrupt political process. Chapter 2 discusses films about the process of government—or about what politicians do once they are elected to office. This chapter (following the lead of Hollywood) puts a special emphasis on the American presidency and on films about presidents, either real or fictional. Some of these films, such as the early *Gabriel over the White House* (1933), suggest that the office makes the man, so that even a vicious criminal, once elected to the presidency, might find himself transformed into an honest and capable leader. Others are essentially celebrations of hero presidents such as George Washington or Abraham Lincoln, while others (especially in the 1990s) produce fantasy visions of ideal presidents, such as the virtuous he-man leaders in *Independence Day* (1996) or *Air Force One* (1997). Nevertheless, numerous films show presidents and other officeholders as sinister, opportunistic, and thoroughly dishonest, often because they have been corrupted by the power of office or by the process they must go through in order to get elected in the first place.

The remainder of the book is then devoted to discussions of films about specific politically charged topics or phenomena. Chapters 3 and 4 deal in different ways with the climate of paranoia and fear that pervaded American society during the Cold War, especially during the peak years of the 1950s. Chapter 3 notes the impact of the anticommunist hysteria of the peak Cold War years of the 1950s on the American film industry. The congressional investigations of purported communist activity in Hollywood led to the development of a blacklist that precluded hundreds of artists from working in the American film industry through most of the 1950s because they were suspected of leftist political inclinations. As a result, any filmmaker with a political message had to tread very carefully during this period for fear of drawing the ire of anticommunist investigators. This chapter discusses films that are directly related to this phenomenon, includ-ing both, films that (mostly well after the fact) criticize the blacklist and those that capitulate to it, as in the sequence of overtly anticommunist films that were produced at the end of the 1940s and beginning of the 1950s. Chapter 4 treats films that deal with the related topic of the Cold War arms race and the resultant fear of nuclear war, a large number of which belong to the science fiction genres of the alien-invasion narrative and the post-apocalyptic narrative.

Chapter 5 shifts to a consideration of films that deal with the role of the media in American political life. These films tend to be extremely critical of the media (especially television), which are often seen as a corrupting force that reduces political debate to superficial sound bytes and that shifts true power from the voters to those who have the wealth and know-how to manipulate the media to their advantage. In short, these films suggest that the media have played an important role in shifting more and more power to fewer and fewer wealthy and unscrupulous Americans. Among other things, this phenomenon raises the issue of class differences in American society, a topic that has been largely avoided in most American political discussions given that most Americans prefer to think of their society as that which grants equal rights and opportunities to all and thus essentially effacing class differences. Of course, these differences still exist, a fact that American films occasionally acknowledge. Indeed, the question of class is central to the films discussed in chapter 6, which deals in particular with the representation of the working class and of organized labor in American film.

Chapter 7 discusses the particularly rich family of films that deal with the Vietnam War and its immediate impact on American society. These films often ask fundamental questions about not only American foreign policy but American democracy as a whole. In so doing, they touch upon a number of topics that resonate with the discussions in earlier chapters such as the roles of the media and of class in American life. Chapter 8 then concludes the book with a discussion of films about American military experience after Vietnam. These films quite often enter into dialogues with the Vietnam War films; they also typically acknowledge the way in which the memory of the Vietnam War has hung over all American military endeavors since that war. At the same time, films about such events as the 1991 Gulf War generally turn away from politics altogether, focusing on the experience of combat rather than the political conflicts this combat is presumably meant to resolve. Such films also often attempt to restore the national identity (so seriously damaged in Vietnam) of the United States as a righteous foe of savage enemies.

This conservative turn in American war films in the early twenty-first century is part of a more general conservative turn in American culture and society as a whole in the wake of the September 11, 2001, bombings of the World Trade Center and Pentagon. Not surprisingly, the reactionary climate of Patriot Act–era America has not proved fertile for the production of oppositional political films. In this sense, the parallels between the political climate of these years and that of the peak Cold War years of the 1950s are extensive. Indeed, conditions in some ways appear even more ominous in the early twenty-first century than in the 1950s. In particular, developments such as the Paramount antitrust case in the 1950s broke the power of the major studios and opened opportunities for the making of new kinds of films, while the trend in the film industry a half century later is toward consolidation, with larger and larger portions of the industry controlled by fewer and fewer powerful corporate entities—as in the 2005 merger of the AMC and Loews theater chains under the ownership of a corporate holding company among whose major investors is the Carlyle Group, a firm with extensive ties to the Bush administration and the Saudi government.

On the other hand, American political documentary films have undergone a genuine flowering during the early years of the new century. Again echoing the 1950s, films such as George Romero's *Land of the Dead* (2005) and James McTeigue's *V for Vendetta* (2005) have suggested the potential for a resurgence in political fiction films, at least in genres such as horror and science fiction. Such developments suggest that there is at least some ongoing potential for the making of genuinely political American films in the future, however many obstacles the makers of such films will have to overcome.

CHAPTER 1

Meet the Candidate: The Political Campaign Film

E lectoral campaigns in the United States have not always been the major media spectacles that they can be in the twenty-first century, but they have been objects of intense public interest from the American Revolution onward. Sometimes, such campaigns are seen almost as sporting events; other times they are actually envisioned as serious contests between competing ideologies. In all cases, they involve an element of individual competition that Americans seem to find fascinating. At the same time, at least since the Watergate scandal of the early 1970s, there has been a growing public cynicism about electoral politics in America, a growing sense that the electoral system is corrupt, inevitably leading to the election of corrupt government officials. The presidential election of George W. Bush in 2000, who lost the popular vote but won the electoral quote under questionable circumstances, did nothing to quell this trend. Nevertheless, electoral politics remain a crucial component of American public life; elections and election campaigns are also a prominent topic of Hollywood film, even if such films have not typically been terribly popular at the box office.

Even before Watergate, films about electoral politics have tended to be skeptical of the political process—though this skepticism toward the process has often been tempered by suggestions that good people can win over a bad system. One thinks of the populist films of Frank Capra that were quite cynical about political bigwigs and insiders, but retained a strong faith in the common people and the ultimate capability of the people to seize control of the political process. Perhaps the most famous of Capra's political films is *Mr. Smith Goes to Washington* (1939), which deals primarily with Washington politics, rather than the electoral process. This film will be discussed in the next chapter. Of Capra's films that deal with electoral campaigns and the electoral process, the best known is *Meet John Doe* (1941), a sort of follow-up to *Mr. Smith Goes to Washington.*

Among other things, *Meet John Doe* is very much a Depression-era film, reminding us that the Depression did not magically end with the close of the 1930s. As it begins, oil magnate D. B. Norton (Edward Arnold) has just taken control of a newspaper, *The Bulletin,* which he transforms into *The New Bulletin,* hoping to use the paper to promote his own political aspirations. Among the staff let go as part of this transformation is a woman reporter, Ann Mitchell (Barbara Stanwyck), whose stories are felt not to have enough fire to attract readers. On her way out, just to show that she can create interest with her writing, she fabricates a story about an ordinary man, John Doe, who is so fed up with the rotten state of things in the country that he has decided to commit suicide by leaping from a tall tower on Christmas Eve as a form of protest.

The John Doe story gains such attention that Henry Connell (James Gleeson), managing editor of *The New Bulletin,* hires Mitchell back on the condition that she run with the story—which means that she has to dig up someone to impersonate the nonexistent John Doe. Times being what they are, there is no shortage of candidates for that task, but Mitchell and Connell ultimately select one Long John Willoughby (Gary Cooper) for the role. A former baseball pitcher who is down on his luck, Willoughby reluctantly agrees to take the job because he desperately needs the money, even though he is an honest man who is uncomfortable with the deception involved.

With Mitchell writing his lines for him, Willoughby/Doe embarks on a highly successful public-relations campaign that strikes a chord with the American public, leading to an upwelling of grassroots support for Doe. Opposition by a rival newspaper and even the governor of the state (a political foe of Norton) is no match for this new movement, which leads to the formation of John Doe Clubs all over the country. These clubs are devoted to the notion that the common people are fine folks and can accomplish a great deal if they just appreciate one another and "all pull in the same direction" to take advantage of their collective strength. However, in a sign of the film's cynical treatment of professional politicians, no politicians are allowed in the clubs for fear they will contaminate them with their own dastardly designs.

Norton, of course, is precisely such a figure, but he uses every resource at his disposal to help the movement along, having his own plans for the burgeoning political power of the seemingly antipolitical John Doe movement. These plans become clear when Norton organizes a national convention of the clubs and attempts to manipulate Willoughby into announcing at the convention the formation of a new John Doe Party and endorsing Norton as the party's first presidential candidate. Warned that Norton is a "skunk" with fascist tendencies, Willoughby quickly understands that the magnate has no sympathy for the common man but merely plans to use the John Doe movement to supplement his connections with corrupt labor leaders and political bosses in his quest for power. Willoughby thus refuses to cooperate and plans to denounce Norton at the convention, but Norton intercedes and denounces Willoughby instead. When his supporters realize that "John Doe" is an impostor, the movement collapses, even though it had brought so much hope to so many who had been disenfranchised for so long.

Willoughby himself sinks into despair, especially after he concludes that Mitchell (with whom he has predictably fallen in love) has merely been using him to win points with Norton. Hoping somehow to bring life back to the John Doe movement, Willoughby decides to commit suicide on Christmas Eve after all. He ascends the tower, but is ultimately dissuaded by Mitchell, who melodramatically crawls out of her sickbed to beg Willoughby not to jump, then collapses in his arms, where presumably she will stay. Meanwhile, a group of former Doe club members join in her effort, promising to try to get the movement going again, if only they can have Willoughby's help. In a final, sloppily sentimental plea that partakes heavily of the holiday setting, a former supporter urges Willoughby to remember the sacrifice of the "first John Doe" (Jesus Christ), who died for the cause of ordinary people so that men like Willoughby would not have to. In the end, Willoughby decides to join the reconstituted movement that presumably will spell the doom of crooked, manipulative politicians like Norton.

The overt sentimentalism of *Meet John Doe* (a Capra trademark) certainly dates the film, but many aspects of it still seem extremely relevant today. In particular, while the film serves as a sort of paean to the potential power of the common people, it also warns that sinister figures like Norton are perfectly capable of using the resources of the media (in this case newspapers and radio) to manipulate the people into placing them in power. Similar points are made in Capra's *State of the Union* (1948), which nicely expresses the director's populist combination of faith in the goodness of the common people with cynicism about the official workings of the political machine. Here, self-made industrialist Grant Matthews (Spencer Tracy) is convinced by political kingmaker Jim Conover (Adolphe Menjou) to seek the 1948 Republican nomination for the presidency. Conover is aided by ambitious, hard-hearted Kay Thorndyke (Angela Lansbury), who not only heads a newspaper syndicate (inherited from her father) but has apparently been having an affair with Conover, who is initially estranged from his wife Mary (Katharine Hepburn). As one might expect from a Hollywood film of the 1940s, much of the focus of this film is on the rekindling of the love between Grant and Mary Matthews after Conover and Thorndyke both conclude that Grant will be electable only if he is at least ostensibly reconciled with his wife. Still, there is considerable emphasis on the political process as well, which is depicted as totally corrupt, driven by individuals interested only in furthering their own power rather than in representing their constituencies.

For a time, the gruff and forthright Matthews is seduced by the lure of the White House into following the admonition of Conover and Thorndyke to back away from an honest explication of his true man-of-the-people beliefs (which are implicitly endorsed by the film and which include such things as working to establish a World Government, albeit one apparently based on the American model). When he begins to deliver speeches filled with double-talk and platitudes (and to make quid-pro-quo deals with the leaders of various special interest groups), his prospects of gaining the nomination seem considerably enhanced. After all, this new stance appeals to the party's power brokers, even if it may be less appealing to common people. As Conover puts it, in a key indictment of the nomination process, "You're not nominated by the people; you're nominated by the politicians." In the end, however, Matthews backs away from this course when he sees that even the virtuous Mary is being forced to compromise her principles in order to support his campaign. He renounces his candidacy (and denounces his backers) in a nationwide radio broadcast, then declares his intention to work as an activist to clean up the political process in both major parties. He and Mary are reunited, and Conover and Thorndyke are left out in the cold.

The cynical view of the political process expressed in *State of the Union* was not particularly unusual for its time. Nor does it really amount to much more than a reenactment of widely held beliefs about American politics. More significant (and unusual) is the inclusion of an adultery motif, though the film is very careful to remain vague about the actual nature of the relationship between Matthews and Thorndyke. There is even a hint that they may never have actually had sex. On two occasions, however, they do nearly kiss, but both times they are interrupted: after all, the Hollywood Code of the time would have seriously frowned upon the representation of an adulterous kiss. The representation of women characters in the film is quite interesting as well. On the surface, Thorndyke is the typical siren-like bad woman who would lead a good man to his doom, somewhat in the mode of the *femmes fatales* of film noir, a genre at its height when *State of the Union* was made. Like Thorndyke, such women were often strong, tough, and wily, though sometimes less unequivocally evil than is Thorndyke, who is represented as scheming and unscrupulous. The film also clearly stipulates that her success is due to the fact that she inherited both her father's newspapers and his intelligence, giving her "a man's brain." In fact, one is tempted to see an allegorical suggestion in her surname: a beautiful but dangerous woman, she is like a rose with thorns; a woman with manly thoughts, she is unfeminine by the standards of the time and thus potentially suspect of lesbianism.

That said, it is also the case that Mary Matthews is a typical Kate Hepburn character and thus one who suggests considerable feminine strength as well. A housewife with two children, she lacks the professional credentials of Thorndyke. She is, however, far from the stereotypical mild-mannered little woman. It is clear in the film that she can match Thorndyke in intelligence and ability, while outdoing her in femininity. Perhaps more importantly, as is usually the case in Hepburn-Tracy film pairings, Hepburn's Mary is at least a match for Tracy's Grant, though he is an unusually strong and capable man in his own right. Thus, in one key scene a first attempt at reconciliation is interrupted by evidence of Grant's relationship with Thorndyke, causing Mary to bolt from the marital bed and to make up a separate bed on the floor. After Grant exhorts her not to be foolish because she will not get any sleep on the floor, she makes it clear that she has no intention of doing so: instead, she takes the bed and relegates Grant to the floor. And it is Grant's own appreciation of Mary's strength, dignity, and virtue that ultimately leads him to disavow the dirty game of electoral politics as currently played, vowing instead to change that game in an effort to give the American people the political system they deserve.

Franklin Shaffner's *The Best Man* (1964) reinforces the notion that presidential nominations are made by politicians, rather than the people, though it does so in a way that now seems a bit dated because of its focus on backroom maneuvering at political conventions. Written by Gore Vidal based on his own stage play, *The Best Man* is a strong critique of dirty politics—with a clear suggestion that those on the right tend to play dirtier than those on the left. In particular, it focuses on a convention of one of the national parties (it never says which) and on the insider wheeling and dealing involved at a time when candidates were often chosen at the convention rather than long before. Going into the convention, the party still has five major candidates, though two of them, Secretary of State William Russell (Henry Fonda) and Senator Joe Cantwell (Cliff Robertson), are the clear frontrunners. Both of these men hope to get an early endorsement from folksy former president Art Hockstader (Lee Tracy), still a major figure in the party, while also hoping to convince one or more of the other candidates to withdraw from the race and issue an endorsement.

The choice between Russell and Cantwell is a very clear one. Russell is a wealthy and cultured man, something of an intellectual. He is also a dedicated liberal, devoted to the cause of civil rights, and clearly a good man, though some suspect that he may sometimes think too much, causing him to be indecisive in a crisis. He has also long been estranged from his wife, Alice (Margaret Leighton), and has apparently engaged in affairs with other women during that time (a huge political liability in 1964). However, he and Alice make a pact to put a good public face on their marriage for political purposes. Cantwell, on the other hand, seems passionately devoted to his wife. A conservative with little enthusiasm for civil rights, he is a ruthlessly ambitious politician, willing to do anything to further his political career, with vague hints that he might eventually become a Hitleresque figure. Cantwell originally gained national recognition by fabricating sensational charges that the Mafia was actually part of a communist conspiracy, thus playing on the anticommunist hysteria of the 1950s, as did numerous politicians of that decade, including at least one, Richard Nixon, who would go on to become president.

As the convention begins, Hockstader has decided to endorse Cantwell, because he thinks Cantwell has the best chance to win in the fall election. However, an early conversation between Hockstader and Cantwell clearly establishes Cantwell's ruthless ambition and his complete lack of any sense of compassion for other people. Here, Hockstader confesses that he is seriously ill and will soon die; Cantwell, caught up in his own scheming, does not even notice. Meanwhile, he tries to strongarm Hockstader (whom he expects to endorse Russell) with evidence that Russell was once in a mental asylum. This move only convinces Hockstader that Cantwell is not the kind of man he should endorse—though more because he thinks the attempt was a stupid political move that showed poor judgment (he had actually planned to endorse Cantwell) than because he finds it reprehensible. Cantwell responds with a threat to make his file on Russell public should Hockstader endorse Russell. As a result, the canny Hockstader does not openly endorse Russell, but instead works behind the scenes to see to it that Russell gets the nomination, though he is hampered by the cancer that eventually leads to his death while the nomination is still in doubt.

Russell's camp, meanwhile, uncovers evidence that Cantwell had been involved in a gay sex scandal while in the army during World War II. It turns out, however, that Cantwell had probably not participated in gay sex but had instead been an informer who led to the court martial of numerous fellow soldiers for such acts. Russell finds this involvement more reprehensible than the gay sex, but he is a man of integrity who chooses not to use the information. He does, however, attempt to use it to prevent Cantwell from using the information about his mental health history. Nevertheless, Cantwell reveals the information about Russell, and seems headed for the nomination after one of the other major candidates, Southern governor T. T. Claypoole (John Henry Faulk)—depicted in the film as a bigoted buffoon (described even by the compassionate Russell as having "all the characteristics of a dog, except loyalty")—drops out and endorses Cantwell. Realizing that he cannot win the nomination, Russell nevertheless outflanks Cantwell by throwing his support behind still another candidate, little-known governor John Merwin (William R. Ebersol). Warned that he knows little about Merwin, Russell expresses confidence that Merwin can win the election and then grow into the office of the president once he is there. Merwin wins the nomination, and Russell gives up his dream of being president—though he does seem to have reconciled with Alice, who is impressed by the integrity he has shown during the convention.

In *The Best Man*, the best man (by most standards) does not win, even if he is at least able to prevent the worst man from winning. Cantwell, how-ever, has at least one good argument: that the information he has uncovered about Russell's past will eventually come to light, anyway, and perhaps hurt the party if he is their nominee. Subsequent events, specifically the 1972 withdrawal of Thomas Eagleton as the Democratic nominee for vice pre-sident when it was revealed after his nomination that he had at one time had a nervous breakdown, seemed to bear out Cantwell's point. The 1972 presidential campaign was a key turning point in American political history: it was during that campaign this Republican candidate Nixon, in his drive toward a landslide reelection to the presidency, committed and/or author-ized so many abuses of the political process that he was eventually forced to resign from office, becoming the first U.S. president ever to do so.

The year 1972 was also the year of Michael Ritchie's *The Candidate*, which remains perhaps the central American film about the electoral pro-cess, embodying insights into the process that still seem current more than thirty years later. Starring Robert Redford as a long shot candidate for the U.S. Senate from California, Ritchie's film was made before the outbreak of the Watergate hotel. Yet *The Candidate* is already a cynical film, born from the growing perception that the idealistic political activism of the 1960s, which peaked in 1968, the year Nixon gained the White House, had accomplished little in the area of electoral politics other than enabling a man like Nixon (widely mistrusted and despised, even before Watergate) to take power.

In *The Candidate*, Redford plays Bill McKay, an idealistic young lawyer-activist who runs a community legal clinic designed to help the poor in rural California. He also happens to be the son of a former governor of the state, which gives him immediate name recognition and electoral viability. In this sense, his career ironically foreshadows the 1974 election of Jerry Brown as governor of California, following in the footsteps of his father Pat Brown, who had served as governor of the state from 1959 to 1967. (Among other things, the elder Brown had the distinction of defeating Nixon in the California gubernatorial election of 1962 then losing to Ronald Reagan in the election of 1966.) On the other hand, in *The Candidate*, popular three-term Republican senator Crocker Jarmon (Don Porter) seems a shoo-in for reelection, so the Democratic party has essentially written off the seat. They therefore recruit McKay to run in the race just so they can at least make a showing. McKay himself is attracted by the fact that he apparently has no chance to win; a situation he believes will give him the freedom to use his candidacy as a forum to say what he truly believes rather than having to play the usual political games. He thus agrees to run, despite his initial agreement with one of his associates at the legal clinic that "politics is bullshit."

Even so, McKay's handlers, led by party functionary Marvin Lucas (Peter Boyle), work to moderate McKay's stance and style from the very beginning. After a rough start, McKay's fresh style and an endorsement from his father, John J. McKay (Melvyn Douglas), help his campaign to pick up steam. He wins the Democratic primary rather easily, then quickly begins to close the gap between himself and Jarmon in the polls. McKay's gathering momentum causes a worried Jarmon to agree to a public debate, while it also encourages McKay's camp to package him more and more like a commodity, limiting his statements to sound bites that will work well with the slick Madison Avenue television ads that are becoming an increasingly large part of their campaign strategy.

After McKay acquits himself well in the debate (despite an unexpectedly frank closing statement that upsets his own handlers), Jarmon begins to run scared. Jarmon's television ads become more negative, focusing largely on McKay's youth, while the senator's campaign rhetoric degenerates into little more than flag-waving and patriotic clichés. With victory now a real possibility, McKay's own campaign increasingly becomes the kind of superficial selling job that he had initially hoped to avoid, trading more on his personal charm and good lucks than on his antiestablishment political beliefs. In one classic scene, as he rides in a car from one campaign stop to another, he begins to mock the prepackaged platitudes of his own recent campaign speeches, ending with an imitation of Nixon's famous victory salute: McKay has become precisely what he was running to oppose.

McKay's conversion from outspoken outsider into political insider becomes complete when he actually wins the election, making him the senator elect. His camp is ecstatic, and his father (a machine politician whose style the younger McKay had formerly disavowed) congratulates him on the victory. "Son, you're a politician," proclaims the former governor—while the look on the son's face makes clear his own discomfort with his new status. Soon afterward, looking like a deer staring into headlights, McKay asks Lucas what is perhaps the key question of the film: "What do we do now?"

This memorable ending is especially relevant to the case of McKay, who began his campaign with no expectation of winning. Thus, he has put very little thought into what he might actually do if elected, a problem that is exacerbated by the fact that the nature of the campaign process precludes any real engagement with the issues if one actually hopes to be elected. But this ending also serves as a sweeping and cynical indictment of the entire political process. In addition to its suggestion of the corrupting effect of running for office, the ending comments on the disjunction between the two parts of the political process. For one thing, getting elected requires different talents and resources than subsequently serving effectively in office. For another, getting elected often requires so many behind-the-scenes compromises and commitments that the newly elected candidate enters office with baggage that virtually precludes him or her from doing a good job in office by serving the public. McKay has managed to get elected relatively free of such encumbrances (though he has cut a couple of deals with former cronies of his father), but the ease with which he was manipulated by the political professionals around him during the campaign makes one wonder just how free of such influences he will be able to remain during his tenure in the senate.

Indeed, this ending represents such a thoroughgoing condemnation of the political process that Ernest Giglio (presumably not entirely seriously) has declared in his book *Here's Looking at You: Hollywood, Film, and Politics* (Peter Lang, 2004) that the ending should be "unlawful for any American youngster to view . . . on the ground that it could destroy whatever is left of the civic virtue." However, we have surely not reached the point where it is desirable to ban cinematic criticism of the political process for fear that viewers will be made excessively cynical about democratic politics—if only because voters have plenty of other reasons to be cynical. *The Candidate*, for example, was released only twelve days after the fateful break-in at the Democratic Party headquarters in Washington's Watergate Hotel.

Of course, that break-in and the subsequent scandal only served to verify suspicions about the political process that had been in place long before Watergate. Still, there is a sense in many post-Watergate films that the scandal has ushered in a whole new era of political cynicism. As Peter Burton (John Cusack), the ambitious (and unscrupulous) young protagonist of Herbert Ross's *True Colors* (1991), puts it, speaking of the post-Watergate political landscape, "It's a brand new day in America, man." And in this new day, he goes on, there is only one rule of conduct: "Don't get caught." *True Colors* is an exploration of this new world of American politics that tracks Burton and his former law-school classmate Tim Gerrity (James Spader) as they come to Washington to pursue careers in government. Burton is a talented young man from the wrong side of the tracks who is determined to succeed in politics at any cost. Gerrity, on the other hand, is a Washington blueblood who eschews electoral politics, choosing instead to work as a prosecutor in the Justice Department. Gerrity genuinely hopes to work for the good, while Burton wants nothing but power (and all that comes with it). Ultimately, he betrays even best friend Gerrity on his rise to the top, landing a job on the staff of Connecticut's Senator Stiles (Richard Widmark) and then solidifying that position by marrying Stiles's daughter Diana (Imogen Stubbs), Gerrity's longtime girlfriend. He even gets Gerrity in hot water with the Justice Department by feeding him fake tips that lead to a bogus investigation of a competitor of Burton's chief financial backer, John Palmeri (Mandy Patinkin), a shady developer with apparent ties to organized crime.

Ultimately, Burton realizes his dream of being elected to Congress within ten years of law school, apparently on a platform that consists of little more than feel-good assurances to his constituents that "tomorrow's looking good." However, he is also arrested on the night of the election as a result of a Justice Department investigation in which Gerrity plays a key role. Burton seems sure to be convicted of racketeering charges, but goes on fighting nevertheless, attempting to portray himself as a man of the people being persecuted by the high and mighty who do not want to see a man like him in office. As the film ends, it remains very much a possibility that he still has a political future, even if his personal life is in shambles. Further, though specific elements of his background help to explain his particular need to succeed, the film ultimately portrays him as a symptom (and perhaps even a victim) of the new amoral world of American electoral politics, a world in which there is no place for a virtuous man like Gerrity.

True Colors includes few details about Burton's actual electoral campaign, though it does make the important point that the high cost of such campaigns is a major cause of corruption in American politics. For an in-depth depiction of a fictional political campaign, one might turn to Robert Altman's *Tanner '88* (1988). Though a television miniseries (on HBO) rather than a theatrical film, this six-hour sequence, scripted by *Doonesbury* cartoonist Garry Trudeau, provides perhaps the most detailed and realistic behind-the-scenes depiction of a fictional political campaign ever put on film—partly because of its length and partly because of its semi-documentary style. The series traces the bid by (fictional) former Michigan congressman Jack Tanner (Michael Murphy) for the 1988 Democratic presidential nomination, beginning with the New Hampshire primary and following through all the way to the Democratic convention in Atlanta. (The cast and crew of *Tanner '88*, literally followed the actual Democratic campaign around the country, intermingling with real political figures as they filmed the series on site.) Tanner begins as a long shot candidate, having been out of politics since 1976, when he retired due to the serious illness of his young daughter, Alex. A soft-spoken, divorced PhD who has been teaching political science in college in the intervening time, Tanner, at first, does not seem a likely bet to win the race against better known and better financed candidates, including Al Gore, Jesse Jackson, and eventual Democratic nominee Michael Dukakis. However, he is handsome and has a quiet sort of charisma, while his thoughtful stance on the issues gives him at least a small initial following.

Tanner is accompanied on the campaign trail by Alex (Cynthia Nixon), now a fresh-faced, nineteen-year-old college student, along with campaign manager T. J. Cavanaugh (Pamela Reed) and other aides. His campaign retinue is also followed by a contingent of journalists, including NBC reporter Molly Hark (Veronica Cartwright), which grows larger as Tanner's candidacy grows more serious. This increased coverage, among other things, makes it more difficult for Tanner to keep secret the fact that he is having an affair with Joanna Buckley (Wendy Crewson), Dukakis's deputy campaign manager. Hark, in fact, reveals this relationship on national television, ending the secrecy and forcing Buckley to resign from Dukakis's campaign. She and Tanner then plan an immediate wedding, but intrusive press coverage causes them to postpone the ceremony until after the election.

Somewhat like Bill McKay, Tanner begins to feel, as his campaign gathers momentum, that he is having to compromise his principles in order to allow himself to be marketed like any other commercial product. In one key scene in the episode "Bagels with Bruce," Tanner complains to real-world Democratic candidate Bruce Babbitt about this predicament. Babbitt, his own candidacy pretty much dead by this time, gives Tanner very straightforward advice about playing the political game: just don't do it. Talk straight, tell the truth, and hope for the best.

Of course, following this advice does not seem likely to lead to success, especially as it comes from a candidate who tried that very strategy and was then very quickly eliminated from the race. Tanner, in any case, does not follow this advice, but becomes more and more of a packaged product manufactured by a team of coaches and consultants as the campaign proceeds. Indeed, he gradually reaches the point where he is almost unable to have a straight conversation with anyone, but instead merely repeats the message points of his campaign speeches.

A long shot candidate, Tanner takes strong and controversial stands (such as strong support for the legalization of drugs), though these stands themselves are orchestrated by his handlers. However, Tanner's campaign takes a sudden serious turn after a trip to Detroit in which he and his entourage visit a ghetto neighborhood to discuss conditions there with the local citizenry. Returning to their cars after hearing numerous horror stories about ghetto violence, they discover a young boy who has been shot and left to die in a vacant lot. Deeply affected by this experience, Tanner decides to make strong and sincere support for social justice, his central campaign theme from that point on—which of course ensures that he will not win the nomination. Nevertheless, he manages to stay in the race right up to the convention, though losing out when Jackson (whom Tanner had earlier insulted in a televised debate) decides to cooperate with Dukakis, sealing the latter's nomination.

Tanner '88 gains realism through cameo appearances by numerous real-world political figures, including Republican presidential candidates Pat Robertson and Bob Dole and Democratic candidates Gary Hart and Babbitt. Numerous journalists and show-business personalities appear as well, further enhancing the documentary feel of the series and foreshadowing the heavy use of cameo appearances that would spice up Altman's 1992 Hollywood satire, *The Player* (1992). *Tanner '88* also looks back to Altman's classic 1975 film *Nashville*, which prominently featured the third-party presidential campaign of Hal Philip Walker (uncannily foreshadowing the later career of Ross Perot), including an important appearance by Murphy as John Triplette, a campaign strategist for Walker. Indeed, two of the eleven episodes of *Tanner '88* occur in Nashville, where Tanner campaigns in the Tennessee primary, gaining attention from an apparent assassination attempt and losing face when his former African American friend, the Rev. Billy Crier (Cleavon Little), endorses Jackson rather than Tanner, partly because of a gaffe by one of Tanner's aides.

Tanner '88 is a subtle and thoughtful exploration of the presidential campaign process that eschews easy answers. It presents presidential candidates as mostly good men caught up in a bad process that turns them into glossy commodities rather than impassioned leaders. Real-world telejournalist Linda Ellerbee (depicted in the film as a longtime friend of Tanner) describes the electoral process during a conversation with the candidate in a way that might be taken as the ultimate theme of the entire series: "Anyone who goes through that whole process and gets to the White House probably is somebody you don't want there."

If Jack Tanner is a liberal Democrat who campaigns largely against the legacy of the Reagan administration, the politician protagonist of *Bob Roberts* (1992) attempts to cash in on that legacy. The film details the rise of Roberts, a right-wing folksinger (played by Tim Robbins, who also directed the film), to fame, fortune, and a seat in the U.S. Senate from the state of Pennsylvania. Like *Tanner '88*, it is filmed in a documentary style; in fact, it is structured around a documentary being made about Roberts, though the film itself is a sort of meta-documentary about the making of that documentary. *Bob Roberts* effectively satirizes the ambition, venality, and hypocrisy of Roberts, a soulless manipulator of the media. He is a pure American demagogue who spouts moralistic slogans but is willing to stoop to any level of deception, and even possibly murder, in a ruthless quest for wealth and power. Roberts has no real political program other than to play on the hatreds and fears of his supporters, providing them with charisma-coated (but content-free) assurances that he will stand up to the evil forces that threaten their way of life. These forces, in line with the general rhetoric of the Republican right, include big government, though they mostly seem to consist of poor people, who for Roberts are poor purely because they are too lazy to work. Roberts's facile diagnosis of all of the important social problems facing America in the 1990s is simple: greed is good, and government is bad.

Bob Roberts is a partisan film that clearly identifies Roberts's conservative agenda as especially compatible with the kind of corruption and vacuity that mark his political campaign. Meanwhile, Roberts's ability to win a major election on the basis of little but conservative clichés and a media-savvy learned from show business is meant to recall the rise of Ronald Reagan to the presidency. Indeed, the film directly links Roberts to the Reagan administration by suggesting that he and his partners were extensively involved in some of the low points of that administration, including the Iran-Contra affair and the wave of savings and loan failures that was enabled by Reaganite deregulation, leading to massive bailouts that contributed to the run-up of huge budget deficits for the federal government. Indeed, the film even suggests links between the Savings and Loan (S&L) crisis of the late 1980s (involving hundreds of billions of dollars of assets) and the Reaganite plan to smuggle illegal arms to Nicaraguan Contras. Roberts and the Broken Dove organization that backs him have apparently been involved in an extensive scheme to borrow money from S&Ls under false premises—money that was never repaid, a fact lost in the shuffle when the S&Ls collapsed. Broken Dove then used this money to buy planes that were employed to smuggle illegal drugs into the United States, selling the drugs on the street to generate even more money that was used to buy arms that were then shipped to the right-wing Contras to support their efforts to overthrow the legally elected government of Nicaragua.

This seemingly farfetched scheme rings quite true in the light of the actual dealings of the Reagan administration in the Iran-Contra affair (through much of Reagan's term in office, advanced armaments were sold to Iran, an avowed enemy of the United States, and the proceeds were illegally diverted to finance acts of insurgency and terrorism in Nicaragua). Meanwhile, that Roberts and Broken Dove ultimately get away with the whole scheme when the Bush administration decides not to investigate, is as bitter an indictment of corruption in government as any that can be found in American film. The depiction of Roberts's corrupt (but successful) campaign for the senate seems intended primarily as a criticism of the lengths to which the political right is willing to go to seize power (a commentary that would gain force in retrospect, given the 1994 "Republican revolution," when right-wing opportunists running on uncannily Roberts-like platforms were swept into Congress and the Senate from districts all over America). But Roberts's electoral success also indicts the entire electoral system and the voters themselves, portrayed in the film as far too easily swayed by slick, but superficial, media campaigns because they are unwilling to do the work to learn the truth about important issues—and even unwilling to face the truth when it is presented to them.

The Democratic party comes in for implied criticism in *Bob Roberts* as well. Roberts's opponent in the senatorial race is the liberal Democratic incumbent Brickley Paiste (Gore Vidal), portrayed as a tired, old man with neither the will nor the ability to combat Roberts's slick and dirty dealing. Paiste (who can be taken as a sort of allegorical representative of the Democratic party as a whole) is a good and honest man, but he seems out of step with the times and unable to relate to most of his constituents. On the other hand, the fact that an honest man like Paiste seems completely unable to cope with the contemporary world of politics is as much an indictment of the political system as of Paiste, suggesting that the system itself is so corrupt and so dominated by media flash that only a cunning and conniving operator like Roberts can succeed within it.

Bob Roberts includes performances of a number of Roberts's songs, many of which are hilarious, highlighted by the music video "Wall Street Rap," a parody of Bob Dylan's "Subterranean Homesick Blues" that glorifies greed and acquisitiveness in a manner that recalls the pro-avarice diatribes of Gordon Gekko in Oliver Stone's *Wall Street* (1987). Indeed, Roberts consistently parodies Dylan, releasing albums with such titles as "The Free Wheelin' Bob Roberts," "The Times They Are a Changing Back," and "Bob on Bob." Further, he attempts to tap into Dylan's rebel image, presenting himself as a conservative rebel, somewhat in the manner of Reagan's 1980 "Washington Outsider" campaign, but this time with a young, hip slant. Meanwhile, Robert's dialogue with Dylan is part of an overall assault on the values of the counterculture of the 1960s, which Roberts portrays as a source of the moral decay he purportedly plans to combat if elected. He particularly campaigns against drug use, which becomes highly problematic when investigative reporter Bugs Raplin (Giancarlo Esposito) uncovers evidence of the pro-Contra drug smuggling scheme.

This evidence is dismissed by the Roberts camp as the ravings of a crazed radical, and they mount an immediate media blitz to discredit Raplin. Unfortunately for Roberts, the story keeps coming up and seriously hampers his senatorial election campaign against Paiste, overshadowing Roberts's earlier, partly successful attempt to discredit his opponent by fabricating evidence of an extramarital affair between Paiste and a teenage campaign worker. Desperate, the Roberts camp concocts an elaborate scheme in which they fake an assassination attempt on Roberts, claiming that he has been crippled by his gunshot wounds. He thus finishes the campaign in a wheelchair, hoping to gain sympathy with voters. In the meantime, the Roberts campaign attempts to kill the Broken Dove story by fabricating evidence to frame Raplin, thus suggesting that Raplin is a madman who cannot be believed because he is clearly willing to do anything to strike against Roberts.

One weakness of the film may be that Raplin, as played by Esposito, does seem a bit unbalanced. Still, Raplin is eventually cleared, thanks to the efforts of his lawyer, Mack Laflin (David Strathairn), but the ploy works: Roberts is elected and Raplin comes to be regarded as an unreliable zealot. Soon after the election, Raplin is murdered, supposedly by a lone right-wing fanatic, but there are hints that the reporter is the victim of a concerted conspiracy to stop his investigation of Broken Dove. Roberts's supposedly moral supporters (many of them looking suspiciously like Hitler Youth) gleefully cheer the news of Raplin's death, and the film as a whole is particularly powerful in its depiction of these followers as willing to do anything in the service of their adored leader, with clear echoes of the followers of Hitler in Nazi Germany. There are also ominous hints that the covert dealings in which Roberts and Hart are involved are part of a vast network of such dealings, engineered by a secret government headed by the National Security Council. Paiste himself believes in the conspiracy, but seems too old and tired to attempt to do anything about it. Meanwhile, real-world events such as the Iran-Contra affair suggest that these seemingly paranoid stories contain more than a grain of truth—and that the American people, like a frog boiled in slowly heated water, have gradually, over time, become so accustomed to illegal and immoral activities on the part of their government that they are perfectly willing to accept such activities as normal. *Bob Roberts* is seemingly effective satire, and Robbins is himself effective in the film as both an actor and a director—supporting the declaration by acclaimed director Robert Altman (who directed *The Player*, a satire of Hollywood in which Robbins starred in the same year) that Robbins has the talent to be the next Orson Welles, a comparison that more than one critic has endorsed. But this satire seemed to have little impact on American voters, ironically demonstrating the apathy of the American populace that is a central theme of the film.

The closing credits of *Bob Roberts* roll to the accompaniment of Woody Guthrie singing "I've Got to Know," the very title of which contrasts with the way in which the voters in the film have so little interest in learning the truth about their government and their elected officials. Perhaps more importantly, the contrast between the true folk singer Guthrie (a legitimate man of the people who serves as an emblem of authenticity) and the manufactured folk singer Roberts (who conscripts folk music in the interest of capitalist greed), suggests a general decline in American popular culture away from the expressions of genuine folk energies toward the production of slick, prepackaged capitalist commodities. By extension, this ending implies that the political process has similarly decayed, from the true populism for which singers such as Guthrie and Pete Seeger supplied a voice, to the faux populism of Roberts, whose real constituency is big business, no matter how folksy he might try to appear to be.

Mike Nichols's *Primary Colors* (1998) shifts the emphasis back to the Democratic party, presenting audiences with a Democratic candidate who, unlike Paiste, has the energy and the will to do the dirty work that is presented as necessary for political success at the end of the twentieth century. Here, protagonist Jack Stanton (John Travolta) is a brilliant and savvy political strategist with a genuine affinity for his poor and (especially) black constituents. Based on the similarly titled 1996 novel by political columnist Joe Klein (though published anonymously), *Primary Colors* is transparently based on Bill Clinton's 1992 run for the presidency. It features Stanton as the governor of an unidentified southern state whose relation to Clinton is made all the more clear by the fact that Travolta goes through the entire film doing his best (though it isn't all that good) imitation of Clinton. Stanton's wife Susan (Emma Thompson), a former law-school classmate of the candidate, is a savvy politician in her own right and obviously has much in common with Hillary Clinton. Billy Bob Thornton plays Richard Jemmons, a self-proclaimed redneck who is also a brilliant political strategist for the Stanton campaign, clearly based on Clinton advisor James Carville.

From here, the one-to-one correspondences between characters in the film and individuals in the actual Clinton campaign become a bit more tenuous. In fact, the connection between Stanton and Clinton is not all that direct in the first place, despite the numerous parallels between their campaigns. Not only does the plot of the film deviate substantially from what actually happened in Clinton's campaign, but Travolta's Stanton is not really all that Clintonesque. In particular, Travolta plays Stanton as a quintessentially Southern good ole boy (or at least as someone who wants to be perceived that way), when in point of fact the Yale and Oxford-educated Clinton was anything but. Indeed, while *Primary Colors* has been widely seen as a commentary on the Clinton campaign, it is more properly viewed as a commentary on campaigns and on the political system in general. It depicts politics as a dirty business in which only those willing and able to play the game (and able to survive having their own dirty laundry aired in public) can possibly survive.

The film begins as Stanton visits an inner-city adult literacy program in New York City and demonstrates a powerful rapport with the poor, mostly black participants in the program. That he wins them over largely through telling a fabricated story about an illiterate uncle (and that he later beds the white woman who runs the program) serves to indicate early on that Stanton might not quite be all that he pretends to be. Yet, throughout the film, he remains a complex figure who seems genuinely devoted to helping the poor and the downtrodden, even though he is also a slick and ambitious politician, willing to stretch the truth in order to accomplish his objectives.

Though dogged by rumors of his past sexual indiscretions, Stanton's campaign begins to pick up momentum as he moves from a relative unknown to a major contender. This narrative of the campaign, meanwhile, is paralleled by the story of Henry Burton (Adrian Lester), the idealistic grandson of a famous civil-rights leader. Burton, who provides the central point of view in the film, is reluctant to become involved in a political campaign, but is convinced to join Stanton's staff after he concludes that the governor is different from the run-of-the-mill politician and that Stanton wants power largely because he wants to be able to help those who do not have the resources to help themselves, including African Americans. For a time, Burton becomes a true believer, dedicated to Stanton's cause, though ultimately he becomes disgusted with the game of politics as a whole.

Burton's disgust comes about after Fred Picker (Larry Hagman), a former governor of Florida, enters the race after Stanton's main rival is struck down by a heart attack and lies near death in a hospital. Picker, who had inexplicably abandoned a promising political career back in 1978, quickly surges ahead when his own astute campaigning creates the popular perception that he is a genuinely good, honest man, and thus a refreshing change in the world of politics. Stanton assigns Burton and another staffer, longtime Stanton friend and supporter Libby Holden (Kathy Bates), to investigate the reasons behind Picker's withdrawal from politics fourteen years earlier. In so doing, they find that Picker was a man of honor who never abused his position as governor. However, they also discover that he had developed a cocaine habit and had even engaged in a brief homosexual affair with the man who procured his drugs for him.

They conclude that this information is not relevant to Picker's qualifications for office, but report it to the Stantons anyway, hoping they will do the honorable thing and agree not to make the information public. Neither Stanton even considers not using the information, partly because they realize that, were Picker to win the Democratic nomination, the Republicans would surely dig up and use the same information. Nevertheless, Holden is so disenchanted with the Stantons' reaction to this news that she ends up committing suicide, now having nothing left to believe in. Stanton, still believing it is the wrong thing to do, but feeling that he owes it to Holden, takes the information to Picker and promises not to use it. Realizing the story will nevertheless come out, Picker decides to withdraw from the race, leaving the way open for Stanton.

Burton, meanwhile, announces that he is resigning because he is no longer comfortable working in the dirty world of politics, but Stanton refuses to accept his resignation. "This is hardball," he explains. "This is it, Henry. This is the price you pay to lead. You don't think that Abraham Lincoln was a whore before he was a president? He had to tell his little stories and smile his shit-eating back-country grin. And he did it just so that he would one day have the opportunity to stand in front of the nation and appeal to the better angels of our nature. And that's where the bullshit stops. That's what it's all about—so we have the opportunity to make the most of it, to do it the right way." Other politicians, he argues, play the dirty game of electoral politics "just for the prize," while he, at least hopes to do some good with that prize if he wins. He then asks Burton the crucial question, "Is there anyone else out there with a chance to actually win this election who'd do more for the people than I would? Who'd even think about the folks I care about?" Stanton promises Burton that he can win, and then make history once in office. A final cut to the inaugural ball then shows that Stanton has won—and that Burton is still on board.

The whole final segment of the film, revolving around the story of Picker, has no basis in fact and nothing to do with the Clinton campaign. It does, however, provide a dramatic focus for the film's ultimate judgment concerning the American political system, which is not all that different (though more detailed) than the judgment of previous films such as *The Candidate*. Granted, Jack Stanton is a far cry from Bill McKay. Far from being an innocent neophyte with no clear idea of what to do after winning election to office, he is an experienced professional politician who has obviously thought long and hard about what he hopes to accomplish after becoming president. But *Primary Colors* does seem to endorse the suggestion in *The Candidate* that running for election and serving in office are two entirely different matters. If anything, the later film may be even more cynical about the electoral process than is the earlier one. Stanton's view of the process (especially his insistence that politics has always been dirty and that even icons of American democracy such as Lincoln played the same game he is playing) is not necessarily endorsed by the film. Still, there is nothing in the film to dispute Stanton's own claim that it is absolutely necessary to be willing to play dirty in order to win elections, and the fact that Burton ultimately sticks with Stanton comes very close to an endorsement on the part of the film. Yet *Primary Colors* retains an idealistic core that at least leaves open the possibility that Stanton, in his pivotal speech to Burton, is not only sincere, but correct. Maybe, just maybe, it is possible for good leaders to win election so that they can do good things in office, even if they have to do bad things to get there.

In this sense, *Primary Colors* may not be so much cynical as it is mature and realistic—even hopeful. It may also be a testament to the complexity of the film, which supplies no easy answers, that some reviewers and critics have seen it as an apology for Clinton, while others have seen it as a hatchet job on a man who was in the midst of a reelection campaign when the film was released. It is certainly the case that Stanton is presented in the film as a flawed man and as much more of a womanizer than Clinton really was, but it is also the case that Stanton's various sexual indiscretions are made to seem unimportant and irrelevant to his qualifications to be president. What is more relevant is his willingness to play hardball politics, but the film does nothing to suggest an alternative to his campaign style. There is no suggestion, as in *State of the Union*, that a few idealistic reformers can fix the system. Indeed, in *Primary Colors* the system is not broken; it just is what it is.

Primary Colors completely rejects the notion, put forth in *Bulworth*, released only a couple of months after *Primary Colors*, that a politician who dared to tell the truth would be such a welcome breath of fresh air that voters would flock to him in droves. *Bulworth* leans decidedly to the left with its strong denunciation of the power of the rich in America. However, the film can also be taken as a slap at the Clinton New Democrats for capitulating to an unfair system in order to gain power. *Bulworth* might almost be a sequel to *The Candidate*, perhaps answering the "what-do-we-do-now" question by showing Bill McKay after a few terms in the senate. Actually, this film focuses on fictional California senator Jay Billington Bulworth (played by Warren Beatty, who also directed the film) as he reaches, in the midst of his 1996 campaign for reelection, a point of despair following a long political career in which he realizes he has accomplished nothing but serve the rich and powerful interests that finance his political campaigns. In the film's first scene (after an opening shot of the Capitol Building, with a telling "DO NOT ENTER" sign in front), Bulworth sits in his Washington office weeping as he listens to the vacuous sloganeering of his own campaign ads, presumably remembering a time when he, a onetime Kennedy liberal, actually stood for something. The point is emphasized by the pictures that decorate the office, featuring civil-rights leaders such as Rosa Parks and Thurgood Marshall, but most importantly (because they foreshadow the ending of the film) Robert Kennedy, Martin Luther King, and Malcolm X, all of whom were slain in the pursuit of their political ideals.

Bulworth has long since abandoned this pursuit. In addition, his marriage is a sham and is wife is cheating on him (though he does not much care, being a noted philanderer himself). With both his personal and political lives now devoid of meaning, Bulworth sees no reason to go on living and has decided that he wants to die. However, rather than commit suicide, he has contracted to have himself assassinated—so that his daughter can collect the massive life insurance policy that he has just acquired from an insurance-industry lobbyist in return for his promise to help kill a bill that would force the industry to offer affordable insurance policies to the poor.

Bulworth travels from Washington to Los Angeles for a weekend of campaigning—during which he has arranged to be killed. With nothing to lose (and perhaps in the midst of a nervous breakdown), he begins to make public statements that reveal the truth of the political process rather than cover that truth with the usual platitudes. These statements apparently gain the attention of Nina (Halle Berry), a beautiful young black woman, though Bulworth does not realize that Nina is actually working for the man who has been contracted to kill him. Influenced by Nina and her friends, Bulworth (whose new carefree attitude has now been supplemented with a liberal dose of alcohol) appears at a big money fundraiser, where he raps a speech in which he excoriates the privileged attendees of the event for their selfishness and even dares to tout socialism as a cure. At the same time, he goes on a one-man rampage that includes extensive criticism of liberals and their usual constituency as well. The press and the media (including Hollywood) also come in for considerable criticism, both in Bulworth's statements and in the way they hound him throughout the film.

By this time, Bulworth's fascination with Nina (who is as intelligent as she is beautiful) has given him a reason to live, so he attempts to cancel his killing. In the meantime, he hides out with Nina's family in South Central and dons ghetto garb while his suit is being cleaned. He then goes on a national television broadcast in those clothes, rapping a stunningly honest critique of the exploitation of the poor by the rich that is largely a repetition of what he has heard from Nina and from a South Central drug lord (Don Cheadle), ending with a declaration that the race problem in America can only be solved by everybody fucking everybody else until we are all of the same mixed ethnicity.

It is never entirely clear during these rants whether Bulworth is finally telling the truth as he sees it or whether he has gone entirely insane, though one implication of this aspect of the film is that a politician would have to be insane in order to tell the truth. However, all seems to work out well. After a series of near disasters, Bulworth and Nina establish a meaningful connection, the contracted killing is off, and Bulworth's personal future is looking up. His political future is looking up as well: his brash, new, in-your-face attitude goes over surprisingly well with the voters, and he wins the Democratic senatorial primary in a landslide. Indeed, his new style is so popular that he even gets a substantial number of write-in votes in the California presidential primary. Apparently, the people were ready for a genuine alternative, having already come to the same conclusion as Bulworth: that Republicans and Democrats are all members of the same club and that the club is run by big business. The South Central drug lord, L.D., is so inspired by Bulworth's speeches that he seems to be changing his ways toward becoming a positive leader for the black community. Then (after a brief moment in which Bulworth seems to be on the verge of reverting to his former self), Bulworth and Nina share a passionate kiss (in front of the flashing cameras of the press), then prepare to enter a car to go off together to begin their new life. Suddenly, though, he is shot down and seemingly killed by an unidentified assailant (apparently hired by the powerful insurance interests whom Bulworth has now turned against—as suggested by the fact that we are shown a shot of the insurance lobbyist atop a building just before the fatal shot comes from there).

This ending is something of a disappointment, if only because Bulworth will now not have to answer the crucial question, posed by Robert Redford's Bill McKay, of what to do after gaining election. But this shocking ending to what has to this point been a largely comic film adds a serious and bitter touch to *Bulworth*'s satire of the political process, suggesting that even if a genuinely original and honest politician were to come along to challenge the system (and even if he were somehow to gain the support of the people in doing so), he would be stopped in his tracks by the sinister forces that hold real power in America. We are, of course, meant to recall the fallen Kennedys, Malcolm, and (especially) King—as evidenced by a shot in which an old onlooker (played by African American writer Amiri Baraka) points to the source of the shot, echoing the famous news photograph taken immediately after the shooting of King. Having lived by the sword of black culture in his efforts to strike against the establishment, Bulworth has now died by that same sword, suffering the fate of America's greatest black leader.

But *Bulworth* is hardly an entirely negative or pessimistic film, despite this ending. The genuine connection made between Bulworth and Nina represents a decidedly hopeful suggestion that people from different ethnic, economic, and even generational backgrounds are all still people, all sharing a common set of needs, hopes, and desires. The film's suggestion that a wild-man politician such as Bulworth becomes would win the support of the vast majority of the voters may even be optimistic to the point of absurdity; then again the film is not a work of realism but a work of satire. As such, it necessarily exaggerates in order to bring its critique of the system into focus. On the other hand, the patent silliness of much of the film dilutes this critique, even if it might have been the only way to get audiences to sit still for such radical statements, or even to get those statements onto film—especially in a major theatrical release from Twentieth Century Fox, part of the media empire of notoriously right-wing mogul Rupert Murdoch.

Perhaps the most problematic aspect of *Bulworth* is its treatment of race, and in particular the appropriation of black culture by Bulworth in a seeming attempt to add shock value to his new political style. Presumably, his budding love for Nina is supposed to make his turn to black culture more authentic, a sign of respect rather than mockery. Still, this notion that black culture is somehow more honest and authentic than mainstream white culture is itself something of a cliché, while Bulworth's rapping performances in ghetto garb represent nothing more than the old tradition of blackface minstrelsy. But this tradition itself has highly racist implications, as it also serves as a kind of emblem of the role of African Americans in American cultural history as a whole: often mocked and despised in mainstream culture, African Americans have nevertheless enriched that mainstream by providing important sources of new cultural energies.

In Bulworth's case, the donning of black disguise is made especially easy because it is merely a disguise, one that, as a rich white man, he can discard at will. In one key scene, he walks the streets of South Central in precisely the kind of gangbanger garb that would make a young black man there an object of suspicion on the part of the police. When he witnesses a white policeman hassling some black boys on the street, Bulworth steps in, physically assaults the officer, showing surprising strength (perhaps from rage) by tossing the cop over the hood of his police car. Bulworth then calmly watches as the enraged cop starts to retaliate then suddenly melts in fear as he matches Bulworth's face to that on a campaign poster that just happens to be conveniently plastered on a wall directly behind him. Bulworth then asserts his power and forces the cop to apologize to the black kids before slinking away with his tail between his legs. That the outcome of this scene would have been so very different had Bulworth not been a powerful white man goes without saying; that this scene is not very believable is pretty obvious as well. Yet the scene is an important one that indicates both Bulworth's genuine sympathy with the poor of South Central and his understanding that he is not really one of them. It also presumably signals Beatty's wish to convey to audiences that Bulworth has been truly inspired by the people of South Central rather than simply appropriating their culture for his own ends.

Bulworth did not, of course, become an inspiration to a new generation of straight-talking, say-what-you-really-think politicians, though it did appear to resonate with American voters' desire for such political candor. However contemporary it might appear, it also participates in a long cinematic tradition, especially looking back to the films of Capra in its assumption that the system is corrupt but the voters can be trusted to do the right thing if given a chance. Chris Rock's *Head of State* (2003) draws upon this tradition as well. Here, a major party (again, the film does not say which) loses both is presidential and vice-presidential candidates when their separate planes crash into each other. The party, already a heavy underdog in the upcoming 2004 election, concludes that it now cannot win. Party boss Senator Bill Arnot (James Rebhorn), who hopes to be elected president, decides that the party can gain some useful equity with voters by running a sacrificial African American candidate in 2004. Obscure Washington D.C. alderman Mays Gilliam (played by comedian Rock, who both directed and cowrote the film) is tabbed for the job, thanks to recent exposure gained when he saved an old woman and her cat from a building that is about to be demolished.

This scenario is pretty unlikely, as are the subsequent events in the film, but that is not really the point. Like *Bulworth*, *Head of State* is a work of satire, aimed at a criticism of our current electoral system through exaggeration. As such, the film works well and got some positive reviews, though it was not particularly well received by audiences. Encumbent Vice President Brian Lewis (Nick Searcy) is a particularly effective butt of the film's satire. Coming off essentially as a combination of Bill Clinton and George W. Bush, Lewis speaks only in platitudes and prepackaged clichés, repeatedly spouting his central slogan, "God bless America—and no place else," which not only effectively satirizes the emptiness of contemporary American political language but also takes a shot at the increasing religiosity of that language. Gilliam predictably functions as the opposite of Lewis, saying what he really thinks and presenting himself as he really is (despite the efforts of his own backers to tone down his image). That Gilliam ultimately wins the election does not suggest that Gilliam's candor would actually work in a real election so much as it enacts a fantasy version of American politics in which such candor *could* work. Meanwhile, the patently unrealistic tone of most of the film (Bernie Mac's turn as Gilliam's embarrassing bail-bondsman brother and vice-presidential candidate is particularly unbelievable) serves to emphasize the vast gulf between the idealized outcome of the film and the real world of American politics.

The broad satire of *Head of State* thus differs dramatically from the realism of *Tanner '88*, perhaps suggesting a decline in the American political process between the elections of 1988 and 2004. A similar suggestion can be inferred from *Tanner on Tanner*, the 2004 sequel to *Tanner '88* that aired on the Sundance cable channel. The sequel features much of the same cast as the original and is again written by Trudeau and directed by Altman. In the sequel, however, Alex Tanner (still played by Nixon, now a prominent star thanks to her role in the vastly popular HBO series *Sex and the City*) is the central figure. She now makes films and teaches filmmaking (apparently at New York University, though that is not made entirely clear). Her latest project is a documentary film entitled *My Candidate*, which follows her father's 1988 presidential campaign, much as *Tanner '88* had done. However, when she shows a preliminary version of the film at the Rough Cut Film Festival in New York, it receives a less than enthusiastic reception. None other than Robert Redford pops out of the audience to critique the film, suggesting that it would be more interesting not to show the campaign process itself but to show Tanner discussing the campaign process with other former candidates who have been through that process. Alex agrees, then heads with her small crew for the Democratic convention in Boston to try to film the needed scenes.

On the trip Alex admits to one of her students (who is in the process of making a documentary film about *her*) that her Guatemalan husband, a reporter, is missing, perhaps abducted and killed by political enemies—adding a note of the kind of seriousness and drama that sets the sequel apart. Meanwhile, her attempts to film interviews and conversations between her father and other political figures veer from one disaster to another. However, she catches lightning in a bottle when she interviews her father on the racquetball court, eliciting a candid and impassioned condemnation of the Bush administration's invasion and occupation of Iraq. This scene alone, filled with the kind of honesty and genuine emotion seldom found in political statements, may be enough to save her film.

Unfortunately, *Tanner on Tanner* takes a dark turn when the camp of Democratic nominee John Kerry approaches Tanner about the possibility of a high post in the new administration. Tanner jumps at the chance, but knows that the scene filmed by Alex on the racquetball court would be a political embarrassment, so he asks his daughter to remove the scene from her film. In the meantime, he makes a series of public statements that toe the Kerry line, turning his back on his own true beliefs. Disgusted with this evidence of the way even a whiff of power has corrupted her father, Alex destroys her film altogether.

If anything, *Tanner on Tanner* presents a darker view of the political process than had its predecessor. Indeed, several of the political figures who make cameos in the film agree that things have gotten worse between 1988 and 2004. Further, through its focus on Alex's filmmaking (which involves, among other things, competition with dozens of other film crews who have also come to the convention hoping for footage), the sequel makes important new points about the increasingly important (and distorting) role played by the media in the political process. It also condemns the media for simply seeking marketable stories rather than asking the kind of hard questions that really need to be asked. In one scene, for example, superstar documentary filmmaker Michael Moore insists that the real villains of his 2004 film *Fahrenheit 9/11* are not the members of the Bush administration who took the U.S. into an illegal and unjustified war in Iraq based on false intelligence, but the members of the media who let them get away with it.

The Bush administration and its political shenanigans are also a topic of another film released in 2004, John Sayles's *Silver City,* one of the most powerful (and underrated) cinematic satires of American electoral politics ever produced. The film follows bumbling, dim-witted rich boy Dickie Pilager (Chris Cooper) as he campaigns to be elected governor of Colorado. Aided by a highly professional campaign staff, a rich campaign coffer, and the connections of his father, Senator Jud Pilager (Michael Murphy), long one of the state's most powerful political figures, Pilager seems sure to be elected, despite his personal limitations (which include an inability to utter a complete, grammatically correct sentence unless it is scripted for him). In this, the parallels between Pilager and President George W. Bush are obvious, though they are made even more so by the way Cooper does a running imitation of Bush's hand gestures and the halting, ungrammatical speaking style throughout the film.

However, there is much more at stake in *Silver City* than a personal lampoon of Bush. For one thing, Dickie Pilager is depicted as a well-meaning true believer who is basically a pawn of his father's political machine and powerful backers. The brains behind the Pilager campaign is political strategist Chuck Raven (Richard Dreyfuss), a Karl Rove-like professional with few scruples, ready to do anything necessary to get his candidate elected. Murphy (though he appears only briefly in the film) is suitably sinister as Pilager's father, while his casting in the role inevitably invites comparison between the oily Jud Pilager and the more naïve Jack Tanner, much to the advantage of the latter. Senator Pilager has no illusions about his son's capabilities; he and his cronies clearly expect to manipulate Dickie as their puppet if he is elected governor. The most powerful of these cronies (and the most sinister figure in the film) is billionaire businessman Wes Benteen (Kris Kristofferson), who heads the vastly wealthy Bentel Corporation and who provides extensive financial support for the political aspirations of the Pilager family. But it is Benteen who is the true pillager. He views the vast natural resources of the American West virtually as his own personal property, to which he feels he is entitled because he is one of the few men with the vision to exploit those resources effectively, exploit being the key word. "It's like a treasure chest waiting to be opened," he tells Dickie. When Dickie stumblingly attempts to suggest that the people might have some right to this treasure, Benteen makes his true, fascistic political vision clear: "The people gotta be grabbed by the horns and dragged to what's good for 'em," he says. Benteen views his political contributions to the Pilagers as part of this effort and an investment on which he expects substantial returns; in particular, he believes having friends in office will help him gain the freedom to pursue his ruthless projects without government interference.

As *Silver City* begins, Pilager and Raven are taping a television campaign ad on the shores of pristine-looking Lake Arapaho, hoping to depict Pilager as an environmentally conscious nature-lover. However, the filming is interrupted when Pilager, fishing from the shore of the lake, hooks a human body that was floating just below the surface of the water. Concerned that even the vaguest association with this event will taint Pilager's campaign, Raven spirits Pilager and his entourage away to an alternative site to continue taping the ad, while he himself calls the police to recover the body, though it is clear that his main concern is to make sure that the body is not linked to Pilager in the press.

Apparently paranoid as well as ruthless, Raven suspects that Pilager's political foes might have planted the body as a dirty trick, so he also hires private investigator Danny O'Brien (Danny Huston), a former reporter, to interview a hit list of suspects and warn them to back off. O'Brien, in fact, is the true protagonist of the film, which from this point becomes a sort of murder mystery as O'Brien's errand for Raven turns into a genuine investigation. O'Brien is not the toughest or most efficient private eye in the world, but he shambles along in the manner of Philip Marlowe in Robert Altman's *The Long Goodbye* (1973), gradually growing in curiosity as a loose collection of clues slowly congeals into a network of connections. In particular, O'Brien discovers that the body in the lake was that of a Benteen employee killed in an on-the-job accident due to unsafe working conditions. The body was then dumped in an old mine shaft that is now used by Benteen's company as an illegal dumping site for toxic waste. That the body subsequently washed into the lake thus has ominous implications that go beyond the outrage of this impromptu burial itself.

In the meantime, O'Brien himself has lost his job, narrowly escaped drowning in the water-filled mineshaft, and nearly been killed by Vincent Esparza (Luis Saguar), an unscrupulous trafficker in illegal Mexican immigrant labor with extensive links to Benteen. More frightening than these harrowing encounters, however, is the likelihood that Pilager will still be elected governor. With Benteen's money and Raven's genius for manipulation of public opinion behind him, how can he lose? Once in office, of course, Pilager's slow wit is likely to make him an easy tool for vicious and powerful men like Benteen, who can literally get away with murder as they go on exploiting immigrant labor and polluting the environment in their unending quest for more and more wealth. Good people who get in the way of the Benteens and Pilagers, meanwhile, are likely to be destroyed—as we see when O'Brien interviews Casey Lyle (Ralph Waite), a former federal mining inspector who was fired and then blacklisted when he tried to expose the environmental contamination being produced by the Silver City mining operation, essentially a joint venture of Benteen and Dickie Pilager.

All in all, *Silver City* is a dark and pessimistic film. As it ends, O'Brien has been able to feed hints of his discoveries to internet journalist Mitch Paine (Tim Roth), and there seems at least some chance that the information might eventually be posted on Paine's website, later to be picked up by the mainstream media, triggering a more thorough investigation. There seems little chance, however, that either Benteen or the Pilagers will be really harmed by any revelations that this investigation might produce. At most, struggling smalltime developer Mort Seymour (David Clennon) might lose everything because he has invested heavily in an attempt to construct an ambitious new project on the former site of the contaminated Silver City mine.

Sayles does add one positive touch to his ending when O'Brien gets back together with former girlfriend Nora Allardyce (Maria Bello), a reporter who has been following Pilager on the campaign trail, attempting to ask tough questions but getting answers so lame that she constantly appears astonished. But this ending is hardly the stuff of Hollywood romance. Allardyce and O'Brien seem headed for a reconciliation almost by default, neither still capable of genuine passion. They were both once idealistic young journalists who believed in the power of the press to do good. O'Brien has abandoned journalism (and has now even lost his job as a private investigator), while Nora, her own newspaper just acquired by the Bentel Corporation, has become cynical about her profession, describing herself as "a part of the entertainment industry." After O'Brien and Allardyce walk away together, any potential romance in their reconciliation is undermined as the film ends with one last snippet of a Pilager speech, followed by a final shot of Lake Arapaho, where dead fish begin to float one-after-another to the previously beautiful surface, with the strains of "America the Beautiful" sounding ironically in the background.

Silver City powerfully condemns the Benteens and Pilagers of the world, but it is just as much a critique of the system that allows them to succeed and of the failure of others to stand up to such figures and put a stop to their exploitation of the American people and America's national resources. This message is driven powerfully home during the closing credits that roll to the music of Steve Earle's "Amerika v. 6.0" a powerful comment on our loss of any genuine belief in the American dream and of the failure of those who should be the opponents of unscrupulous men like Benteen and misguided men like Pilager to provide any real opposition. Per Earle's song, such opponents are now, like O'Brien and Allardyce (or Brickley Paiste), too tired, frustrated, and beaten down to keep up the fight in any but the most perfunctory of ways.

Of course, the exhaustion of officeholders also suggests that even those in power often lack the energy to fight the system. Then again, officeholders may also lack the motivation, as the system of which they are now a part. Numerous American films have explored the careers of politicians after they are elected to office, often suggesting that even the most idealistic and well-meaning candidates can be either corrupted by power or simply beaten down by the system. Such films about the workings of government are described in the next chapter.

CHAPTER 2

Inside Politics: The Process of Government in American Political Film

Oliver Stone's *JFK* (1991) was one of the most controversial films of the 1990s. It is also one of the best-known political films in the history of American cinema, combining elements of the post-Watergate political thriller with real-world political events in a particularly effective way. In particular, *JFK* narrates the efforts of New Orleans District Attorney Jim Garrison (Kevin Costner) to demonstrate that the 1963 assassination of President John F. Kennedy was in fact the result of a vast conspiracy involving not only the Mafia and right-wing anti-Castro Cubans, but defense contractors, the FBI, the CIA, virtually the entire American Military Intelligence community, and even Vice President Lyndon Johnson. From the casting of likeable nice guy Costner in the central role to the construction of the entire narrative as a dramatization of the conspiracy theory, the film is clearly sympathetic to Garrison's position, which is only to be expected, given that the script for the film was partly based on Garrison's best-selling book, *On the Trail of the Assassins* (1988). Elaborately researched and presented in a documentary style, *JFK* presents a case that was convincing enough to stimulate the U.S. Congress to attempt to reopen the investigation of the assassination, though these efforts essentially came to nothing. The film is also an impressive achievement in storytelling, weaving together a vast amount of information and loosely connected strands into a compelling drama that never wavers during its three-hour-plus run. It was nominated for eight Academy Awards, including best picture and best director, though it won only two, for best cinematography and best film editing.

The film sets up its theory by beginning with a clip of President Dwight Eisenhower's famous parting warning against the growing power of the "military-industrial complex." The film then establishes that Kennedy, as Eisenhower's successor, ran afoul of this sinister entity through a variety of actions, ranging from his refusal to support an all-out invasion to Cuba to his plan to withdraw all American forces from Vietnam before that conflict ever involved American troops in a major way. The film then turns to the assassination, which seems surrounded by disturbing questions, most of which are quickly dismissed by the Warren Commission that was assembled to investigate the assassination, which declares that Lee Harvey Oswald (played in the film by Gary Oldman) acted entirely alone in killing the president, even though this conclusion requires the acceptance of a number of unlikely propositions and the dismissal of a number of seemingly important pieces of evidence.

Convinced that the truth of the assassination is being covered up, Garrison begins his own investigation, justified by the fact that numerous personages connected to the assassination, including Oswald, had New Orleans connections. Garrison encounters considerable opposition, including the bashing of his investigation in the media. His family receives threatening phone calls, and his family life is seriously disrupted as wife Liz (Sissy Spacek) urges him to give up the investigation. Most law enforcement agencies inexplicably refuse to cooperate with this investigation, Garrison's tax returns are audited by the IRS, and he is asked to resign from the National Guard. Meanwhile, several potentially important witnesses are killed under suspicious circumstances, and Garrison at one point narrowly escapes an attempt on his life. In the meantime, Martin Luther King and Robert Kennedy are assassinated as well, strengthening Garrison's conviction that sinister forces are afoot in America, perhaps leading toward a fascist takeover of the government.

Garrison pursues his case doggedly, despite the obstacles he encounters, finally bringing an indictment against New Orleans businessman Clay Shaw (Tommy Lee Jones) for conspiracy to kill Kennedy. Garrison presents a seemingly compelling case, though the judge refuses to allow him to introduce some of his most important evidence. When Shaw is acquitted of the charge, Garrison vows to continue the fight as the film ends. He would, however, never succeed in proving his case in court, though many of the questions he raised remain unanswered to this day. Seen by many as an irresponsible portrayal of an unproven theory as if it were fact, *JFK* was celebrated by many others as a powerful and important film that stimulated much-needed debate concerning the mysteries that still surround the assassination. On the other hand, some of the film's more ominous implications about the real nature of modern American society and the American political system have been largely ignored. Still, if the film's suspicious view of government as driven by dark forces well beyond the view of the electorate seriously calls into question many fundamental assumptions about American electoral democracy, that view is also very much in accord with much post-Watergate political cinema.

In its focus on the assassination of a president, *JFK* participates, if in a peripheral way, in a long line of films featuring American presidents, who are, after all, the superstars of American politics. To a large extent, such films had, before *JFK*, tended to treat presidents as heroic figures, focusing on such icons of American democracy as George Washington and Abraham Lincoln. Even during his lifetime, Kennedy himself had already been the subject of one such film when Leslie Martinson's *PT 109*, released just months before the assassination, detailed Kennedy's heroism in World War II. *PT 109* is typical of many films about presidents, in that, it focuses on a specific event rather than presenting a full-scale biopic of its central character. For example, numerous films about the Revolutionary War or the Civil War feature important appearances by George Washington and Abraham Lincoln.

In fact, there has been no major biopic proper about Washington, though the 1984 television miniseries *George Washington* (with Barry Bostwick in the title role) gives an account of Washington's life through the Revolutionary War, while the follow-up, *George Washington II: The Founding of a Nation* (1986), follows Washington through his presidency. Among other founding fathers, Benjamin Franklin has appeared in a number of films, including his own self-titled biographical television miniseries on CBS in 1974. Thomas Jefferson is the central figure in the Merchant-Ivory production *Jefferson in Paris* (1995) (with Nick Nolte in the title role). This film focuses on Jefferson's tenure in Paris as the American minister to France in the late 1780s, with the growing tensions that would lead to the French Revolution as a political background. However, the film is more interested in Jefferson's personal life than in politics, and *Jefferson in Paris* is primarily a love story detailing the beginning of the long romantic liaison between the widower Jefferson and his teenage slave, Sally Hemings (Thandie Newton)—a liaison the nature (and even existence) of which is still disputed by historical scholars. That Jefferson, both, owned slaves and campaigned against slavery is clear, though the film does not really take him to task for this obvious contradiction.

Lincoln comes in for even more extensive coverage in American film. One of the finest films based on American presidents is John Ford's *Young Mr. Lincoln* (1939), which, like *PT 109*, focuses on the younger years of a president-to-be. Strictly speaking, not an exploration of the workings of government, this film focuses on Abraham Lincoln during his days as a young lawyer in private practice rather than on his political career. Highly fictionalized, *Young Mr. Lincoln* is an unabashedly patriotic tribute to the young Lincoln as a paragon of wit, wisdom, and homespun craftiness. It features Henry Fonda in the title role, wearing heavy makeup that makes his face look remarkably like a young, unbearded version of the craggy visage we all know so well. It also includes several bits of American patriotic iconography, such as an Independence Day parade early in the film that even includes veterans of the Revolutionary War—thus providing a subtle link between Lincoln and the founding fathers. Finally, while the film focuses on Lincoln's younger days, before he became prominent in politics, it does include several hints of his future achievements, especially in a final scene in which he symbolically sets out to walk to the top of a hill.

In the film, Lincoln is just starting his law career when he finds himself defending two brothers from a backwoods family that reminds him very much of his own. Charged with murder, the brothers appear through most of the film to be guilty, so much so that, soon after the killings, they are nearly lynched by the townspeople of Springfield, Illinois, where Lincoln has just set up practice. Then, in a key moment, Lincoln intercedes, using a combination of courage, physical strength, folksy charm, and rhetorical skill to calm and disperse the mob. He then uses these same qualities to defend the two brothers in their murder trial. In addition, he uses his great deductive intelligence, to save the day by identifying the true murderer.

However much a celebration of Lincoln as an icon of American greatness, *Young Mr. Lincoln* is a complex film with moments of genuine darkness. The lynch-mob scene is the most obvious of these, reversing Capraesque populism to show a single great and good man overcoming the pettiness and viciousness of the common people. Lincoln's clownish performance in the trial, in which he pretends to be a simple-minded country bumpkin, is also more suggestive than it might first appear. There is never any doubt that Lincoln's aw-shucks act is just that, and it comes as no surprise that he ultimately wins the day. However, his performance suggests an element of showmanship that foreshadows his later political success, while at the same time indicating that even the great Lincoln had to be a showman in order to succeed.

Lincoln, of course, is one of the greatest (perhaps *the* greatest) figure in American political history, and he has often been featured on the screen. *Young Mr. Lincoln* was preceded by *Abraham Lincoln* (1930), the first sound film by legendary director D. W. Griffith (starring Walter Huston in the title role). It was also quickly followed in 1940 by *Abraham Lincoln in Illinois* (1940), a more extensive biopic that takes Lincoln up to his departure for the White House, though it still does not cover his presidency. Lincoln has figured in numerous films since then, though his life has probably been explored most fully in the 1988 television miniseries *Lincoln*, based on Gore Vidal's novelization of Lincoln's life. As of this writing, Lincoln is the central character in a project currently under development by Steven Spielberg, based on the biography by historian Doris Kearns Goodwin.

Henry King's *Wilson* (1944), now little known, was the first major full-scale presidential biopic. Focusing on President Woodrow Wilson, it is a lavish, big-budget production with the same producer (Darryl F. Zanuck) and screenwriter (Lamar Trotti) as *Young Mr. Lincoln*. Though not a box office success, it achieved some critical success, receiving ten Academy Award nominations, winning four, but losing in the important categories of best picture and best director, much to the frustration of Zanuck. *Wilson* is an impressive period piece that features elaborate sets and costumes that help to establish the film's historical setting. It is, however, rather ponderous and slow-moving as it traces the career of Woodrow Wilson (played by Alexander Knox) from 1909, when he left the presidency of Princeton University to enter politics, subsequently experiencing a meteoric rise that saw him become the governor of New Jersey in 1910 and the president of the United States in 1913. The film traces, though rather superficially, his presidential career, as he introduces a number of reforms while struggling to keep the United States out of World War I. Reelected in 1916 on a platform of staying out of the war, he nevertheless takes United States into the war in 1917 under circumstances that are, according to the film, beyond his control, forced by German provocations. The latter parts of the film are devoted to Wilson's central role in the peace negotiations that followed World War I, focusing especially on his devotion to the concept of the League of Nations, a concept that failed partly because the United States never entered the league. As a result of this refusal, Wilson leaves office at the end of the film a broken and defeated man, nearing death.

Wilson is weak as a historical epic, spending more time on the protagonist's private life than on the crucial historical events in which he was centrally involved. In fact, it is less interested in historical accuracy than in glorifying Wilson. As a result, Wilson in the film always looks good, while his critics and opponents either appear evil or do not appear at all. Most important, *Wilson* almost entirely elides the very real controversy that surrounded Wilson's reversal of policy on the U.S. participation in World War I. It dismisses criticism of the move as not worthy of consideration and leaves out altogether the important critique of that move on the Left, a critique that is captured in capsule form in the satirical biographical sketch of Wilson included in John Dos Passos's novel *1919* (1932), which depicts Wilson as a tool of big business.

However, there is a political message in the film, which in a number of subtle ways depicts Wilson as the predecessor of Franklin Roosevelt, so that its celebration of Wilson can be taken as an expression of support for Roosevelt's New Deal. Roosevelt's opponents, in fact, complained that the film was propaganda in support of Roosevelt's fourth term. Most centrally, the film's depiction of the controversy over the League of Nations represents a clear plea for the United States to learn from that episode and to pursue a more enlightened policy in support of world peace after World War II, which at the time of the film's release had turned strongly in favor of the Allies and already seemed to be nearing its final phases.

Roosevelt himself would become the subject of a major biographical film in *Sunrise at Campobello* (1960). Starring Ralph Bellamy in the lead role, *Sunrise* is largely a celebration of Roosevelt's strength and courage in overcoming polio to become a great national leader. The HBO made-for-TV film *Warm Springs* (2005) covers much of the same ground, but in a more dramatically effective way. The message here is that Roosevelt (Kenneth Branagh) rose to greatness not in spite of his infirmity, but because of it. By struggling to overcome polio and helping others to do the same, Roosevelt—once a privileged young dilettante—gains the strength, courage, and compassion that would make him one of the great presidents of the United States. In the meantime, to other made-for-TV films, *Franklin and Eleanor* (1976) and *Franklin and Eleanor: The White House Years* (1977), also provided coverage of the life of FDR, with emphasis on the important contributions made to his career by wife Eleanor.

Oliver Stone's underrated *Nixon* (1995) may be the finest work of cinematic art of all films about presidents. It is also one of the few attempts at a full-scale presidential film biography. Here, Lincoln is repeatedly identified as a hero and inspiration of the problematic title character (played by Anthony Hopkins), but Nixon and the honest, courageous Lincoln ultimately stand in sharp contrast to one another. The film begins with the 1972 break-in by White House operatives of the Democratic Party offices in the Watergate Hotel in Washington, D.C. The remainder of the film then centers on the aftermath of this break-in, leading to Nixon's resignation from office in disgrace. Along the way, Nixon's life and career are filled in via a series of flashbacks that together seek to explain what drove him both to become president and to make the mistakes that drove him from office. The film relates the expected problematic aspects of Nixon's career, such as his opportunistic rise to fame as a communist hunter and his escalation of the war in Vietnam (including the illegal invasion and bombing of Cambodia in the early 1970s). All in all, the film is surprisingly sympathetic to its protagonist. Stone's Nixon is brilliant and talented, but troubled and tormented, a man who seems as much a victim as a villain, an outsider who never quite fits in within the upper echelons of Americas power elite, even as president.

For one thing, Nixon is depicted as the product of a loveless childhood that was made even more difficult by the deaths of two brothers by tuberculosis. Nixon thus grows up craving approval, while at the same time feeling that anything and everything he has might be taken away at any moment. In the meantime, despite all of his wheeling and dealing, he is something of an innocent, frequently shocked as he learns more and more about the inner workings of power in America. Among other things, Nixon is haunted, after his defeat in the presidential election of 1960, by the specter of John F. Kennedy, who seemingly had everything Nixon lacked: a large and loving family with extensive connections in the corporate and political worlds, great personal wealth, good looks, charm, charisma, and a first-rate education. His feelings are summed up late in the film as he speaks to a portrait of Kennedy hanging in the White House: "When they look at you they see what they want to be; when they look at me they see what they are." Even Nixon's election to the presidency in 1968 is tainted because it is enabled by the assassination of Kennedy's young brother, Robert.

Nixon is troubled even more by the assassination of John Kennedy, partly because Nixon, while president, is constantly dogged by dark hints that he had better not go in certain directions (such as bringing an early end to the Vietnam War) or he might be next. There are also repeated hints that Nixon, while vice president in the 1950s, had been involved in a secret plot against Cuba that was inherited by Kennedy and might have ultimately led to the Kennedy assassination. Then, in one key scene, shortly before the November 1963 assassination, Nixon is approached by a group of wealthy right-wingers who are interested in having him run for the presidency again in 1964. When he declines, saying that no one could possibly defeat Kennedy in 1964, a Cuban American in the group ominously asks, "What if Kennedy doesn't run in '64?" especially as he himself had a vague awareness of the possibility of an assassination plot. Horrified by the obvious hint, Nixon rushes to report the conversation to FBI director J. Edgar Hoover. Hoover simply dismisses the report as inconsequential, with a clear suggestion that even he may in one way or another be in on the assassination plot.

Nixon is pervaded by an air of suspicion that sinister forces are at work in America, a motif already familiar from Stone's *JFK*. Here, however, this notion becomes especially poignant through the film's suggestion that Nixon, whatever other dastardly deeds he might have been capable of, was decidedly not a part of these sinister forces, even if they did sometimes use him as a pawn in order to achieve their purposes. All of this is summed up in a scene (based on an event that actually occurred) in which Nixon, alone and with no entourage, confronts a group of student dissidents at the Lincoln Memorial. When he suggests to them that even he does not have unlimited power to achieve things within the system, one of them suggests that he seems to view the system as a wild animal, out of control. He realizes she is right and, whisked away by his handlers back to a waiting limo, he staggers as if in a trance, realizing that the system—which he sums up as consisting of "the CIA, the Mafia, those Wall Street bastards"—is indeed like an uncontrollable beast that even the president cannot tame.

Ultimately, however, it is Nixon's own insecurity and paranoia that do him in, leading to the Watergate break-in and subsequent cover-up. The film ends as events surrounding the Watergate scandal spiral out of control, seemingly driving Nixon to the brink of madness as the pressure builds on his presidency. Eventually, in August 1974, he resigns from office (to prevent his almost certain removal by Congress), and we then see actual news footage of Nixon and wife Pat as they leave the White House and fly away by helicopter into retirement. Nixon was a much despised president, but there is no gloating in the film over his demise. Instead, his final downfall is treated as a tragedy, as the fall of a potentially great man due to his own inherent flaws and due to his inability to cope with certain forces that are larger than himself. In this, he resembles one of the great fallen men of American film, Charles Foster Kane, and *Nixon* in fact contains a number of allusions to *Citizen Kane*. The tragic element is further emphasized as the *Nixon* closes with actual news footage of Nixon's 1994 funeral, featuring speeches by then-president Bill Clinton and presidential hopeful Bob Dole.

Nixon is clear in its vision of a corrupt American system whose villains are not individuals but secret and sinister forces that transcend the power of any one person. In Niels Mueller's *The Assassination of Richard Nixon* (2004), set during the Watergate investigation of 1974, struggling salesman protagonist Sam Bicke (Sean Penn) comes to a similar diagnosis of the system. Having lost his wife and children and a series of jobs, Bicke concludes that his life is falling apart because "the whole system has a cancer" that makes it impossible for the little man to succeed. On the other hand, as his life and his mind become increasingly unraveled, Bicke begins to focus more and more on then-president Nixon (much in the spotlight due to Watergate) as the source of the cancer. He thus concocts a plot to hijack a plane and fly it into the White House, planning to kill Nixon in the process. Bicke, however, is himself killed in the attempt, and the plane he tries to hijack never gets off the ground.

Viewed through *Nixon*, Bicke's identification of Nixon as the key oppressor of the little man is highly ironic, given that Stone's protagonist, despite his successes, feels deep inside that he is a little man much like Bicke, buffeted by forces more powerful than himself. Indeed, one could argue that the title of the film reinforces this irony. It is, in fact, Bicke who is assassinated (he dies from a self-inflicted gunshot wound), so that the title in a sense conflates Bicke with Nixon. Bicke also bears more than a passing resemblance to Travis Bickle, the unhinged protagonist of Martin Scorsese's 1976 classic *Taxi Driver*, and Penn's Bicke even looks and talks a bit like Robert De Niro's Bickle. *Taxi Driver* was, in fact, probably an influence on the final product, though it should also be noted that

The Assassination of Richard Nixon is based on the true story of Samuel Byck (an apparent model for Bickle), who died in a real 1974 hijack/assassination attempt. Meanwhile, given the events of September 11, 2001, Bicke's plan to destroy a national monument by crashing into it with a hijacked plane has a special resonance for the post-9/11 audiences of *The Assassination of Richard Nixon.*

Nixon, predictably, given his unique tenure as president, has been a fascination of American film at least since Robert Altman's *Secret Honor* (1984), a one-man show in which Philip Baker Hall plays a solitary Nixon, descending into near madness while brooding and soliloquizing on his life and career. Altman's Nixon, like Stone's, is something of a tragic figure. The same cannot be said for the Nixon of Andrew Fleming's *Dick* (1999), a comic farce in which two teenage girls (played by Kirsten Dunst and Michelle Williams) accidentally stumble on incriminating information about the Watergate burglary. They then feed the information (becoming, of course, the "Deep Throat" of Watergate lore) to reporters Bob Woodward and Carl Bernstein (Will Ferrell and Bruce McCulloch) after becoming disgusted by Nixon's uncouth behavior (and cruelty to his dog Checkers). *Dick* essentially plays out as a comic follow-up to the taut Watergate drama *All the President's Men* (1976), making a ridiculous figure of Nixon (played by Dan Hedaya in a spot-on imitation), though it might also be noted that Woodward and Bernstein (among many others) are ridiculous figures here as well.

Collectively, the various Nixon films can be taken as an indication of the diminished nature of the American presidency by the 1990s. At the same time, this same sense that presidents were not what they used to be, fueled an interest in fantasy visions of idealized presidents beginning in that decade. For example, Roosevelt's successor, Harry S. Truman, is presented in a 1995 HBO made-for-television film as a common man of the people, honest and competent, but capable of moments of greatness when required. As such, it presents us with a picture of a fantasy president, standing in contrast to conniving Nixon. *Truman* (featuring Gary Sinise in the title role) is a competent, no-bells-and-whistles biography that eschews cinematic flourish in favor of simple storytelling. This approach makes the film seem a bit flat, but it is appropriate, given Truman's growing reputation at the time as an honest, no-nonsense politician (in contrast to common assumption that politicians of the 1990s were dishonest and self-serving). The film is also careful to work in all of the various well-known anecdotes about Truman, providing moments of recognition that enhance its verisimilitude. We see, for example, the famous "The Buck Stop Here" sign on Truman's desk, as well as the moment after Franklin Roosevelt's death when Truman, about to become the new president, asks Eleanor Roosevelt if there is anything he can do for her. She responds that she should rather be asking what she can do for him. "You're the one who is in trouble now," she says. We also see the famous moment after his victory in the 1948 presidential election when Truman holds up a premature newspaper headline announcing "DEWEY DEFEATS TRUMAN."

The 1990s also saw an increase in the production of films about fictional presidents, though these films are perhaps best read against a long legacy of fictional films about figures in American government. However, while the high stakes of presidential actions can make for effective drama, until the 1990s films about the process of government tended not to focus extensively on presidents, as if such figures were too sacrosanct to be fictionalized on film. Perhaps the best-known American film about the process of government that does not focus on the presidency is Frank Capra's *Mr. Smith Goes to Washington* (1939). One of the most beloved films of the American cinema, *Mr. Smith Goes to Washington* is the seemingly affirmative story of the triumph of one virtuous man over a corrupt political system. However, like much of Capra's work, the film has a dark edge, especially given that these evil forces in the film are essentially composed of the entire American political system. Indeed, the film suggests a basic cynicism toward the American political system (and the American media, which work, in the film, to support that system) of a kind that many Americans tend to think has only come about in the 1990s, or at least since Watergate.

Mr. Smith Goes to Washington begins after the death of a U.S. senator, leaving it up to Governor Hubert Hopper (Guy Kibbee) to appoint a replacement. Hopper is very much in the pocket of political boss Jim Taylor (Edward Arnold), but Taylor's choice for the new senator is so patently unpopular that Hopper balks and instead takes the advice of his own children and appoints Jefferson Smith (James Stewart), leader of the Boy Rangers (a version of the Boy Scouts), to the post. However, all seems well because Smith is a clear political naïf; he seems unlikely to cause much trouble in Washington, a crucial consideration given the fact that legislation of great importance to Taylor will soon come before the Senate.

However, Smith's naiveté includes a genuine belief in the principles of American democracy, as stated by figures such as George Washington, Thomas Jefferson, and Abraham Lincoln. He thus takes his new job ser-iously and refuses to be a mere puppet. With the help of his experienced secretary, Clarissa Saunders (Jean Arthur), he gradually begins to learn his way around Washington politics. When he discovers that a proposed federal dam project is a mere case of graft designed for Taylor's profit, Smith staunchly opposes the project, only to find that he himself is sud-denly accused of dishonesty. Moreover, he is shocked to find that his main accuser is the other senator of his own state, Joseph Payne (Claude Rains), an old-time friend of Smith's father and a man Smith has greatly admired.

All seems lost after an investigating committee, acting on forged evidence, recommends that Smith be expelled from the Senate. However, he takes the floor and begins a heroic filibuster to forestall his ouster, hoping that the truth can meanwhile come to the fore. But Taylor, who controls most of the media in their home state, makes sure that Smith's efforts are portrayed negatively in the press, meanwhile suppressing the efforts of Smith's supporters (mostly Boy Rangers) to get out the truth. Finally, the exhausted Smith collapses on the floor of the Senate, ending the filibuster. However, Payne, reminded of his own former idealism and of his former friendship with Smith's father, comes to the rescue and confesses his own involvement in Taylor's scams. Smith is cleared, Taylor's machinations are revealed, and Smith and Saunders, madly in love, prepare to live happily ever after together.

The obvious sentimentality of this typical Capra ending aside, *Mr. Smith Goes to Washington* clearly suggests that American politics are inescapably corrupt and that only an uncontaminated outsider can ever hope to bring integrity to the system. At the same time, the fact that Smith must be rescued at the end by Payne serves as a warning that lone individuals cannot really hope to overcome the system and that some help from the inside is required. That this help is in fact forthcoming adds a positive note to what might have been a cynical film indeed. The film is thus ultimately ambivalent about the American political system. Moreover, despite the celebration of individualism that runs through the film (and through all of Capra's work), it is in many ways ambivalent about the myth of American individualism, as well. The audience is encouraged to identify with the hero, who stands virtually alone against the world as an icon of individualism; at the same time, because Smith needs help from a powerful insider to succeed, viewers are subtly cautioned not to let their identification with him lead them to believe that they themselves could successfully stand against the establishment.

Mr. Smith Goes to Washington has remained a central work of the American cinema for more than sixty years, though its somewhat old-fashioned attitudes have sometimes made it the object of humor—as in animated television comedies such as *The Simpsons* and *Family Guy* that have based episodes on the film. In addition, the 1992 Eddie Murphy vehicle *The Distinguished Gentleman* is essentially a comic remake of *Mr. Smith Goes to Washington*—with a significant update in attitude. Here, Murphy plays Thomas Jefferson Johnson, a charming con man and petty criminal who manages to get himself elected to Congress in a scam after the sitting Congressman dies—while having sex with his mistress. However, once in Washington, Johnson discovers that his own questionable ethics are nothing in comparison to those of his fellow Congressmen, though he manages, with the help of a couple of insiders, to strike a few blows for the good before his own background is revealed and his political career is ended.

The Distinguished Gentleman is more cynical than *Mr. Smith Goes to Washington* in that, it takes corruption in government for granted, as a matter for jokes, rather than outrage. However, many earlier films take corruption in government for granted as well. For example, George Cukor's *Born Yesterday* (1950) features Broderick Crawford as millionaire junkman Harry Brock, whose business involves (among other things) government contracts. One character in the film is Congressman Norval Hedges (Larry Oliver) who has been bought and paid for by Brock, though the film makes little of the Brock-Hedges connection, seeming to take for granted that such corruption exists, even at the highest levels of government. Meanwhile, the film is essentially a romantic comedy that focuses on the attempts of the gruff and abusive Brock to educate his beautiful but uncultured fiancée, "Billie" Dawn (Judy Holliday), so that she can be more presentable in the high circles in which he now travels. In this sense, the film is a vague reworking of the central theme of George Bernard Shaw's play *Pygmalion,* made into the classic film *My Fair Lady* in 1964. Billie now stands in for Liza Doolittle, a role Holliday plays with an over-the-top zeal that is the highlight of the film. The Henry Higgins role, meanwhile, is played by bespectacled newspaper reporter Paul Verrall (William Holden), a sort of poor man's intellectual. Predictably, love blooms between Billie (who turns out to be highly intelligent) and Verrall, who in the end wins her away from Brock because he, unlike Brock learns to appreciate that Billie is much more than a stereotypical dumb blonde.

The matter-of-fact cynicism about politics exhibited by *Born Yesterday* makes it seem, thematically, almost like a film of the 1990s. It was thus a perfect candidate for a remake. Unfortunately, Luis Mandocki's 1993 version of the film pales in comparison to the original, partly because the performances of the new cast, headlined by Melanie Griffith as Billie, are flat and uninspired in relation to the superb original performances. Meanwhile, the political corruption theme of the remake remains secondary and does little to update the treatment of politics in the original film. Perhaps the most interesting aspect of the remake is that Hedges (now a senator) is played by actor/politician Fred Dalton Thompson, who, ironically, would himself be elected to the senate from Tennessee the year after the film was released.

Neither version of *Born Yesterday* seems particularly concerned about the political corruption that both accept as an inherent part of the American system, while *Mr. Smith Goes to Washington* seems confident that the system is fine if only the right individuals are elected to office. Other films have been even more optimistic about this possibility, suggesting that the responsibilities of high office can themselves have a positive transformative effect on those elected to serve. The prototype of such films is Gregory La Cava's *Gabriel over the White House* (1933), in which an entirely vicious and unscrupulous criminal manages to get himself elected president, but then becomes a noble leader once in office. In particular, he is inspired to do good by the influence of the angel of the film's title, with implications that the same angel might have inspired previous presidents, such as Abraham Lincoln. Ultimately, even if one interprets the angel allegorically, the film is a reassuring patriotic declaration, in the troubled times of the Depression, that God is on the American side and will not let the country go wrong. Less hokey and more ambivalent is Preston Sturges's *The Great McGinty* (1940), in which, support from a mob boss (Akim Tamiroff) helps street bum Dan McGinty (Brian Donlevy) to become the crooked mayor of a large city, then governor of the state. However, once in the governor's mansion, McGinty is humbled by the power of his new office and decides to go straight. However, in doing so, he must cross his powerful former backers that leads to his political downfall. He has to flee the country and his wholesome new wife and kids, whom he apparently now loves, though he acquired them for political purposes. He ends up working for the same boss (who also has to flee the country after he attempts to assassinate McGinty for turning against him) as a bartender in a "banana republic." The message here is clear: the responsibilities of high office might cause a crooked politician to go straight, but honesty does not pay, at least not in politics, though this message is carefully limited to state, rather than national politics, thus avoiding a declaration that might have been regarded as unpatriotic.

Other films have been even more cynical about the possibility of overcoming corruption in the political process. The prototype of such films is Robert Rossen's *All the King's Men* (1949), based on Robert Penn Warren's 1947 novel of the same title. Here, an honest and forthright young yokel by the name of Willie Stark (Broderick Crawford) finds himself stymied in his attempts to gain political office, but then rises to power as the governor of his state when he learns to play the political game, depicted here as a dirty game indeed. Anticipating Jack Stanton of *Primary Colors* (1998), Stark justifies the corruption of his campaign on the basis that his election will allow him to do good things in office. He does, in fact, accomplish a great deal, but he is ultimately unable to avoid using the same ruthless and dishonest tactics as governor that he had used as a candidate.

All the King's Men is loosely based on the career of Louisiana politician Huey Long, an interesting enough figure in American political history to have been the subject of two made-for-television films: *The Life and Assassination of the Kingfish* (1977, with Ed Asner as Long) and *Kingfish: A Story of Huey P. Long* (1995, with John Goodman in the title role). The former features a serious Long, focusing on the shooting and death of Long, with highlights of his life related as flashbacks; the latter depicts Long as more colorful, clownish figure, but dangerous when angered. Both strive to depict Long as the complex figure he was, and neither really takes a stand on whether he was a great man of the people or just a Southern-fried would-be American Hitler. In any case, Long rose from humble beginnings to become the governor of his state in 1928, at the young age of 34.

After one four-year term as governor, he was elected to the U.S. Senate, where he began to lay the groundwork for a 1936 presidential bid. He was, however, assassinated (under circumstances that remain murky to this day) in the halls of the Louisiana Capitol Building in 1935. He had just turned forty-two years. Long was a complex and enigmatic politician. A populist who consistently campaigned as an advocate for the common man, he was accused of cronyism and suspected of corruption, though not to the extent depicted in the film. His advocacy of educational reforms, public works projects, and social programs designed to redistribute American wealth and thus ease the burden of the Depression on the poor was felt by many to be too radical, though his populist platform made him a beloved figure among the people of his state to this day. Thus, in Harold Becker's *City Hall* (1996), idealistic political consultant (and deputy mayor of New York City) Kevin Calhoun (John Cusack) hails from Louisiana and frequently (and proudly) describes himself as coming from Huey Long country. Calhoun hopes to make New York mayor John Pappas (Al Pacino), whom he admires greatly, president some day. Ironically, it is political corruption in New York City that is the main subject of the film (and that ultimately derails Pappas's aspirations to higher office), while the Long-inspired Calhoun is presented as a paragon of virtue.

To many, Long's ideas often smacked of a sort of homegrown socialism, though his political enemies tended to try to compare him to the fascism that was emergent in Europe as he came to Washington. *All the King's Men,* however, barely addresses the question of Stark's ideology, concerning itself instead with his personal shortcomings. It begins with Stark as a semi-literate "hick" living in rural Kanoma County in his unidentified state. Fed up with the corruption of the local political machine, he runs for county treasurer as an anticorruption candidate, focusing on graft in the recent construction of a new school. Stark's campaign is crushed by the county's political bosses, who are not above employing violence and intimidation to prevent his election. Fed up with politics, he turns to the study of law, struggling and with the aid of wife Lucy to get through stacks of law books and eventually to get his degree. He then returns to local prominence when shoddy construction at a school causes an accident that kills and mangles a dozen children, demonstrating the validity of his earlier charges.

This new prominence brings Stark to the attention of the state's political bosses, who are concerned that their gubernatorial candidate is in trouble in the upcoming election because his opponent seems sure to carry the "hick" vote. They convince Stark to run for governor as a third-party candidate, hoping he will draw off enough of these rural votes to assure their candidate of election. Stark runs a spirited and impassioned campaign, especially after he realizes midway that he is being played for a stooge. In fact, he puts a real scare into the statewide machine, though he ultimately loses. Four years later, he returns as a seasoned politician, running a suspiciously well-financed campaign that sweeps him into the governor's mansion. He subsequently exercises unprecedented power while in office, but is dogged by rumors of bribery and corruption, while descending more and more into drinking and womanizing.

Stark is nearly undone when his adopted son Tom (John Derek) is involved in an auto accident that leads to the death of a young woman passenger. The young woman's father insists that Tom had been driving under the influence of alcohol at the time of the accident, but his public campaign to demand an investigation is cut short when he suddenly disappears. When the man is later found beaten to death, Judge Monte Stanton (Raymond Geenleaf) who had earlier resigned from Stark's cabinet to protest the corruption of the administration, leads a campaign to have Stark impeached. He is impeached, though Stanton is removed from the fray when he commits suicide after Stark digs up evidence of corruption early in the judge's own career. Stark, backed by strong popular support, manages to win in the subsequent impeachment trial in the state senate and to stay in office. Afterward, he addresses an adoring crowd of supporters on the steps of the state capitol, only to be assassinated immediately afterward by Dr. Adam Stanton (Sheppard Strudwick), judge Stanton's nephew, bringing his career to a sudden close.

The real Long's own apparent assassin was a Dr. Carl Weiss, also the nephew of a judge who was a political opponent of Long. Other aspects of *All the King's Men* mirror Long's career rather closely as well, though many do not. The film is a stinging indictment of the political process. Stark starts out as an honest man; he then finds that in order to succeed in politics, he must become dishonest. The absolute-power-corrupts-absolutely plot spirals downward from there, as Stark gains more and more power (dreaming even of the White House) and becomes more and more corrupt. On the other hand, the film is both superficial and inaccurate if taken literally as a portrayal of the career of Huey Long. The film and its message in fact suffer from that connection, which tends (given Long's unique place in American politics) to suggest that Stark's experience is unusual, either because his state is particularly corrupt or because he himself is particularly flawed and susceptible to corruption.

Under pressure from congressional investigators as a purported haven for communists, Hollywood tended to shy away from criticisms of the political system during the 1950s. Even John Ford's *The Last Hurrah*

(1958), a potential follow-up to *All the King's Men* that is critical of the growing power of money in American politics, treats its machine politician protagonist in a positive light. This protagonist is Frank Skeffington (Spencer Tracy), a big-city mayor who is preparing to run for his fifth term in office. Skeffington (whose career is based on that of flamboyant, longtime Boston mayor James Michael Curley) is the son of impoverished Irish immigrants; he has risen to the top through talent and hard work, and the film hints that he may have had to step on a few toes (or even broken a few heads) in order to do so. But he is a very effective mayor who genuinely works to improve the lives of the city's common people, though in doing so he has encountered powerful enemies among the city's patrician upper class. The city's Catholic Cardinal is also a professed political enemy (for reasons that are never specified), though the Irish Catholic Skeffington has long enjoyed strong support from the city's Catholic voters.

Early in the film, Skeffington acknowledges that his campaign style (which involves old-fashioned activities such as shaking hands and kissing babies) will soon be obsolete, to be replaced by media-based television and radio campaigns. But rather than adjust, he announces his intention to retire after one more term as mayor. Unfortunately, he tries to get one too many elections out of his old-fashioned campaigning style, and he loses the election that is portrayed in the film—to an opponent who has no ideas or opinions of his own, but who will clearly serve as a puppet of the powerful interests who finance his expensive television-based campaign.

This indication of the growing importance of the media in politics and the consequent increase in the cost of political campaigns is insightful; it is also almost prescient in its understanding that this change in the political landscape will put more and more power in the hands of the rich and privileged and make it increasingly difficult for a poor man such as Skeffington to rise to the top. There is also a suggestion that growing educational and economic opportunities mean that the truly talented members of the working class can probably find success in other fields more easily than in politics. Ultimately, however, the political commentary in this film is very low key. The focus is on Skeffington, whose rough-hewn rectitude (especially as conveyed by Tracy) makes him a very sympathetic protagonist. The film then ends on a sentimental note as Skeffington collapses from a heart attack and eventually dies in the wake of his electoral defeat—marking also the end of an era in American politics.

The next major American film to critique the political process was Otto Preminger's *Advise and Consent*, released in 1962. An inside look at the workings of the U.S. Senate, *Advise and Consent* is still widely regarded as one of the most important (and most realistic) films ever to have been made about American politics. The film begins as an ill and aging U.S. president (played by Franchot Tone) appoints former University of Chicago professor Robert Leffingwell (Henry Fonda) to replace the recently deceased secretary of state. Leffingwell, however, has offended numerous members of the senate during his more recent career in government, so the ratification of the nomination by the senate is anything but a foregone conclusion. The film shows the inside maneuvers that occur as Senate Majority Leader Robert Munson (Walter Pidgeon), a member of the president's party, attempts to steer the nomination through the senate, despite strong opposition led by South Carolina Senator Seabright Cooley (Charles Laughton), a wily old Southern politician with a grudge against Leffingwell.

Munson manages to get the nomination reviewed in a subcommittee chaired by Utah Senator Brigham Anderson (Don Murray), who is believed to be supportive of Leffingwell's nomination. Much of the film concerns the subsequent subcommittee hearings that get dirty when Cooley produces a witness who testifies that Leffingwell had been a member of the Communist Party during his days at the University of Chicago. The witness, Herbert Gelman (Burgess Meredith), also claims to have been a student of Leffingwell's and to have failed Leffingwell's class when he refused to participate in a communist cell of which Leffingwell was a member. Meredith's brief performance is brilliant, made more poignant by the fact that Meredith himself had been accused of communist sympathies by the House Un-American Activities Committee (HUAC), seriously curtailing his career in film through the 1950s. However, Gelman is still recovering from a nervous breakdown, and his testimony (which includes numerous inaccuracies and even apparent outright lies) is easily demolished by Leffingwell.

The problem for Leffingwell is that there is a grain of truth in Gelman's testimony. The nominee has never been a member of the Communist Party, but he did briefly participate in meetings of a communist group (attended even more briefly by Gelman) while in Chicago. When Cooley is able to find a witness to corroborate that fact, Leffingwell's nomination seems doomed. Surprisingly, however, the president stands behind the nominee. He is a dying man and he wants to go out with confidence that the secretary of state will continue the advances he has made in foreign policy during his term as president. Munson therefore agrees to continue to do what he can, though by this time Anderson is convinced that the nomination cannot go through.

By this time, however, someone has begun to blackmail Anderson with threats to reveal that he had been involved in a brief gay liaison while serving in the army in Hawaii during World War II. The identity of the blackmailer is never revealed, though there are hints that it might be Wyoming Senator Fred Van Ackerman (George Grizzard). An unscrupulous hatchet man who has been supporting the nomination in the hope of winning points with the powers-that-be that will further is own political career. Ultimately (after a quick trip to New York where he encounters his old lover in a gay bar, probably the first such bar to be shown in mainstream American film), Anderson commits suicide. The nomination then clears his subcommittee and moves on to the senate, where it receives a tie vote. Just as it looks as if Vice President Harley Hudson (Lew Ayres) is about to vote to break the tie in Leffingwell's favor, word comes that the president has just died, making Hudson president. As the film ends, Hudson declines to support the nomination, because he prefers to name his own secretary of state. Anderson has died and many have suffered—all for naught.

Fonda's understated performance as the studious Leffingwell makes it clear that the nominee is a good and thoughtful man who would probably be a fine secretary of state. The film as a whole, however, makes it clear that such qualifications are necessarily not enough in the sometimes rough world of Washington politics, where even a hint of minor youthful indiscretions (especially if they involved communism or homosexuality) can destroy lives and careers. But *Advise and Consent* is itself a good and thoughtful film that eschews easy answers to the questions it raises about the political process. Leffingwell is intelligent and well-meaning, but he has his flaws. He does, for example, lie during the conformation process, and he is almost brutal in his cross-examination of Gelman—though it is clear that he is virtually forced into these moves by the process itself. Cooley, on the other hand, is almost the opposite: seemingly mean, spiteful, and vindictive, he evolves into a more positive figure who apparently believes he is doing the right thing. Finally, Leffingwell's strongest supporter in the senate is Van Ackerman, probably the most negative character in the entire film, making it clear that Washington politics can seldom be separated into simple good vs. bad oppositions.

Nevertheless, *Advise and Consent* is clear in its contempt for the red-baiting, anticommunist purges of the 1950s, and it should be noted that Preminger was one of the directors most responsible for breaking the associated Hollywood blacklist. Preminger's film *Exodus* (1960) represented one of the first major challenges to the blacklist by openly crediting Dalton Trumbo (a member of the Hollywood Ten) as its screenwriter, while, in addition to Meredith, *Advise and Consent* features blacklisted actor Will Geer (as the Senate Minority Leader) in his first Hollywood film since going on the blacklist in 1951. But the content of *Advise and Consent* suggests, among other things, that the anticommunist hysteria of the 1950s (surely one of the ugliest episodes in American political history) was not entirely a thing of the past in 1962.

Advise and Consent directly anticipates *The Best Man* (1964), which involves many of the same themes and even stars Fonda as the Secretary of State. Meanwhile, Rod Lurie's *The Contender* (2000) is in many ways an update of *Advise and Consent* in that it also focuses on congressional review of a presidential appointment. However, by the time of *The Contender* American politics has moved beyond the destructive Cold War paranoia about communism that is central to *Advise and Consent.* Instead, the concern with sexual conduct that serves as a sort of sidebar to the Preminger film has now taken center stage, with the accompanying suggestion that in some ways American politics has gotten even meaner and pettier in the four decades between the two films. The echoes of the spiteful impeachment of President Bill Clinton over his involvement with Monica Lewinsky are quite clear here.

In *The Contender*, Democratic President Jackson Evans (Jeff Bridges) is in the middle of his second term in office and thus nearing the end of his presidency. The vice president has recently died, and Evans feels that he has a chance to cement his legacy through his appointment of a successor. Accordingly, he tabs Ohio Democratic senator Laine Hanson (Joan Allen) for the job, even though another leading contender, Virginia governor Jack Hathaway (William Peterson) has recently made headlines for heroically attempting (though unsuccessfully) the rescue of a woman whose car ran off a bridge. From this point, however, politics rears its ugly head, and the confirmation process very quickly gets dirty. The congressional committee charged with reviewing the appointment is headed by one Sheldon Runyon (Gary Oldman), a sanctimonious Republican with a grudge against Evans, who originally beat him out for the presidency. Runyon, aided by earnest freshman Democratic congressman Reginald Webster (Christian Slater), uncovers apparent evidence (including photos) of Hanson's participation in a frat house orgy when she was a freshman in college, then endeavors to use that evidence to block the nomination.

Confronted with the evidence in a committee hearing, Hanson does not deny her involvement in the frat-party orgy, but instead steadfastly refuses to comment on the allegation on the grounds that it is inappropriate for the committee to be asking questions about such personal matters. This is especially the case because Hanson knows evidence of such youthful indiscretions would be taken far less seriously were she a man, and she feels that it is important to stand on principle against this kind of double standard, even if it wrecks her chance to become the first woman vice president (and potentially president). As she herself puts it late in the film, "Principles only mean something when you stick to them when it's inconvenient."

Things get nastier and nastier as the hearings proceed, while Runyon becomes a truly sinister figure of all that is wrong with American politics, partly because he is not actually all bad and has a certain humanity that prevents him from becoming a mere caricature. He seems to believe what he is saying when he hammers Hanson for her liberal stance on such issues as abortion rights, going so far as to call her a child murderer. For her own part, Hanson is given evidence that Runyon's own wife had an abortion twenty years earlier, but decides to stay on the high road and refuses to use the information. Runyon, meanwhile, maneuvers behind the scenes with Hathaway, his own preferred candidate for the office. Perhaps surprisingly, Evans sticks by Hanson through it all, even though she refuses to discuss the allegations about her past sexual conduct even with him. Ultimately, Evans seems to give in and agrees to switch to Hathaway, but only if Runyon gives Hathaway such a strong public endorsement that it will be impossible for him to oppose Hathaway's nomination that would cause even more embarrassment for the president. Once that statement has been made, Evans (in a development that may be just a bit *too* convenient) reveals evidence that Hathaway actually paid the woman to drive off the bridge so that he could save her and become a hero. Hathaway is arrested for negligent homicide, and Runyon's judgment is thrown seriously into question.

Nevertheless, tired of the ugliness of the confirmation hearings (which include revelations that she had an affair with her current husband when he was still married to her then best friend), Hanson finally asks Evans to withdraw her name from consideration for the nomination. Evans then goes before Congress, where he surprises even Hanson by announcing that he refuses to withdraw her name and excoriating the Congress for its treatment of her. Addressing Runyon directly, he pointedly asks, "Have you no decency, sir?" Having thus linked Runyon to the discredited Senator Joseph McCarthy (whose notorious reign of anticommunist terror quickly came to an end after he was asked the same question by U.S. army attorney general Joseph Welch in a 1954 hearing), Evans then demands an immediate roll call vote on Hanson's nomination so that each member of Congress will have to stand up before the American people (in whose decency he expresses great confidence) and take a position.

The film ends here, though there is a clear implication that Hanson will be confirmed. By this point, *The Contender* has become a surprisingly complex film. Runyon has become a thorough villain, despite the fact that he believes in what he is doing. Evans, on the other hand, comes off as a man of integrity and as a genuinely courageous leader, even if he is also a savvy politician who is willing and able to play hardball, despite his affable public image. Evans may be more interested in beating Runyon and in furthering his own legacy than in helping women, but he nevertheless does the right thing when the chips are down. Meanwhile, his statement of faith in the American people almost looks back to the populism of a Capra. The real hero of the film, though, is Hanson who shows such integrity in refusing to answer Runyon's inappropriate charges—especially after we learn late in the film that the charges are not even true and that she did not, in fact, participate in the orgy. She is thus genuinely standing on the principle that women appointees should not be subjected to questioning such as Runyon's and that she must avoid setting a precedent that would make such questioning seem a normal part of the process in the future. One cannot help but wonder, however, if this unflinching integrity would really serve her well in the White House.

There are, *The Contender* suggests, still good people in politics—and these people even stand a chance of rising to the top of the American government, while shifty and unscrupulous operators such as Runyon (or McCarthy) will ultimately be undone by their own ambition and ruthlessness. As part of his final inspirational speech, Evans quotes Napoleon to the effect that "to get power you need to display absolute pettiness; to exercise power you need to show true greatness." Lurie's film, to an extent, challenges this notion as, by the end of the film, Hanson seems on her way to becoming the first woman vice president of the United States, despite the fact that she staunchly maintains her integrity and refuses to play petty political games. On the other hand, part of her success can be attributed to the fact that Evans plays these games for her, and *The Contender* gives us a look at an American president who provides high-minded leadership in public but is not above Machiavellian manipulations behind the scenes.

Evans is nevertheless an admirable figure, and his depiction in *The Contender* topped off a decade of films that presented a variety of fantasy visions of the American president, though some of these paradoxically demythologized the presidency itself. In Peter Segal's action comedy *My Fellow Americans* (1996), both the president and vice president are characterized as unscrupulous felons, but their nefarious plots are thwarted by honest former presidents Russell Kramer and Matt Douglas (played by Jack Lemmon and James Garner, respectively), who manage to work together despite their political differences to remove the two criminals from office. In the process, Kramer and Douglas learn important (and humbling) lessons about the effects of their policies on ordinary citizens, and even decide to run together on the same ticket in an effort to retake the White House, though at the end of the film they are still squabbling over who will be the candidate for president and who for vice president. *My Fellow Americans* participated in a sequence of cantankerous-old-man comedies that were popular in the decade, ranging from *Grumpy Old Men* (1993), which also featured Lemmon, to *Space Cowboys* (2000), which also featured Garner. But it also enacted the fantasy of powerful politicians learning wisdom from the common folk and then leaping into action to put that new wisdom to use for the common good.

Ivan Reitman's *Dave* (1993) is a romantic comedy that imagines one of the common folk suddenly thrust into the White House directly—and acquitting himself quite well there. Actually, the film begins with a rather cynical view of politics, with president Bill Mitchell (Kevin Kline) shown as a self-serving jerk who spends much of his time philandering with young female members of the White House staff. To make matters worse, Mitchell's distraction by his extracurricular activities means that his sinister Chief of Staff Bob Alexander (Frank Langella), who has designs on ascending to the presidency himself, is left with much of the responsibility of actually running the country. Meanwhile, to help cover up the president's infidelities, he and his staff decide to hire a look-alike to divert attention from the real president.

This position is filled by struggling temp agency owner Dave Kovic (also Kline), a dead ringer for the president who already supplements his income by making appearances as a Mitchell impersonator in venues such as car dealerships. However, Kovic's relatively harmless attempts to draw the press away from the real Mitchell suddenly become more serious after the president suffers a stroke while having sex with a White House staffer (played by Laura Linney). As the president lies in a coma, Alexander decides to cover up his condition by having Kovic pose as Mitchell full-time. In the meantime, he concocts a plot to frame the virtuous vice president, Gary Nance (Ben Kingsley), forcing him to resign. Kovic/Mitchell will then appoint Alexander as the new vice president, after which it will be announced that the president has suffered a decapacitating stroke, allowed Alexander to ascend to the presidency.

Possibly named for secretary of state Alexander Haig (who famously claimed to be "in control" at the White House after the 1981 assassination attempt on President Ronald Reagan and who in fact served as the White House Chief of State at the end of the Nixon presidency), Alexander assumes that the good-natured Kovic will be easily manipulated. However, as Alexander's machinations become more and more ominous, Kovic rebels, eventually showing strength by demanding Alexander's resignation. Kovic, seeming to gain substance from the office he now holds, even introduces important new jobs legislation, before bowing out by faking his own stroke, then switching back with the real Mitchell in the ambulance on the way to the hospital. By this time he has also fallen in love with beautiful first lady Ellen Mitchell (Sigourney Weaver), long estranged from her husband due to his philandering. As the film ends, Mitchell has died, Nance has become president, and Kovic has decided to enter local politics in Washington, D.C. And, needless to say (this being a Hollywood comedy), he and Ellen seem headed for a happy life together.

Dave enacts the common everyman fantasy of surely being able to run the country better than the actual president. If it thus brought the presidency down to earth, Roland Emmerich's science-fiction action flick *Independence Day* (1996) went in the other direction, giving us a larger-than-life president whose purview extends to outer space. Here, an alien invasion of the earth is defeated through the leadership of exemplary American president Thomas J. Whitmore (Bill Pullman), a former war hero who had served as a fighter pilot in the 1991 Gulf War. Especially in the latter part of the film, President Whitmore's rhetoric of defiance strongly anticipates the "bring it on" rhetoric of the Bush administration's "war" on terrorism. Moreover, the film essentially endorses this rhetoric, depicting Whitmore's turn from compromising politician to staunch military commander as a decidedly positive development that makes Whitmore the kind of strong leader that many Americans want. Whitmore—a young, handsome, charismatic former war hero—is a President much more in the mold of John Kennedy than of either Clinton or Bush. Thus, in terms of the film's function as an Americanist fantasy, one might also consider Whitmore as a kind of fantasy President. Not only does he provide strong and dramatic leadership in a terrible national crisis, but he is also depicted (in contrast to the popular perception of politicians in the 1990s) as a figure of absolute virtue, a dedicated family man who is, we are reminded at least twice in the film, virtually incapable of telling a lie. From this point of view, it is even possible to see his initial tendency toward political compromise as a virtue, his shift to a more hawkish attitude in the wake of the alien attacks simply indicating the way in which he is able to change his leadership style to match the situation at hand.

It is also crucial to the film that Whitmore is able to provide strong leadership not only for the United States but for the world too. Remarkably, once he gives the go-ahead for a plan to lower the alien shields via a computer virus, Whitmore has no trouble at all in eliciting the complete cooperation of military forces around the globe, even with the global communications system on the fritz. In fact, he seems to be able to give instructions directly to troops in the field, even without going through their governments. The American government is, in fact, the only one we see in the film, making it the de facto government of the world. Much of the value of the film as an Americanist fantasy, then, comes from its vision of the United States as the unquestioned leader of the entire world, able to make policies that all other nations will follow without question or resentment. And rightly so, because—in this film at least—American leadership saves the day.

The immediate response of military forces around the world to Whitmore's call to action is not very realistic, even in such a crisis, but then *Independence Day* is not a film that is much concerned with realism. This is a film designed to entertain with spectacular action and touching moments of human emotional contact; as such, it is not designed to stand up to a great deal of thoughtful scrutiny. Nevertheless, there is one fascinating element of the film that should be closely analyzed, and that is the contradictory nature of its self-conscious effort to serve as an American national allegory. The Americans of the film are completely outgunned, faced with a foe far superior to them in firepower and technological know-how. As such, the film is perfectly in keeping with what is widely regarded as a typical American tendency to root for the underdog. The problem, of course, is that in the global political situation of the real world, the United States is not an underdog, but the most powerful nation on the planet. In the real world of geopolitics, the United States does not occupy the position of underdog as depicted in the film. Instead, the real United States is very much in the position occupied in the film by the alien invaders, facing numerous smaller nations around the globe from a position of vast military and technological superiority—and often using force to impose its will on smaller and less powerful nations.

Wolfgang Petersen's *Air Force One* (1997) joined the fantasy sweepstakes with its vision of a tough, action-hero president (played by Harrison Ford) who personally defeats a gang of cartoonishly evil Russian hijackers. Actually, the hijackers are described as ultranationalist neocommunist Russians from Kazahkstan—which shows just how muddled and basically unintelligent this film really is. On the other hand, the film (apparently unintentionally) introduces a severe complication into its seemingly simplistic good vs. evil vision: the hijackers are acting in response to a raid by U.S. commandos in which their own leader was "apprehended" and taken away to Russia, potentially suggesting that the good guys and bad guys in this film are basically doing pretty much the same thing. But the opposition between Ford's staunchly virtuous president (a former Medal of Honor winner who fights to protect both family and country) and Gary Oldman's fanatical terrorist leader is probably far too stark to allow this complication to occur to very many viewers of the film.

The prominence of such heroic fictional presidents in American film in the 1990s suggests a nostalgia for the days of the imperial presidency, when real presidents appeared to be larger-than-life figures. Those days, however, were over, opening up the presidency for treatment in all sorts of films, many of which specifically revolved around the diminished nature of the office. For example, members of the first family became the focus of screen comedy in films such as *Guarding Tess* (1994), *Chasing Liberty* (2004), *First Daughter* (2004), though the first of these (a sort of comic follow-up to the 1993 thriller *In the Line of Fire*) contains thriller elements as well. Several other thrillers of the 1990s revolved around corruption in high places, including the White House. These thrillers thus looked back to the paranoid political thrillers of the 1970s, but also showed a distinctly 1990s form of cynicism toward government and fascination with conspiracy (two elements perhaps best represented in the American culture of the 1990s in the popular television series *The X-Files*).

The action-thriller plot of Dwight Little's *Murder at 1600* (1997) revolves around the murder of a young White House staffer who had been having an affair with the president's son—and possibly simultaneously with the president himself. The success of this plot depends not only on the audience's acceptance that such shenanigans go on in the White House (the Clinton-Lewinsky scandal is again an obvious backdrop), but also on its ability to believe that President Jack Neil (Ronny Cox) and the secret service might have been involved in the murder and subsequent cover-up. As it turns out, Washington, D.C., homicide detective Harlan Regis (Wesley Snipes) and secret service agent Nina Chance (Diane Lane) are able to unravel the mystery and reveal that the president and the secret service are innocent. Instead, the entire scheme was the work of the president's national security advisor, Alvin Jordan (Alan Alda), who had hoped (because of their disagreements over foreign policy) to discredit the president and force him to resign. With Jordan's plot foiled (and Jordan himself killed by secret service agents when he tries to shoot the president as a last resort), the film then ends with an extra cynical twist when the White House covers up the whole plot for fear it will reflect badly on Neil's presidency.

In *Absolute Power* (1997), cat burglar Luther Whitney (played by Eastwood, who also directs) breaks into the palatial home of wealthy magnate Walter Sullivan (E. G. Marshall). While gathering jewels and cash from Sullivan's private vault, he witnesses an adulterous encounter between the young and beautiful Mrs. Sullivan (Melora Hardin) and Allen Richmond (Gene Hackman), the president of the United States. When the rough sex between Richmond and Mrs. Sullivan turns ugly, two secret service agents burst in, shooting and killing the woman. The White House, under the leadership of sinister Chief of Staff Gloria Russell (Judy Davis) naturally (at least this film seems to assume that it is natural) attempts to cover up the whole matter and, eventually, murder Whitney when they realize he had been a witness. Whitney, however, triumphs. Both secret service agents wind up dead, while Russell is arrested. Richmond is killed by Sullivan, but manages to make it look like a suicide. And Whitney is reunited with his long-estranged daughter Kate (Laura Linney).

In addition to such fantasy films and thrillers, Rob Reiner's *The American President* (1995) showed a turn toward unprecedented realism in the depiction of the day-to-day activities of the president, even if the president himself remains something of an idealized figure. Here, Michael Douglas stars as President Andrew Shepherd, a virtuous and well-intentioned leader who has somewhat lost his way, allowing his upcoming reelection campaign to take precedence over his own political principles. Shepherd is a widower whose wife died before his election to the presidency, a fact that seems to have contributed to his election by gaining him a certain amount of sympathy from the voters. This sympathy runs out, however, when the lonely president meets and falls in love with Sydney Ellen Wade (Annette Bening), a high-powered Washington lobbyist working for a liberal environmentalist organization. The relationship between Shepherd and Wade becomes big news, especially after Senator Bob Rumson (Richard Dreyfuss), an unscrupulous rival in the opposing party, tries to boost his own campaign for the presidency by suggesting that the affair between Shepherd and Wade is immoral and inappropriate. Rumson's attempt, however petty, is highly successful, especially after he unearths a thirteen-year-old photograph of Wade participating in a demonstration in which an American flag was burned in protest of the failure of the U.S. government to take strong action to try to end the brutally racist practice of apartheid in South Africa.

Shepherd attempts to ignore Rumson's charges, not wishing to dignify them with a response. Instead, he concentrates on his own efforts to get Congress to pass a comprehensive new crime bill that he hopes will be the lynchpin of his reelection campaign. Unfortunately, he has had to make so many compromises to ensure passage of the bill that it now lacks most of its original power that included strict new gun control legislation. Even at that, Shepherd is forced, in order to get his crime bill passed, to make a political deal that leads to the defeat of an important piece of environmental legislation for which Wade has worked long and hard. This last move leads to the seeming end of Shepherd's relationship with Wade, a development that causes him to step back and look long and hard at the extent to which he is betraying his own principles in his quest for reelection. In response, he appears at a news conference at which he finally answers Rumson's sniveling charges, while at the same time announcing his new determination to use all of the power of the presidency to work to pass a crime bill restored to its original power as well as the environmental bill to reduce carbon emissions. As the film ends, Shepherd is newly energized as a political leader—and (of course) restored to the arms of the idealistic Wade, who realizes he has now become a man she can respect and admire, as well as love. Even the president's professional staffers, led by White House Chief of Staff A. J. MacInerney (Martin Sheen), are reenergized, seeming suddenly to remind why they had originally wanted to get into politics in the first place.

Though the relationship between Shepherd and Wade is central to the plot of *The American President*, the film is anything but a romantic comedy. It shows the president making difficult decisions and dealing with complex issues in conjunction with his staff. It also provides a powerful reminder that, however unique his position, the president of the United States is still a human being. He is, however, a very special human being in a difficult position that challenges his humanity. For one thing, he must sometimes order actions that lead to the deaths of innocent people.

When he authorizes the bombing of a site in Libya in retaliation to the Libyan bombing of a U.S.-built defense facility in Israel, Shepherd is intensely aware that the action is more than symbolic and that innocent Libyans (who had nothing to do with the attack on Israel) are likely to be killed. One of the most interesting aspects of *The American President* is the way in which Shepherd's courtship of Wade is made difficult by his position—not just because so many eyes are watching, but because he is accustomed to dealing with the outside world only through the mediation of his staff. Thus, when he wants to order flowers to be sent to Wade, he decides to make the call himself in order to make it more personal. He has no idea how to go about it, however, and even when he finally reaches a florist, he discovers that he has left all his credit cards back in his home state of Wisconsin. He also discovers that he is unable to convince the florist that he is really Andrew Shepard: she concludes that he is a crank caller.

The American President was remarkable at the time for the extent to which it explored the inside workings of the White House, though this aspect of the film would eventually be eclipsed by *The West Wing*, a popular and widely acclaimed television series that ran on NBC from 1999 to 2006. *The West Wing* was created and largely written (in its first four seasons) by Aaron Sorkin, who had written the screenplay for *The American President*, and the family relationship between the film and series is obvious. *The West Wing*, centering in its first seasons on the administration of President Josiah Bartlet (Martin Sheen), presents us with a president who is both idealized (at least from a liberal point of view) and humanized. Bartlet is a brilliant man, a winner of the Nobel Prize in Economics. He is also honest, erudite, and compassionate, though these qualities do not prevent him from being a canny politician who has never lost an election in his rise from economics professor, to congressman, to governor of New Hampshire, to the presidency. He seems to be a sort of compendium who combines the best characteristics of several previous Democratic presidents, especially Franklin Roosevelt, John Kennedy, and Bill Clinton. But Bartlet is also a very human character. He is absentminded and physically frail, suffering secretly from multiple sclerosis, the revelation of which leads to a public scandal in the second and third seasons of the show. He loves his wife and young-adult daughter very much and is intensely loyal to those who work for him, though his strong personal feelings for his family and his staff sometimes get in the way of his ability to make tough decisions.

This staff is, in fact, the heart of the show, and brilliant young staffer Sam Seaborn (played by Rob Lowe) was originally envisioned as the lead character in the series. However, the show very quickly became an ensemble piece in which several other staffers were equally important, while Bartlet himself became a more prominent character than had originally been envisioned. One of the keys to the success of *The West Wing* is the extent to which the White House functions in the series as a sort of idealized workplace, where gifted and talented people work hard at important jobs, meanwhile providing each other with extraordinary support and encouragement. However, many felt that the show declined dramatically after Sorkin departed at the end of the fourth season, leading to more emphasis on dramatic plots rather than the personal interactions of the staff. By the end of the seventh season, Bartlet had served out his two terms in office, and his successor, Congressman Matt Santos (Jimmy Smits) had been elected the first Hispanic president. But declining ratings also led to the cancellation of the show before Santos's term in office ever got underway.

The West Wing has been widely praised for the realism of its behind-the-scenes depiction of the day-to-day activities of the president and his staff, a characteristic that was enhanced by the presence of several former White House staffers as technical advisors on the program. An inside look at a different aspect of political life in Washington can be found in the HBO television series *K Street* (2003), from producers George Clooney and Steven Soderbergh. Named for a Washington, D.C., street that is home to numerous lobbying and political consulting firms, the series follows a new such firm (Bergstrom Lowell) as it struggles to get a foothold in the cutthroat world of Washington politics. Featuring largely improvised dialogue and shot in a quasi-documentary style that is reminiscent of HBO's earlier *Tanner '88*, the series gains realism from the fact that its fictional characters, headed by Bergstrom Lowell operatives Maggie Morris (Mary McCormack) and Tommy Flannegan (John Slattery), interact extensively with real-world political figures. It gains its ultimate realism, however, from the fact that well-known political consultants James Carville and Mary Matalin play themselves as the leading figures in the firm of Bergstrom Lowell.

The engagement of *K Street* with real-world Washington politics was made even more intense by the fact that the show generally aired within ten days of taping, allowing it to cover extremely current events, almost in the mode of a weekly news program. Sometimes, the show even impacted current events. For example, the very first episode (originally aired on September 14, 2003) features a scene in which Carville and Paul Begala (another former Clinton advisor) help Vermont governor and presidential candidate Howard Dean prepare for an upcoming debate with other Democratic presidential hopefuls. Given that the debate is sponsored by the Congressional Black Caucus, Carville anticipates that Dean will be asked about his ability to relate to black constituents given the very small number of African Americans who live in his home state. He suggests that Dean respond to such a question by pointing out that living in a state with numerous black residents does not guarantee an ability to relate to them.

"Otherwise," Carville tells Dean to say, "Trent Lott would be Martin Luther King." When the actual debate occurs (the real debate occurred on September 9), Dean does use the line, which gets a big laugh. In the actual presidential campaign, Dean used this quip repeatedly, indicating the blurring of the line between fiction and reality that is the distinguishing feature of *K Street*.

The realistic day-to-day political drama provided by the operations of the firm were apparently intended to provide the heart of the program, though the principal plot strand of the series has to do with an FBI investigation of the firm, primarily because of its dealings with the Center for Middle East Progress, a somewhat mysterious entity whose apparent function is to promote a better image of the Arab Middle East in the United States. Indeed, as the first (and only) season ends, Bergstrom Lowell has been effectively shut down by this investigation. *K Street* is also marked by numerous subplots, most of which are never resolved, partly because the series was canceled after only ten episodes. To an extent, however, this open-ended narrative complexity is appropriate, in that it mirrors the complex and confusing world of Washington politics. On the other hand, many of these plots, which revolve around such motifs as Morris's lesbian love affair and Flannegan's penchant for pornography and prostitutes, seem to have been conceived not for realism but in an effort to add drama to the show and to attract a larger viewing audience. Chief among the narrative elements that seem designed to spice up the show include the presence of the mysterious Francisco Dupré (Roger Guenveur Smith), who is hired by the firm in the first episode at the behest of the firm's principal investor, Richard Bergstrom (Elliott Gould). We never quite learn who Dupré is or what his motivations are. The eccentric (and perhaps insane) Bergstrom, meanwhile, stays holed up in his Brooklyn apartment throughout the run of the series, repeatedly watching the 1945 film *Mildred Pierce* on a small television set. However, as the last episode ends and with the firm shut down, Bergstrom inexplicably arrives at the airport in Washington, D.C., on a mission whose purpose is never revealed.

There are vague suggestions in *K Street* that the FBI investigation of Bergstrom Lowell may be partly a politically motivated witch hunt. There is, of course, a legacy of such witch hunts in Washington, the most recent of which involved the impeachment of President Bill Clinton for a minor sexual peccadillo. The most important of these overblown, opportunistic investigations, of course, involved the congressional investigations of communist activity in the United States in the late 1940s and 1950s. These investigations were aimed first and foremost at the government itself, though the Hollywood industry itself was also a central target. It is not surprising, then, that these investigations had a major impact on American film, a phenomenon that is explored in the next chapter.

CHAPTER 3

Communism, Anticommunism, and the Blacklist: McCarthyism and American Film

N o account of American political film can be complete without a discussion of the tremendous impact of the Cold War on American film (and American society) from 1945 to 1990. In many ways, the Cold War and related phenomena were the central facts of American political life for most of the second half of the twentieth century. It is thus not surprising that many American films have dealt with these phenomena in one way or another. However, the relationship between the Cold War and American film was significantly complicated from the late 1940s to the mid-1960s because much of the anticommunist hysteria of that period was directed at Hollywood itself. This phenomenon significantly impacted the kinds of films that were made in Hollywood during that period, including films that deal with the international politics of the Cold War itself. In addition, a number of American films either react to or specifically deal with the anticommunist purges that swept Hollywood at the peak of the Cold War.

Beginning with a series of hearings before the HUAC in the late 1940s, Hollywood was identified as a major haven for communists and communist sympathizers, not so much because the charge was true as it was sensational and drew tremendous publicity to the anticommunist cause. In addition, Hollywood had some of the most progressive labor unions in America, and the attempt to link Hollywood labor activism to communism was part of a broader effort in the 1940s and 1950s to roll back the advances made by American organized labor in the 1930s. Playwright and screenwriter Lillian Hellman has entitled her memoir of this period in Hollywood history *Scoundrel Time* (Little, Brown, 1976), indicating that the investigation into Hollywood was reprehensible—but also suggesting that Hollywood's reaction to the HUAC investigations was itself less than admirable. For one thing, many individuals who were called before the committee decided to cooperate and even to inform against friends and associates in order to get themselves off the hook. For another, rather than fighting the trumped-up charges, the Hollywood studios largely bowed to them, proving their "loyalty" to America by blacklisting Hellman and more than 300 other screenwriters, directors, producers, and actors who came under suspicion in the investigations, even if no charges against these individuals were ever proved.

Central to the anticommunist purges that swept Hollywood, especially in the 1950s, was the case of the Hollywood Ten, a group of writers, directors, and producers (including Alvah Bessie, Herbert Biberman, Lester Cole, Edward Dmytryk, Ring Lardner, Jr., Howard Lawson, Albert Maltz, Samuel Ornitz, Adrian Scott, and Dalton Trumbo) that was called to testify before HUAC in 1947. As detailed in the 1976 documentary film *Hollywood on Trial*, these individuals refused to cooperate with HUAC, feeling that the committee's questions about their political beliefs represented an illegal violation of their constitutional rights as Americans. They were subsequently charged with contempt of Congress, arrested, and sent to federal prison. Ironically, Cole and Lardner shared their term in Danbury Federal Prison with John Parnell Thomas, the former HUAC chair who had spearheaded the investigations into Hollywood, but was subsequently convicted of fraud.

Hollywood on Trial also details the opportunistic reaction of Hollywood's right wing to the climate of fear and intimidation provoked by the HUAC investigations and the subsequent blacklist. In this sense, the film's principal villain is Ronald Reagan, whose various filmed comments endorsing the purges and blacklist reveal an opportunistic political savvy that would later propel him to the presidency. The documentary also notes that, during this period, Hollywood produced a number of rather outrageous anticommunist films—including R. G. Springsteen's *The Red Menace* (1949), Gordon Douglas's *I Was a Communist for the FBI* (1951), and Edward Ludwig's *Big Jim McLain* (1952)—produced at least in part, to demonstrate a repudiation of the leftist inclinations with which the film industry was being charged.

The Red Menace begins with a young couple driving melodramatically through the night, obviously terrified. We soon learn that the couple, Bill Jones (Robert Rockwell) and Nina Petrovka (Hannelore Axman), is being pursued by a mysterious and terrifying "them." The rest of the film then flashes back to the events that led to this terrible predicament, revealing that (of course) the couple's pursuers are none other than the Communist Party, which turns out to have a terrible presence all over America.

Petrovka, as it turns out, is a longtime party operative, while Jones is an ex-GI who was lured into the party out of frustration with the American system after he was fleeced of his last $2500 by an unscrupulous real estate firm.

The film's voiceover narrator adds to the air of melodrama (and near hysteria) that pervades the entire film, which purports to reveal the shocking tactics of the Communist Party as it attempts to ensnare unsuspecting innocents, then to brainwash them into sharing its devotion to atheism and totalitarianism. If brainwashing does not work, they are not above turning to "bloodshed and terror." We learn that the party employs gangs of thugs who beat up and even murder those who stray from the party line, though in some cases they employ more subtle techniques, driving party dissidents to suicide instead. Luckily, there is hope, as when one woman long-used by the party as a sexual lure, manages to escape the party and return to respectability by fleeing back home to her mother and the kindly priest, Father O'Leary (Leo Cleary). Jones and Petrovka apparently escape the clutches of the party as well, driving all the way from California to Texas, where a sympathetic sheriff takes them under his wing and advises them to get hitched and have a couple of real American kids to raise with real American values. The film then cuts to a shot of the Statue of Liberty as the stirring strains of "America (My Country 'tis of Thee)" sound in the background.

Big Jim McLain features John Wayne in the title role as an investigator working for HUAC, along with his partner, Mel Baxter (a young James Arness in his pre-Matt Dillon days). After a brief indication of how hard it is to root out commies in influential positions (college professors are especially bad, apparently), most of the film deals with HUAC hearings that are scheduled to be held in Hawaii to investigate communist activity there. McLain and Baxter are sent ahead by the committee to gather information and to compile a list of witnesses that should be called to testify at the Hawaii hearings. Predictably, they find communists lurking under every rock and pineapple, though hard evidence is difficult to obtain because the communists are so clever and conniving, not to mention ruthless and murderous, which discourages anyone from testifying against them. They are also part of a sophisticated, efficient, well-organized, and well-funded international "conspiracy to enslave the common man"—as well as to undermine the American government.

Such depictions of communists (however different they are from the reality of the weak and bumbling American Communist Party at the time) are not surprising in this film, which was made in cooperation with HUAC itself and which was clearly an effort on the part of Hollywood to curry favor with the committee and to curb the public perception (promulgated by the committee since the late 1940s) of Hollywood as a haven for dangerous reds. For its own part, HUAC needed for communists to be perceived as a powerful and formidable foe in order to justify their own ongoing activities.

Unfortunately for HUAC, this film is so bad and so overt in its efforts at propaganda that it could not possibly have been convincing to anyone who was not already convinced of HUAC's claims about the danger of communist subversion in America. Wayne himself, however dedicated he might have been to the film's anticommunist mission, seems awkward and uncomfortable in the lead role, especially in the scenes involving a feeble, romantic subplot in which McLain meets a woman doctor in Hawaii (played by Nancy Olson), sweeps her off her feet and convinces her to marry him. She happily drops her medical practice and agrees to move back with him to Washington, D.C., as any obedient 1950s wife should. All is not well, however. For one thing, Baxter is found dead soon after he and McLain begin their work in Hawaii. Subsequently, the Hawaii police manage to get enough evidence to arrest three communist agents for manslaughter in the death of Baxter, which apparently occurred due to a bad reaction to the sodium pentothal with which they injected him in an effort to get information about his mission. The communists are subsequently indicted for murder (this film is not concerned with logical inconsistencies like the fact that they are arrested on one charge and indicted on another) and seem sure to be convicted. The HUAC hearings do not go so well, however. All the suspected communists called to testify plead the fifth amendment that leaves the committee unable to make charges stick against any of them. McLain stalks off, disgusted that such vile creatures, intent on subverting the constitution, would hide behind it. Luckily, a subsequent patriotic visit to the U.S.S. *Arizona* memorial at Pearl Harbor cheers him up considerably as he prepares to fly back to the mainland with his new woman in tow.

Of the anticommunist films produced at the beginning of the 1950s, *I Was a Communist for the FBI* is probably the best and most entertaining, even though it is based on the same stereotypes about communists as the other films in this group. In particular, this film comes closest to realizing the dramatic potential of communists as film villains—at least for a certain kind of over-the-top melodramatic film. Here, protagonist Matt Cvetic (Frank Lovejoy) is a stalwart and heroic American who has been forced to suffer years of abuse on all sides and rejection even by his own family because of his public persona as a member of the Communist Party in Pittsburgh. For their own part, the commies are vile and despicable in the mode of comic-book villains, willing to do virtually anything to destroy the American way of life and to deliver the United States into the hands of the Soviet Union as a "slave colony." Dramatic interest is added in the person of young, beautiful Eve Merrick (Dorothy Hart), a teacher at the high school where Cvetic's son is a student. The idealistic Merrick is one of many communist teachers who has infiltrated the Pittsburgh schools, but is soon disillusioned by the party's cold-blooded quest for power. When she thus resigns from the party and threatens to reveal their schemes to the Pittsburgh school board, Merrick is ordered killed by a communist hit squad—but saved (in some fairly effective action scenes) by the heroic intervention of Cvetic. In the end, Cvetic himself testifies before HUAC and tells them all he knows from his nine years working underground in the party. He is thus publicly redeemed and restored to his family, who shed tears of joy. The film then ends with a shot of a bust of Lincoln, with the patriotic strains of "The Battle Hymn of the Republic" sounding in the background.

All of this might be fine were it not for the fact that the film purports to be an accurate portrayal of the operations of the Communist Party, even though many of the stated "facts" (as when it is stipulated that the communists have murdered hundreds of their own members in the United States who have strayed from the party line) are entirely manufactured and have no basis in reality. Indeed, the film precisely reverses reality on many accounts, as when the Communist Party's admirable (if largely ineffective) contribution to the struggle for racial justice in America is presented as a fraudulent maneuver designed to foment discord in American society. On the other side, the film's presentation of the persecution suffered by Cvetic because he is a known communist inadvertently suggests an intolerance of dissent in American society. More importantly, Cvetic's heroism is largely a Hollywood fantasy. The real Matt Cvetic, who indeed worked undercover within the Communist Party for seven years, was fired by the FBI in 1950 because he was judged to be unreliable due to his heavy drinking, then later sold his story to the *Saturday Evening Post* in an attempt to cash in. Indeed, it is now widely acknowledged—and documented in Daniel Leab's book *I Was a Communist for the F.B.I.: The Life and Times of Matt Cvetic* (Pennsylvania State University Press, 2000)—that Cvetic was an unscrupulous and self-serving opportunist who, unable to dig up any real dirt on the Communist Party despite his years undercover, presented almost entirely falsified testimony—a fact of which the FBI was apparently aware but chose to ignore because his stories of communist perfidy helped their cause.

In retrospect, *I Was a Communist for the FBI* serves not as an exposé of the Communist Party but as a revelation of the extent to which the FBI and its network of paid informants were willing to go to promote the notion of a communist threat, real or imagined. To an extent, the same can be said for all the overtly anticommunist films of the period that collectively now seem informed by a misplaced paranoia and a lack of concern with the facts that make them seem more demonstrations of the dangers of arrant anticommunism than dramatizations of the evils of communism.

Meanwhile, that such films seemed perfectly believable to many at the time, documents the level of anticommunist hysteria that reigned in American society at the time.

Among other things, *I Was a Communist for the FBI* nicely illustrates the way in which anticommunist films of the early 1950s, with no basis on reality upon which to construct their narratives, instead based their portrayal of communists on the portrayals of fascists in the antifascist thrillers of the 1940s. Perhaps the best example of this transfer in the role of symbolic villains directly from fascists to communists occurs in Samuel Fuller's noir thriller *Pickup on South Street* (1953), which follows directly in the footsteps of antifascist thrillers such as Edward Dmytryk's *Cornered* (1945), Henry Hathaway's *The House on 92nd Street* (1945), or Orson Welles's *The Stranger* (1946), but focuses on communists, rather than fascists, as sinister enemies of the American way of life.

Actually, *Pickup on South Street* seems a rather lackluster effort in comparison with some of Fuller's other films, including the zany offbeat cult classics *Shock Corridor* (1963) and *The Naked Kiss* (1964). Yet, even this film is interesting in the way it combines the noir crime drama with the Cold War spy thriller. In the film, pickpocket Skip McCoy (Richard Widmark), deftly lifts the wallet of Candy (Jean Peters), a woman on the subway, only later to discover that the wallet holds a microfilm containing U. S. government secrets that Candy was unknowingly delivering to a gang of Soviet spies for her ne'er-do-well boyfriend, Joey (Richard Kiley). The plot of the film is uninteresting and highly predictable: McCoy outwits (and outfights) Joey and the evil commies, winning the heart of Candy, which is, of course, a heart of gold, despite her checkered past. McCoy wins a clean slate with the cops, as well, finally getting them off his back. In the end, Candy and McCoy leave the police station with his record wiped clean, presumably headed for a new life together.

In short, the plot, at least in its outline, is pure cliché. The commie spies are clichés as well, seemingly driven not by ideology, but by pure evil, thus providing an apparent example of the virulent anticommunism that informed so many films of the period. However, the anticommunism of *Pickup on South Street* may be more complex than it first appears. The film's most rabid anticommunist, for example, is a police informer by the name of Moe (Thelma Ritter). Despite her seeming willingness to do anything for a buck, Moe does have certain values that she refuses to compromise. In particular, she refuses to do business with commies, preferring death at the hands of Joey to helping them locate McCoy. Yet Moe's anticommunism is incoherent and confused. When Joey asks her why she hates commies so much, she replies, "What do I know about commies? Nothing. I know one thing: I just don't like them." Joey then shoots and kills her, apparently verifying her antipathy toward communists. However, Joey is not really a communist, but merely an opportunist trying to make a buck any way he can. He is, in short, a capitalist. Meanwhile, the virulence with which Moe detests communists, despite knowing absolutely nothing about them, tends to cast American anticommunism as little more than mindless bigotry and fanaticism.

If this scene makes the casting of communists as villains less simplistic than it might first appear, the casting of Skip McCoy as the film's hero is problematic as well. In some ways, McCoy is the typical film noir flawed hero. For example, he has a great deal in common with Harry Fabian, the protagonist of Jules Dassin's *Night and the City* (1950), a role that had also been played by Widmark. But McCoy lacks the basic rectitude that tends to inform the film noir flawed hero. He, for one, is perfectly willing to deal with the commies until he develops a personal grudge, and his manhandling of the beautiful-but-dumb Candy—which tends to alternate between punching and kissing so brutal that it is not much different from the punching—goes well beyond the norm, even for a genre in which women often receive rough treatment. And, of course, McCoy's characterization as hero is further destabilized by the casting of Widmark, who, his roles in *Night and the City* and Elia Kazan's *Panic in the Streets* (1950) notwithstanding, was best known to film noir audiences as the crazed psycho-killer of such films as *Kiss of Death* (1947) and *Road House* (1948), not to mention his role as a loathsome bigot in *No Way Out* (1950). In *Pickup on South Street*, McCoy seems to teeter on the brink of insanity for virtually the entire film, leaving the question of whether he has really become stable and respectable at the film's end, very much open.

Such complexities clearly separate *Pickup on South Street* from simplistic anticommunist films such as *I Was a Communist for the FBI* or *Big Jim McLain*. Fuller's reasonably successful incorporation of anticommunist themes into the format of the noir thriller illustrates the extent to which such themes were perhaps more effective in films in which they were secondary to other themes. Fuller's film is also an important forerunner of the Cold War spy thrillers that became so prominent in American film, especially after the success of the James Bond film franchise, beginning with *Dr. No* (1962). Of course, Bond's foes are not always Russians or communists, but are often supervillains that take the films into the realm of science fiction.

Other popular genres have sometimes allegorized the phenomenon of anticommunism as well. For example, Fred Zinneman's classic Western *High Noon* (1952) has often been read as a veiled satire of McCarthyism. Zinneman's film includes the requisite good guys, bad guys, and gunplay, but it also explores a number of ethical and political issues, giving it a depth sometimes lacking in the genre. The action takes place in the town of Hadleyville (perhaps recalling Mark Twain's Hadleyburg, bastion of bourgeois corruption and conformity), a formerly wild and dangerous town that Marshal Will Kane (Gary Cooper) has tamed, making it a good place to live and raise a family. One of his major accomplishments in this regard was the arrest and conviction, for murder, of local bad man Frank Miller (Ian McDonald), sent away to state prison five years earlier. But, as the film begins, Miller has just inexplicably been pardoned and is now headed back to Hadleyville to seek revenge on Kane; Miller is due to arrive on the noon train, thus the title of the film. But Hadleyville has been peaceful for so long that most of Kane's deputies have been let go, and most of the townspeople have grown comfortable and complacent. The town is thus ill equipped to deal with the threat posed by Miller and his allies, who come to town and gather at the train depot to await his arrival.

Kane, like the blacklisted artists who were abandoned by the official Hollywood community, is thus left to stand alone against the forces of evil, whether they be HUAC or the Miller gang. As Peter Biskind puts it in his book *Seeing Is Believing: How Hollywood Taught Us to Stop Worrying and Love the Fifties* (Pantheon, 1983), "once the Millers were equated with HUAC or McCarthy, the craven townies became friendly witnesses." He then quotes the film's screenwriter, Carl Foreman, to the effect that the film was about "Hollywood and no other place but Hollywood" (p. 48). One could even argue that Miller's resurgence after his earlier defeat by Kane associates HUAC and McCarthy with the fascism that had been presumably defeated a few years earlier in World War II.

Perhaps the most direct contemporary reaction to the Hollywood black-lists was the film *Salt of the Earth*, the first and only film produced by Independent Producers Corporation, a group of leftist filmmakers orga-nized specifically to try to find a way to make socially responsible cinema within the repressive climate that was sweeping Hollywood in the McCarthy years. Aided by funding from the International Union of Mine, Mill, and Smelter Workers, blacklisted director Herbert Biberman, produ-cer Paul Jarrico, and writer Michael Wilson were able to produce a remark-able film that is important in American film history for a number of reasons. For one thing, *Salt of the Earth*, despite its low budget and mostly amateur actors, is a genuinely fine film, a compelling piece of social drama that makes important political points while telling an engaging story built around convincing and genuinely human characters. The social history of the film is also important. Made by a strongly committed group of film-makers who were not beholden to any Hollywood studios or other interests within the capitalist establishment, *Salt of the Earth* may be the purest example of leftist film in the entire history of the American cinema, though it is actually rather moderate in its politics. At the same time, the reaction of the capitalist establishment to the film was also significant. Furious efforts were made to suppress the film, and the filmmakers were hounded by

HUAC, the FBI, and the CIA during the making of the film. After the film was completed, theaters all over the country, reacting to government and corporate pressure, refused to show the film. The film thus reached only a very limited audience, though it was rediscovered in the 1960s, finally going into general release in 1965.

Salt of the Earth deals with the efforts of Mexican American zinc miners in New Mexico to battle against the exploitative practices of their employer, Delaware Zinc, Inc., thereby hoping to achieve better working and living conditions. In addition to the obvious emphasis on class, the film also deals centrally with the unfair treatment of the miners and their families on the basis of ethnicity. In particular, the company pursues a carefully planned program of ethnic discrimination, systematically treating Anglo miners far better than Mexican ones, thereby hoping to win the loyalty and obedience of the Anglo miners, who are still exploited despite this preferential treatment. *Salt of the Earth* is also particularly strong in its treatment of gender; the wives of the miners play a crucial role in their fight for justice, while the miners, in the process, learn important lessons about their own tendency toward gender-based discrimination.

The film focuses in particular on Mexican American miner Ramon Quintero (impressively played by Juan Chacon, an actual miner) and his wife, Esperanza (played by Rosaura Revueltas, a professional Mexican actress who was driven out of the United States as the film neared completion, subsequently to be blacklisted in Mexico). However, this focus is far different from that of the typical Hollywood film; the emphasis is not on the private problems of the Quinteros as unique individuals, but on their representative problems as members of a larger community. As the film proceeds, ethnic discrimination and unsafe working conditions finally drive the Mexican miners to declare s strike, with the support of the International Union of Mine, Mill, and Smelter Workers. They are also supported by many of the Anglo miners, who stand beside their Mexican brothers. Though the men are reluctant to get their wives involved, the women eventually provide important support to the picket line, bringing food, drink, and supplies to the men as they picket the entrances to the mine and try to keep out scabs.

The company, supported by the sheriff (played by blacklisted actor Will Geer) and his armed thugs, makes every effort to break the picket line. At one point, they arrest Ramon, beat him so badly that he has to be hospitalized for a week, then take him to jail for a month. While he is in jail, Esperanza gives birth to their third child. Finally, the company gets a court injunction ordering the miners to cease picketing. Having little choice, the men agree to obey the order; however, as the order mentions only striking miners, it does not apply to their wives. The women therefore replace the men on the picket line and keep the strike going, despite the continuing efforts of the company to intimidate them. At one point, the leaders of the women are taken to jail. Esperanza is among them, taking her baby with her, though Ramon eventually takes the child home with him. The picket line holds, however, as women from miles around rush in to fill the spots left by the arrested women. Soon, the women in the jail mount such a protest that the sheriff releases them just to get rid of them. In the meantime, however, Ramon and the other husbands of the jailed women are forced to do the domestic chores normally done by their wives, thus learning better to appreciate the difficulty of the work their women do.

Nevertheless, when the women are released, tensions flare between Esperanza and Ramon, who is feeling threatened by her newfound strength and independence. In response, Esperanza delivers what is probably the central political statement in the film, noting that the mine company's oppression of Ramon is driving him to oppress her in turn, but that a better response would be to work to do away with oppression altogether rather than simply passing it along. Ramon is at first unconvinced by her arguments. Tired of the domestic routine, he and several other men decide to go away on a hunting trip after the women are released. Ramon, however, soon realizes that he has been wrong to resent Esperanza's efforts in support of the strike. He leads the men back home, where they find that the sheriff's deputies, in a further attempt to break the strike by intimidating its leaders, are evicting the Quinteros from their company-owned housing. In a classic scene of leftist activism, an angry crowd of workers and wives from miles around gathers at the house and forces the deputies to abandon the eviction. A company official, looking on, concludes that the company had better settle the strike "for the present." The miners and their families thus win at least a temporary victory, thanks to the solidarity they have shown in standing together against the company and its official supporters. Ramon thanks the crowd for their help, acknowledging them as "sisters and brothers." Esperanza, meanwhile, envisions a day when such localized efforts will lead to a better world in which her children, "the salt of the earth," will inherit it.

Salt of the Earth is impressively lucid in its delineation of the central labor struggle within the larger context of the capitalist system. It is also highly effective in its depiction of the role played by gender and ethnicity within that system. It avoids clichés, presenting the miners and their families as realistic human beings who are neither romanticized nor heroicized. This realism is also aided by the film's basis in fact, the struggle of Mexican American miners in the Southwest having been among the most important labor struggles of the 1950s.

Elia Kazan's *On the Waterfront*, also released in 1954, stands as a virtual antithesis to *Salt of the Earth*. For one thing, Kazan's film was a well-financed work of mainstream Hollywood cinema with an A-list cast. For another, it presents labor unions as deeply corrupt and as working against the true interests of their members. Perhaps most importantly, it was made by a director who cooperated with HUAC and thus saved his career, as opposed to Biberman, whose career was ruined by his refusal to cooperate with what he saw as an illegal and un-American enterprise.

On the Waterfront details the scene on a New Jersey waterfront, where most of the longshoremen who keep the docks running, live and work under miserable conditions. However, the film focuses its critique of these conditions not on the shipping companies who employ the workers but on the local longshoremen's union, which is headed by gangster Johnny Friendly (Lee J. Cobb). This corrupt union exploits the workers, rather than representing them. Friendly and his minions rule the entire waterfront, exploiting both the workers and the shipping companies for their own profit. Marlon Brando probably deserved the best actor Oscar he won for his performance in the film, but in general the film is a highly overrated compilation of Hollywood stereotypes, though it admittedly harnesses these stereotypes in a fairly effective way.

As the film begins, the longshoremen's union is being investigated by the State Crime Commission, presented in the book as a force for righteousness. The investigation is made difficult by the reluctance of everyone on the waterfront to testify against Friendly, but young Joey Doyle, an agitator for union reform, has agreed to cooperate with the commission. Friendly orders his lieutenant, Charley Malloy (Rod Steiger), to take care of Doyle, and Charley engages his brother, Terry (Brando), an ex-boxer who "could have been a contender" had he not been mismanaged, to lure Doyle to a rooftop from which he is thrown to his death. Terry, not having realized that Doyle was to be killed, is seriously disturbed by this development but takes no immediate action. Most of the rest of the film involves the efforts, initiated by Joey's pure-as-the-driven-snow sister, Katie (Eva Marie Saint), an innocent convent-educated college student, to bring Joey's killers to justice and thus break Friendly's hold on the waterfront. Initially, Katie gets little support, but the dedicated efforts of Father Barry (Karl Malden), a local priest, eventually convince one of the longshoremen, "Kayo" Dugan (Pat Henning), to testify before the Crime Commission. Dugan makes a statement before the commission but is quickly killed by Friendly's thugs. Concerned by Terry's lack of loyalty, Friendly orders his death as well, and Charley is killed for protecting his brother. Furious, Terry plans to kill Friendly, but Barry convinces him instead to testify before the commission, and his testimony is instrumental in initiating the cleanup of the union, just as, presumably, the testimony of Kazan and Schulberg before HUAC helped in the "cleanup" of Hollywood.

In its concern for the exploitation of workers, *Waterfront* clearly participates in a central concern of the political left. However, its presentation of a corrupt union as the principal villain in this exploitation leaves largely unexamined the role of the shipping companies, even though the profits of these companies from this exploitation are acknowledged in the film to be far greater than those realized by the corrupt officials of the union. Positive figures such Katie Doyle and Terry Malloy are, in their separate ways, political naïfs who have no understanding of the role played by the capitalist system in the exploitation of workers. Their perspective helps to reduce the film to a simple opposition between good individuals and evil individuals, with little emphasis on class as a category of collective action.

Widely promoted as a daring and hard-hitting exposé of labor union corruption, *On the Waterfront* can also be seen as a shameless bit of self-promotion and opportunism that rides the tide of antiunion sentiment in the 1950s while providing a rationale for the friendly testimony of Kazan and Schulberg before HUAC. It is true that East Coast dockworkers unions were indeed well known for their corruption in the 1950s. Yet the West Coast unions, led by such figures as Harry Bridges, were known for their courageous defiance of capitalist exploitation and their strong advocacy of the rights of their members. If Kazan and Schulberg had wanted to be courageous, they could have told the story of Bridges and other admirable leftist union leaders. But their decision to focus on unions as forces of evil (and on government informers as battlers for justice) provided a much easier and more lucrative road to Hollywood success.

Daniel Taradash's relatively obscure *Storm Center* (1956) is one of the more direct and overt of the criticisms of McCarthyism that appeared in American film of the 1950s, as opposed to films such as *High Noon* (1952), which left itself available to anti-McCarthyism interpretations, but muted them through its wild west setting. At the same time, in its depiction of a potentially sinister side to small-town America, *Storm Center* looks back to films such as Fritz Lang's *Fury* (1937). The film focuses on Alicia Hull (Bette Davis), a small-town librarian who has devoted most of her life to work in the town library and to using it to further the educational development of the town's children. When the town council, caught up in a wave of anticommunist hysteria, demands that a book entitled *The Communist Dream* be removed from the shelves because of its political content, Hull at first complies, then returns the book to the shelves, feeling that its removal was a violation of her personal integrity and the principles of American democracy. For that act, she is immediately fired, despite her long service, and replaced by her friend and former assistant, Martha Lockridge (Kim Hunter). However, the town judge, Robert Ellerbe (Paul Kelly), believes that Hull has been unfairly treated and calls a town meeting to discuss the issue. Unfortunately, this move backfires when Paul Duncan (Brian Keith), Lockridge's boyfriend, seizes the opportunity to further his own political ambitions by denouncing Hull as a dangerous communist, winning the sympathy of the townspeople.

To this point, *Storm Center* is a fairly realistic account of the climate of fear and suspicion that reigned in America in the 1950s. However, the film then takes a series of unlikely turns that undermine its political message. When Hull is ostracized by most of the townspeople after the hearing, one of the children she has befriended, Freddie Slater (Kevin Coughlin), is so incensed that he sets fire to the library. As the townspeople watch the building burn, they suddenly realize the error of their ways and reinstate Hull to her former position so that she can supervise the building of a new library, which will presumably pursue more democratic policies in its choice of books. This easy resolution thus weakens the film's message and elides the fact that individuals such as Hull did, in fact, lose their jobs all over America during the 1950s, few of them recovering their positions so easily.

Storm Center is thus ultimately far less successful as a critique of communism than Charlie Chaplin's near-contemporary *A King in New York*, a film that was made in Britain and released there in 1957, during Chaplin's period of political exile from the United States. Because of its powerful critique of American culture and society, the film was not released in the United States until 1975. Nevertheless, it remains one of the leading film commentaries on the anticommunist witch hunts of the 1950s. Though the film was released five years after Chaplin was driven back to Europe by political persecution in America and three years after Joseph McCarthy was censured by the Senate and thus passed the peak of his power, the anticommunist hysteria that the film critiques was still very much in force in 1957. Moreover, the film's commentary on American anticommunism is supplemented by a scathing critique of American popular culture as a whole, which suggests that McCarthyism was not a short-term aberration from the American way, but a quintessentially American phenomenon, part and parcel of the consumerist culture of modern America. The film, which carries numerous autobiographical resonances and can be read as Chaplin's direct response to his shoddy treatment by American authorities in the midst of the anticommunist purges, is Chaplin's most overt and radical political critique of American society.

A King in New York begins with an on-screen caption announcing that "One of the minor annoyances of modern life is a revolution." It then proceeds to show scenes of a revolution underway in the fictional European country of Estrovia, though the revolutionaries, largely in business dress, are clearly depicted as bourgeois rather than middle-class. King Shahdov (Chaplin), the country's monarch, flees to America in the wake of the revolution, taking with him the contents of his country's treasury. However, he is not out for personal gain but hopes to use the money to finance his long-term dream of creating a utopian society based on the wealth made possible by cheap and abundant nuclear power, produced by plants that he himself has designed. Shahdov (the name is perhaps a sly illusion to the 1953 U.S.-engineered coup that placed Shah Reza Pahlavi on the throne in Iran, presumably as an anticommunist measure) initially seems excited about the democratic possibilities of America, despite his own royal background.

Soon after Shahdov arrives in America, however, his former prime minister, Voudel (Jerry Desmonde) absconds to South America with the royal funds, leaving Shahdov, accompanied by his loyal aide, Ambassador Jaume (Oliver Johnston), penniless in New York. The early scenes of the king's stay in New York primarily concern his attempts to deal with the constant barrage of American popular culture with which he finds himself bombarded wherever he turns. Hounded by the press wherever he turns, he encounters an environment saturated with commodified images. Rock-and-roll music and women's magazines are among the satirized forms, though the most powerful commentary is reserved for film and television. These scenes include a particularly effective one in which Shahdov and Jaume attend a film but leave in disgust after viewing the coming attractions, a series of parodies of trailers for films of various current American genres, including a tale of gender confusion, a Western, and a film noir. The comment on the current state of American film is clear. Even more powerful is the film's critique of television, as Shahdov finds himself followed everywhere by Orwellian telescreens. There is even a screen (complete with windshield wiper to clear away any collected moisture) over the bathtub in his hotel room. As in Orwell, the telescreens can transmit as well as receive images, suggesting the element of surveillance that pervaded the paranoid American society of the 1950s. When the king attends a dinner party to which he has been lured by the beautiful Ann Kay (Dawn Addams), he finds much of Ann's conversation at the party puzzling, especially when she suddenly lapses into the discourse of deodorant and toothpaste commercials. Shahdov later learns that the entire party (heavily populated with rich, but vulgar Americans) has been broadcast, Candid-Camera-like, on television via a hidden camera for the television show "Ann Kay's Real-Life Surprise Party."

At first, the king is horrified to learn that his conversation at the party (during which he was induced to perform the to-be-or-not-to-be soliloquy from *Hamlet*) has been broadcast. However, the show is a big hit, and the king (in a comment on the fascination of American culture with European royalty) is soon showered with offers to appear on other programs and, especially, to endorse various commercial products. At first, he resists such offers, feeling them vulgar and beneath his dignity. However, when there proves to be no market for his nuclear power plans in America (the Americans already have plans of their own), the king is desperate for cash. He eventually begins to accept the offers and soon becomes, despite his incompetent performances, a successful media star. Image, after all, is everything, and he is, after all, a king. In the meantime, apparently in the process of a divorce from his wife (with whom he had made a merely political marriage), he attempts to become romantically involved with Ann Kay, though she resists his advances, preferring to act as his agent and to keep their relationship on a professional, if friendly, basis.

Trying to learn more about America, the king visits a progressive school (with the press still dogging his every move) where he and encounters a precocious ten-year-old, Rupert Macabee (played by Chaplin's son, Michael), in the act of reading Karl Marx. Rupert makes an impassioned radical speech against oppression and authority of all kinds, engaging in, and clearly winning, a debate with the king when the latter tries to claim that in a democracy like America, authority is not a bad thing but merely the will of the people. Rupert warns the king that should he attempt to test the system, he will find that freedom in America has strict limits indeed. He especially rails against the lack of freedom of movement across borders, in an obvious reference to the fact that Chaplin—labeled an "undesirable alien" at the instigation of FBI head J. Edgar Hoover because of his political beliefs—had been denied a visa to reenter the United States after a trip abroad in 1952.

Eventually, Rupert runs away from the school to avoid questioning by federal authorities, who are investigating his parents, suspected communists, for HUAC. The king finds the boy on the street and takes him in, befriending him. While with the king, the boy decides to admit that he is a communist, not because he necessarily accepts communist views, but because he feels that American society forces everyone to accept some label or other, much in the mode of brand names. Again, image is everything. In the meantime, the boy's parents refuse to name names before the committee and are imprisoned on charges of contempt of Congress. Rupert is retrieved by federal marshals, and the king, because of his involvement with the boy, is himself called to testify before HUAC, as Chaplin had once nearly been.

Despite some riotously funny comic mishaps (in which, among other things, the king inadvertently sprays the committee with a fire hose), the king goes over well in the committee hearings, suggesting the vacuousness of the hearings, which clearly parallels the film's portrayal of the emptiness of American popular culture. Shahdov, as a king, already has a convenient label and is cleared of all suspicion of communist sympathies. But in the film's most powerful comment on the human consequences of the HUAC investigations, Rupert does not fare so well. Browbeaten by federal authorities who entice him to cooperate by offering freedom for his imprisoned parents, the boy eventually agrees to name names. When the king again encounters him, he is a broken shell of his former combative self, torn by guilt over his testimony. The king, having had enough of America and on the way to a reconciliation with his wife, is about to return to Europe but assures Rupert that he hopes to have him and his parents over for a visit soon, though the schoolmaster hints that there may be "complications" to such an arrangement, suggesting that the boy and his parents, because of their political affiliations, may not be allowed to travel abroad. In the end, the king flies to Europe to stay, having declared that "it's too crazy" in America.

The initial American critical response to *A King in New York* was, predictably, negative. Moreover, as Charles Maland notes in his book on Chaplin (*Chaplin and American Culture: The Evolution of a Star Image*, Princeton University Press, 1989), American reviews often went out of their way to emphasize, not entirely accurately, that foreign reviews of the film had been negative as well (321–25). Actually, British reviews of the film were largely favorable, but the film remains one of Chaplin's least known and appreciated works. Still, viewed on its own terms, it is a powerful piece of satire, one of the best film commentaries on both McCarthyism and the popular media. It is also unusual in that it notes the complicity between these two phenomena rather than simply seeing the film and television industries as victims of McCarthyism.

It would be nearly twenty years after its European release before *A King in New York* could be released in the United States, partly because developments such as the Watergate scandal had discredited the kind dirty tricks of government to which Chaplin had earlier fallen prey. Mostly, however, the passing of time had simply eased the air of anticommunist hysteria that had pervaded American society in the 1950s. Indeed, Chaplin (then a longtime resident of Switzerland) had returned to the United States for a visit in 1972, when he was given an honorary Academy Award for his historic contributions to the development of film as an artistic medium. At the awards ceremony, he received the longest standing ovation in the history of the Oscars, both as recognition of his artistic achievements and as a sort of belated apology for the political repression to which he had fallen victim.

The less repressive political climate of the second half of the 1970s also allowed Hollywood to begin to take on the legacy of anticommunism more directly than ever before. For example, although enlivened by numerous comic moments, Martin Ritt's *The Front* (1976) is a poignant and powerful story of the McCarthyite blacklists that blighted the American entertainment industry in the 1950s. Here, Woody Allen is entirely convincing in the lead role of Howard Prince, an underachieving schlemiel who finally gets his chance to be somebody when successful television writer Alfred Miller (Michael Murphy), a friend and former schoolmate, asks Prince to front for him so that he can continue to sell scripts even though he has just been blacklisted as a communist sympathizer (which he, in fact, is). The character of Miller clearly refers to distinguished playwright Arthur Miller, who had himself come under suspicion in the anticommunist purges of the 1950s and who courageously satirized those purges in his classic play about the Salem witch hunts, *The Crucible* (1953).

In *The Front*, Prince agrees to accept Miller's proposition, and the arrangement is so successful that he soon begins to front for other black-listed writers as well, making a good living from his 10 per cent cut of their fees. He also begins a romantic relationship with beautiful television pro-ducer Florence Barrett (Andrea Marcovicci), so that all in all his prospects look bright. In the meantime, comedian Hecky Brown (played by Zero Mostel, blacklisted in 1950) is fired from the television show for which Prince "writes," on evidence of minor involvement by Brown in communist activities (apparently in an attempt to seduce a woman who was a commu-nist). However, Brown is given a chance to redeem himself by spying on Prince, and, with his once thriving career now in ruins, he agrees to do so, though with great misgivings.

As the film nears its conclusion, Prince is called to testify in a private executive session before a subcommittee of the HUAC. The network urges him to cooperate, assuring him that the committee merely wants a pro forma statement of his loyalty to America and opposition to communism. By this time, political pressure has also forced Barrett to leave the show, and Prince, though apolitical, is growing increasingly offended by the intrusions of the committee into the lives of innocent Americans. Nevertheless, he is tempted to cooperate with the committee to a point, if only to protect the writers for whom he is fronting. Then, as the time for Prince's testimony nears, Brown commits suicide, as did real-life performer Philip Loeb (blacklisted for such "atrocious" activities as signing a petition to end segregation in professional baseball), on whom the character of Brown is partly based. Prince then goes before the committee determined to defeat their questioning with clever evasions, but their insistence that he name names (including that of Brown) makes him furious. He denounces the committee's activities, tells them to go fuck themselves, and angrily leaves the room. In the final scene, he is being taken to prison for contempt, a hero to Barrett and to a crowd of demonstrators who are protesting on his behalf.

The Front is convincing in its presentation of the destruction of the lives of innocent Americans during the McCarthyite purges. It is also convincing in its portrayal of the political climate of fear and intimidation that allowed such destruction to continue for years, despite its obvious injustice and illegality. The film is particularly good in its portrayal of the activities of HUAC as a pure quest for power, with the attempt to defend America against communism as a mere pretext. Of course, much of the authenticity of the film probably arises from the fact that many of its principals were themselves victims of the blacklist, including director-producer Ritt and screenwriter Walter Bernstein, who was also the author of *Inside Out: A Memoir of the Blacklist*, an important memoir about the blacklist (Knopf, 1996). In addition to Mostel, cast members Herschel Bernardi, Lloyd Gough, and Joshua Shelley were also blacklist victims.

While *The Front* deals with the plight of television writers in New York, Philip Saville's relatively obscure *Fellow Traveller* (1989) focuses on the experience of a left-wing screenwriter to dramatize the impact of the McCarthyite anticommunist purges on Hollywood. The central character, Asa Kaufman (Ron Silver), is a former member of the Communist Party who has subsequently become a successful screenwriter but who is forced to flee to England to avoid a HUAC subpoena, having already refused attempts of FBI investigators to convince him to identify other leftists working in Hollywood. In London, Kaufman manages to land work writing scripts for a children's television series based on the legend of Robin Hood, though he has to hire a washed-up British writer to front for him because his visa does not allow him legally to work in Britain.

Kaufman adjusts, though with some difficulty, to this dramatic decline in his professional position, sometimes fantasizing about subtly turning his Robin Hood scripts into commentaries on the repressive conditions prevailing in America. At the end of the film, he is joined by his wife and children in London, where they begin to try to build a stable life for themselves. In the meantime, Kaufman's personal traumas are exacerbated when he learns that prominent actor Clifford Byrne (Hart Bochner), a lifelong friend, has committed suicide. Later he discovers that Byrne's suicide followed the actor's decision to cooperate with HUAC and name names. One subplot involves Kaufman's association in London with Sarah Atchison (Imogen Stubbs), Byrne's British former lover, who is now heavily involved in the peace and disarmament movement in London, an activity Kaufman is unable to join because of his own delicate status in Britain. Another subplot refers back to Kaufman's growing psychological stress under the pressures of the repressive climate in Hollywood in the early 1950s, an experience that led him to seek psychoanalysis with Dr. Jerry Leavy (Daniel J. Travanti), a progressive analyst who supposedly sympathizes with left-wing causes. It turns out, however, that Leavy is funneling information gained from sessions with his leftist patients directly to the FBI and that this information was crucial to the identification of both Kaufman and Byrne as targets for investigation. Through this and other motifs,

Fellow Traveller does a good job of indicating both the pervasiveness of the anticommunist investigations that swept America in the 1950s and the human cost of those investigations. At the same time, the film downplays the real political issues involved, focusing on the private problems of individuals such as Kaufman and Byrne and downplaying the genuine political commitment of many Hollywood leftists.

Fellow Traveller was a minor film that got little attention. The same can be said for Karl Francis's *One of the Hollywood Ten* (2000), which deals with the efforts of blacklisted director Herbert Biberman to make the independent film *Salt of the Earth* (1954). Thus, Irwin Winkler's *Guilty by Suspicion* (1991) remains the most prominent Hollywood film to deal directly with the anticommunist witch hunts and blacklists that struck the film industry in the late 1940s and 1950s. Thus, while some critics have complained that *Guilty by Suspicion* is nothing more than a stale would-be revelation of facts that are already well known, it is clear that Hollywood has never dealt sufficiently with the trauma of the McCarthy era and that, much remains to be done. Unfortunately, *Guilty by Suspicion* is a rather flat piece that fails sufficiently to explain the historical background of the events it describes. Instead, in its attempt to dramatize the human suffering caused by the anticommunist purges, it focuses on the personal tragedies of a few individuals, at times becoming a story more of private angst than of public persecution. In addition, the film's focus on the persecution of individuals who were never really communists tends to suggest that it was perfectly acceptable to persecute real communists.

Guilty by Suspicion focuses on hotshot director David Merrill (Robert De Niro), who returns to Hollywood after a few months in Paris to find the entire town swept up in anticommunist hysteria. Given that the Hollywood witch hunts had been going on since 1947, the apparent suddenness of this development in not very realistic, but it presumably increases the sense of terror that the film seeks to portray as endemic in the film industry. Merrill discovers that he, having innocently attended a couple of Communist Party meetings more than a decade earlier, has just been named as a communist sympathizer in the testimony of screenwriter Larry Nolan (Chris Cooper). This fact, together with Merrill's own refusal to name close friends, such as screenwriter Bunny Baxter (George Wendt), quickly results in Merrill's exclusion from employment in the film industry, despite his former status as the "golden boy" of powerful producer and studio executive Darryl Zanuck (Ben Piazza).

Hounded by FBI agents, unable to find a job, and virtually friendless, Merrill is eventually forced to take up residence in a small apartment with his ex-wife, Ruth (Annette Bening), and their young son, Paulie (Luke Edwards). As the pressure builds on Merrill to testify, Zanuck offers him the opportunity to direct a major new film if he will only cooperate with the committee. Finally, he agrees, then goes to Washington, only to have a change of heart in the hearing room and lambaste the committee for their sinister inquiries. He is then dragged away from the microphone. Inspired by Merrill's example, Baxter, who had also agreed to testify, simply takes the fifth amendment and refuses to answer any questions. Merrill thus wins a moral victory but is charged with contempt of Congress, facing a possible prison term. The film then ends with on-screen text announcing that "thousands of lives were shattered and hundreds of career destroyed by what came to be known as the Hollywood blacklist."

The inclusion of the real-world figure Zanuck as a character in *Guilty by Suspicion* adds a certain air of realism to the film, though by far the most realistic treatment of McCarthyism in Hollywood film appears in George Clooney's much praised *Good Night, and Good Luck* (2005), which garnered five Academy Award nominations (including best picture and best director). Clooney's film is also probably the finest film to date to deal directly with the phenomenon of McCarthyism, though it does not deal with the anticommunist purges in Hollywood. In particular, it focuses on the historic televised clash between McCarthy and distinguished CBS news commentator Edward R. Murrow that occurred after Murrow critiqued McCarthy and his methods on his *See It Now* weekly news show in March of 1954. *Good Night, and Good Luck* (the title comes from Murrow's well-known sign-off phrase) is shot in black and white and incorporates a great deal of actual footage from contemporary television programs, giving it an extremely authentic 1950s feel that is further enhanced by the fact that it sticks very closely to the known facts in telling its story.

Ultimately, *Good Night, and Good Luck* is as much about the rise of television as a political force in America in the 1950s, as it is about McCarthyism. Indeed, the film begins in 1958 with a broadcasting industry function at which Murrow is being honored in the wake of the broadcast of the last episode of *See It Now*. Murrow himself delivers an address in which he harshly condemns the medium of television for providing escapist entertainment that insulates audiences from reality rather than helping them to learn about it and deal with it. He also warns that this situation may lead to dire consequences for the nation if something is not done to change it before it is too late.

The film then cuts to 1953 and proceeds to narrate Murrow's encounter with McCarthy, which is thus cast as an example of the kind of responsible, engaged television that, by 1958, had largely disappeared. Actually, Murrow had originally run afoul of McCarthy and his ilk in October 1953, when he ran a *See It Now* episode that criticized the air force for stripping a Lieutenant Milo Radulovich of his commission because he had refused to sever relations with his own father, who was suspected (without actual substantiation) of being a communist. Radulovich was reinstated by the air force soon after the broadcast, which garnered considerable public sentiment for Radulovich and contributed to a growing public sense that the anticommunist purges in Washington had gotten out of hand.

Murrow then takes on McCarthy himself in the landmark March 1954 program in which he charges McCarthy with making dishonest, irresponsible, and unfounded statements to further his own political agenda. Invited by CBS to answer Murrow's criticisms, McCarthy responds on *See It Now* three weeks later, attempting to smear the much-respected Murrow as a communist sympathizer. The real Murrow was good on television; McCarthy was not—and his unfounded charges against Murrow only served to prove Murrow's point about McCarthy's dishonesty and irresponsibility. Both Murrow's criticisms and McCarthy's response work to McCarthy's disadvantage and contribute to his downfall when he was eventually censured by the Senate in December of 1954. On the other hand, the film also makes it clear that CBS, Murrow, and supportive producer Fred Friendly (played by Clooney) experienced considerable pressure from McCarthy and his supporters (such as Hearst columnist Jack O'Brian)—pressure that apparently drove CBS commentator Don Hollenbeck (played in the film by Ray Wise), a Murrow supporter, to suicide.

Of course, as the film also indicates, McCarthy's downfall was even more directly related to the televised Army-McCarthy hearings, in which the U.S. army investigated charges that McCarthy had improperly pressured the army to give favorable treatment to David Schine, an associate of McCarthy's chief counsel, Roy Cohn. During these hearings, McCarthy attempted to turn the tables by charging that the defense industry and possibly the army itself had been infiltrated by communists. In a famous exchange, he claimed (without presenting evidence) that Fred Fisher, a young man who worked in the Boston law office of Joseph Welch, the army's attorney general, might be one of these infiltrators. Welch himself responded, in a moment often considered the beginning of the end for McCarthy: "Have you no sense of decency, sir? At long last, have you no sense of decency?"

Documentary footage of that moment is featured in *Good Night, and Good Luck*, and the fact that the Army-McCarthy hearings were televised, no doubt contributed to their impact, furthering the film's suggestion of the potential power of television—and its criticism that this power has not often been used for the public good. Indeed, the latter part of the film traces the decline of Murrow's television career that began soon after the McCarthy incident, implying that this incident and other controversies—and subsequent decreasing support for Murrow from CBS head William S. Paley (Frank Langella)—might have contributed to that decline. On the other hand, the film also notes the contribution of simple economic pressures as sponsors turned away from responsible news programs such as *See It Now* and toward more popular programming, including game shows such as *The $64,000 Question*, themselves ultimately central to the scandals outlined in the later film *Quiz Show* (1994).

Of course, the political climate of the Cold War years involved more than the twin fears of communist subversion and anticommunist repression. Particularly important to the texture of American life was the fear of literal attack by the Soviets and their allies, an attack that would likely lead to an all-out nuclear war. This fear was reflected in American culture in a number of ways, perhaps most prominently in science fiction film. Those films are discussed in the next chapter.

CHAPTER 4

Science Fiction and Nuclear Fear: The Cold War in American Film

I t is no accident that science fiction rose to an unprecedented prominence in the 1950s, at the height of the Cold War. I have discussed the reasons for this prominence and its terms in my book *Monsters, Mushroom Clouds, and the Cold War* (Greenwood Press, 2001). For now, it is sufficient to say that science fiction was one of the key genres of Cold War film, especially in the 1950s, when science fiction films often responded directly to the public anxieties of the time. For example, the alien-invasion films of the 1950s directly reflected anxieties associated with the Cold War, when the general American population was encouraged by its own government to adopt a siege mentality and to expect invasion from sinister enemies at any moment. Similarly, the numerous post-apocalyptic disaster films of that decade expressed fears of what many saw as an almost inevitable nuclear war between the United States and the Soviet Union. The latter films were also closely related to an important family of more realistic dramas about the possibility of nuclear war that are only vague science fictions.

Among the science fiction films of the 1950s, most closely and obviously related to the anxieties of the Cold War were the numerous alien-invasion films produced during the decade. The popularity of alien-invasion films in the 1950s was no doubt partly due to the fact that such films could be set in a perfectly normal earth environment, thus saving the expense and technical difficulty of depicting alien settings. But the prominence of such films was due to the embattled sense that many Americans felt during the decade. In the science fiction films of the 1950s, the earth, surrounded by a potentially threatening universe, became a consistent metaphor for the

United States, surrounded by a potentially threatening world. Emerging from World War II, the most powerful and richest people on earth—Americans—suddenly found themselves supplanting the British as the central bearers of the banner of Western democracy worldwide. Thus, Americans were confronted not only with the red menace of the Russians (and the opposed red, white, and blue menace of McCarthyism), but with the red and brown and yellow and black menace of all those Third World hordes who had formerly been held in check by the global power of the British Empire. Little wonder that Americans felt so paranoid in the decade, and little wonder that this paranoia often found expression in films dealing with alien invasions.

Numerous alien-invasion films of the 1950s allegorize the communist threat without mentioning it directly. Others are much more direct—and correspondingly more paranoid—about the communist menace. Thus, films such as *Invasion U.S.A.* (1952), *Red Planet Mars* (1952), and *The 27th Day* (1957) overtly thematize the anticommunist paranoia of the 1950s in ways that now seem a bit dated, if not downright bizarre. Thus, in *The 27th Day*, alien invaders distribute devastating antipersonnel weapons among several humans, who subsequently learn how to use the weapons so that they will only kill off "every enemy of peace and freedom." It turns out, fortunately, that there are only a few thousand such enemies, most of them found among the leaders of the Soviet Union. Thus, the doomsday weapon wipes out the bad guys and ushers forth a new era of peace and prosperity for the vast majority of the earth's population, which in this film is virtually everyone who is not a Soviet apparatchik.

Perhaps the weirdest (and worst) of all of the anticommunist alien-invasion films of the 1950s was Harry Horner's *Red Planet Mars*, in which the earth is metaphorically invaded and taken over by Martians, who are led by no less than Jesus Christ (maybe), leading to a new age of global Christian religiosity under the guidance of the president of the United States. In the film, American scientists, using technology first developed by a Nazi superscientist, apparently make contact with Mars, learning that an extremely advanced civilization has established a utopia there via advanced technology. This technology, in fact, makes earth's technology seem obsolete, a fact that immediately leads to the collapse of the world's capitalist economies, while the evil Soviets look on and gloat. Then, suddenly, the Martian messages turn spiritual, announcing that the real secret to their success has been their faith in God and their adherence to the message of Christ. This announcement triggers a global outburst of religious hysteria, though the film does not really explain why most of the earth's inhabitants, who are not Christians, would be so enthusiastic over this announcement. In fact, most earthlings unaccountably conclude that the messages are coming from Christ himself, and the film takes it for granted that the earth's population, even the non-Christian majority, would immediately and unequivocally accept the bizarre notion that Christ is alive and well and living on Mars. Russian peasants return to religion with a particular vengeance, despite the scenes of pure Cold War propaganda in which dozens of them are mowed down by Soviet machine guns as they kneel to pray. In fact, they manage to overturn the Soviet government and to install the patriarch of the Russian Orthodox Church as the new leader of the Russian government, a fact that is treated as a positive movement toward world peace in the film that apparently does not know very much about the Russian Orthodox Church or its contempt for the West.

In fact, the world seems headed for a new era of Christian utopia, led by the president of the United States. Of course, there is no hint that such a development might be greeted by the non-Christian majority of the world's inhabitants as decidedly dystopian, nor is there any explanation of how the world is going to recover from the economic collapse that has just been triggered by the "Christian" messages from Mars. Indeed, by this point, the film has completely forgotten (and therefore does not explore the implications of) the fact that the wave of religious hysteria that it depicts so positively has already destroyed, not only communism, but capitalism as well.

Invasion U.S.A. is a sort of companion piece to *Red Planet Mars* in that neither film is really science fiction in the usual sense; both are fantasies driven by Cold War-inspired anti-Soviet paranoia. *Invasion U.S.A.* begins as several individuals, including TV newsman Vince Potter (Gerald Mohr) and an attractive woman, Carla (Peggie Castle), hang out in a New York bar. There is also a strange figure in the bar known only as Mr. Ohman (read, omen). Suddenly word comes that the enemy has attacked, and the rest of the film shows evil communist invaders murdering, raping, and pillaging their way across the United States, aided by a liberal dose of atomic bombs dropped by their air force. These invaders, though identified in the film as communists, are never specifically identified as Soviets, though the actors playing them occasionally make vague efforts at effecting Russian accents. Actually, the invaders look and sound a lot like German Nazis; indeed much of the film consists of old combat footage from World War II.

In the course of the film, most of the people who had been in the bar are killed as a result of the invasion and of the "bitter struggle against the forces of evil." Meanwhile, romance ludicrously blooms between Carla and Vince, though he is eventually shot down by a fat communist soldier, and Carla has to throw herself out the window to avoid being raped by the same soldier. All is again well, however. As Carla hurtles earthward, the people in the bar suddenly regain consciousness: it has all been a mere illusion produced by Ohman, who has hypnotized everyone in the bar to teach them a lesson about preparedness. They learn the lesson well, and all agree to change their ways, devoting themselves henceforth to preparing Americans for an all-out war against communism.

The conception and execution of *Invasion U.S.A.* are so silly that one is tempted to wonder if the filmmakers were producing a sly spoof. After all, the film was produced by Albert Zugsmith, who later produced Orson Welles's diabolically clever *Touch of Evil* (1958), a masterpiece of film art masquerading as lurid drivel. But *Invasion U.S.A.* director Alfred E. Green was no Orson Welles, and, alas, the film is probably just what it pretends to be. Even at that, it (inadvertently) leaves an awkward question hanging at the end. After all, if the film's hysterical warnings about the dangers of communist aggression turn out to be hallucinations produced by hypnosis, does this really mean that we should take such warnings seriously, or does it mean just the opposite?

The 27th Day, Red Planet Mars, and *Invasion U.S.A.* are extreme cases, but more mainstream science fiction films reflected Cold War anxieties via alien invasions as well. Typical here is the much-admired *Invaders from Mars* (1953), which focuses on young David Maclean (Jimmy Hunt), who sees a Martian saucer land, but can get none of the adults around him to believe him when he reports the landing, especially as the saucer has taken refuge underground. Then David watches in horror as his parents, two policemen, and various other adult authority figures turn into robot-like zombies, manipulated by the Martians using a mind control device. David thus becomes the prototype of the alienated individual, all alone in his knowledge of an alien invasion, crying out fruitless warnings to an unheeding world.

Fortunately, David's isolation, however terrifying, is relatively short-lived. He discovers rather early on, two adult authority figures, medical doctor Pat Blake (Helena Carter) and astronomer Stuart Kelston (Arthur Franz), who accept his story with surprising ease. Kelston's credibility is especially high, and he has no trouble getting the military to accept his warnings, even though General Mayberry (William Forrest), the highest ranking officer in the area, has been taken over by the Martians. From this point on, *Invaders from Mars* is a relatively straightforward combat film. The invaders and their human robots attempt to blow up the local rocket plant and, along with it, a new advanced rocket that is capable of reaching Mars. The military responds by surrounding the landing site with tanks and artillery; soldiers then invade the system of underground tunnels in which the Martians have taken refuge by digging their way through the earth with "some kind of ray." The medical authorities cooperate as well, quickly discovering that the affected locals are being controlled by electronic devices implanted in their brains by the aliens. After a few close calls and tense moments, the army, led by Colonel Fielding (Morris Ankrum), manages to plant a "demolition charge" in the Martian saucer, at the same time rescuing David and Dr. Blake, who have just been taken captive. As the saucer attempts to take off, it explodes into smithereens, awaking David, who, it turns out, has apparently been dreaming the whole thing. Yet, as the film ends, David looks out the window and sees yet another saucer landing off in the distance.

Somewhat in the same vein as *Invaders from Mars* is Don Siegel's alien-invasion classic *Invasion of the Body Snatchers* (1956), one of the signature films of the 1950s. Interestingly, though, this the-aliens-are-already-among-us statement (based on Jack Finney's 1954 novel of the same title but also reminiscent in many ways of Heinlein's 1951 novel *The Puppet Masters*) reflects fears of both communism and capitalism. In the film, local physician Dr. Miles Bennell (Kevin McCarthy) returns home to the small California town of Santa Mira after a trip to a medical convention. At first, the once peaceful town seems very much as it has always been, but Bennell quickly begins to encounter signs that something sinister and strange is afoot. After numerous local citizens (all of whom, interestingly, are women or children) begin to claim that their friends and loved ones have been replaced by impostors, Bennell eventually learns that these replacements have been grown from alien seed pods that have blown in from outer space and that are now engaged in a quest to take control of the entire planet.

The film features a romantic subplot involving the renewal of a former courtship between the divorced Miles and his old girlfriend, Becky Driscoll (Dana Wynter), who has just returned to town after her own divorce. Through much of the film, Miles and Becky struggle to escape from the town so that they can go for help, meanwhile watching everyone in town, especially the town's authority figures, gradually being replaced. Surrounded by an army of emotionless replacements, Miles and Becky become images of American individualism, fighting to maintain their own distinctive identities and their ability to experience human emotion. Scenes in which masses of townspeople pursue the two lone surviving individuals make the film's privileging of the individual over the community quite clear. Eventually, even Becky is replaced, leaving Miles as a lone (and alienated) Jeremiah, crying out in the California desert. He finally manages to escape to a neighboring town, where he is initially thought insane and hospitalized. Indeed, director Don Siegel originally envisioned the film ending with Miles's warnings still being ignored, so that he turns to the audience and warns them they will be next. However, the studio insisted on tacking on a more upbeat ending, so, as the released version of the film comes to a close, an accident victim is brought into the hospital, having been struck by a truck containing giant seed pods. The psychiatrist who has been interviewing Miles suddenly realizes that Miles's story is authentic. He quickly calls the federal and state authorities, who send out an urgent alert that will presumably lead to the defeat of the pod people. The ending is thus doubly reassuring in that it allows Us to overcome Them, while at the same time identifying such suspect figures as psychiatrists, the military, and the federal government as the principal agents of that victory.

But *Invasion of the Body Snatchers* is ultimately more troubling than reassuring. The replacements, who look the same as everyone else, but feel no emotion and have no individuality, directly echo the era's most prevalent stereotypes about communists. Thus, the repeated assurances given Miles by the replacements that his life will be far more pleasant if he simply goes along with the crowd and learns to live without emotion can be taken as echoes of the supposed seductions offered by communist utopianism. On the other hand, the film also draws upon the decade's more general concern about the difficulty of telling the difference between Us and Them. It demonstrates a typical 1950s doubleness by offering the alternative interpretation that the pod people represent, not communism, but the conformist forces (including anticommunism) within American society itself. The film can also be taken as a critique of anticommunist hysteria, rather than as an enactment of it. By this reading, the film suggests that the notion of communists secretly taking over various aspects of American life (as envisioned by anticommunist alarmists like Senator Joseph McCarthy) is about as likely as tiny seeds blowing in from outer space, then developing into large pods that grow perfect replicas of specific human beings, whom they then do away with and replace. In this view, the film suggests that the communist conspiracy warned against by McCarthy and others is incredibly farfetched, the stuff of B-grade science fiction.

Star Kevin McCarthy (whose shared surname with Senator McCarthy provides an additional irony) has stated in an interview that he himself felt that the pod people were reminiscent of the heartless capitalists who work on Madison Avenue. Indeed, if communism was perceived by many Americans of the 1950s as a threat to their cherished individuality, capitalism itself was often perceived in much the same way. While the burgeoning capitalist system of the 1950s produced unprecedented opportunities for upward mobility in America, this highly complex system also required, for its operation, an unprecedented level of efficiency and standardization. Thus, if the 1950s represented a sort of golden age of science fiction film, the decade was also the golden age of American homogenization, as efficiency-oriented mass production techniques pioneered by industrialists such as Henry Ford reached new heights of sophistication and new levels of penetration into every aspect of American life. While television helped to homogenize the thoughts and dreams of the rapidly expanding American population, General Motors, the great industrial power of the decade, achieved unprecedented success in the business in which Ford's techniques had originally been developed. At the same time, Bill Levitt's Long Island suburb of Levittown brought mass production to the housing industry, ushering in the great age of suburbanization, perhaps the single most important step in the commodification of the American dream. The 1950s were also the golden age of branding and franchising, as standard brands, aided by television advertising, installed themselves in the collective American consciousness, while chain franchises spread across the nation, informed by the central driving idea of homogeneity—selling identical products in identical ways at thousands of identical franchises across the country. Thus, if Levitt's vision helped to homogenize the American home, Kemmons Wilson's Holiday Inn chain made identical lodgings available to Americans wherever they drove on the nation's rapidly expanding (and more and more homogeneous) highway system in their increasingly powerful, standardized automobiles. Similarly, Ray Kroc made homogeneous food available on the road when he took the fast-food production techniques pioneered by the McDonald brothers and made standardized hamburgers an indispensable part of everyday cuisine in America.

In short, the pod people of *Invasion of the Body Snatchers* can be seen as an allegorical representation of either passionless, interchangeable communist drones or mindless shoppers brainwashed by advertising into the consumption of standardized commodities. In either case, the film partakes of the classic Cold War fear of psychological and behavioral manipulation. The same, in fact, might be said of *Invaders from Mars*, with its vision of high police and military officials taken over by alien mind control devices. Thus, David Seed, in his book *American Science Fiction and the Cold War: Literature and Film* (Edinburgh University Press, 1999) finds this film the "most politically explicit" of the alien "conspiracy" films of the period; he argues that the mind control motif in the film can be related to contemporary revelations over the supposed brainwashing of American POWs in Korea by their communist captors (p. 133). This aspect of the film, of course, links it to any number of the espionage thrillers that were produced during the Cold War.

Among such thrillers, most directly related to the motif of the Korean brainwashing is John Frankenheimer's Cold War classic, *The Manchurian Candidate*, perhaps the central Cold War political thriller among all American films. Based on a novel by Richard Condon, *The Manchurian Candidate* grows out of one of the central elements of Cold War anxiety: that diabolical communists were somehow able to "brainwash" innocent Americans, transforming them into communists or communist sympathizers. Indeed, the term "brainwashing" was first used in the United States to explain the fact that an extraordinary percentage (perhaps as many as one-third) of American prisoners of war in the Korean conflict of 1950–1953 ended up defecting to the communist side. The term quickly became a part of the American popular imagination, partly because the notion of communist brainwashing was actively promoted in the press, especially in the writings of Edward Hunter, a journalist who was later revealed to be a CIA propagandist working undercover (and thus engaged in a brainwashing project of his own).

The Manchurian Candidate draws upon suspicions concerning the brainwashing of American POWs in Korea, centering on the fictional capture and brainwashing of an American patrol in Korea in 1952. However, it gives the motif an additional twist by envisioning an intricate plot in which the communists plan to use the brainwashing of this patrol to seize control of the American presidency. In particular, Chinese and Russian scientists (with pictures of Mao and Stalin in the background) work to condition the members of the captured patrol to believe that they were never captured but were instead saved by the heroic actions of Staff Sergeant Raymond Shaw (Laurence Harvey). This process (which takes only three days) is so successful that, upon their return to America, Shaw is awarded the Congressional Medal of Honor on the recommendation of the patrol's commanding officer, Captain Bennett Marco (Frank Sinatra), who is himself promoted to Major.

Meanwhile, in a move that does not really make much sense, Shaw seems to have been carefully selected for this role because he is the stepson of John Yerkes Iselin (James Gregory), a McCarthyesque red-baiting senator who hopes to parlay his fabricated exposés of communist infiltration of the U.S. government into his party's vice-presidential nomination in the upcoming elections. Then again, numerous things do not quite make sense in this film, which seems intentionally to seek to produce an air of strangeness. For example, at one point Marco meets a woman on a train. They have a dialogue that sounds so strange that one suspects it is designed to trigger Marco's programming. For example, the woman, Eugenie Chaney (Janet Leigh), wants to be called Rosie—and she insists on praising the beauty of the Maryland landscape, even though they are passing through Delaware at the time. After meeting Marco, who seems on the verge of a total breakdown due to the aftereffects of his brainwashing, Rosie immediately breaks off her engagement and takes up with him. But her role in the film ends there, and we are left merely to ponder the possibility that she might not be on the level.

Iselin is a buffoon who is essentially the puppet of Shaw's manipulative mother (played by Angela Lansbury), but that is largely the point. Mrs. Iselin, we eventually discover, is actually a communist agent, while her son has been programmed via brainwashing to assassinate the party's presidential candidate, Benjamin K. Arthur (Robert Riordan). Iselin will then presumably to propelled to the presidency, where he will be a dupe of his wife and her communist backers. However, the plot begins to go wrong when Marco's conditioning begins to fade and he starts to suspect that his implanted memories of what happened in Korea are false. After a period during which he seems to be on the verge of a complete breakdown, Marco eventually manages to overcome his programming and to deactivate Shaw's programming as well. However, Shaw has by this time already committed three murders due to this programming, including that of Senator Thomas Jordan (John McGiver), a prominent liberal who had sworn to block Iselin's vice-presidential nomination. As a result of Jordan's removal, Iselin is able to secure that nomination, but Shaw, deprogrammed by Marco, foregoes the killing of Arthur and instead shoots down both his mother and Senator Iselin. He then takes his own life as Marco rushes in to try to stop him. The plot is thus foiled—unless the plot was really to get rid of the Iselins all along and Marco has himself been programmed (perhaps Rosie is his controller?) to maneuver Shaw into killing them.

The Manchurian Candidate is a complex film that seems to endorse contemporary anxieties about communist brainwashing, while at the same time suggesting that anticommunist zealots are actually playing into the hands of the very communists they purport to oppose. Meanwhile, that the signals used to activate Shaw's programming are sometimes delivered via television also speaks to contemporary fears that the still relatively new medium might itself have considerable potential as a brainwashing tool. Indeed, television sets seem unusually ubiquitous in this film, which suggests, fairly early on, the growing role of television in American politics. In addition, the fact that President John F. Kennedy was assassinated (ostensibly by a man who had recently spent time in the Soviet Union) a year after *The Manchurian Candidate* was released gave the film new prominence, fueling speculation that Lee Harvey Oswald might have been programmed, like Shaw, to commit the assassination. This connection seemed so direct that Sinatra actually bought the rights to the film and kept it out of circulation for years after the Kennedy assassination.

Ultimately, however, *The Manchurian Candidate* may be most important not as a film about assassination or brainwashing but as a cynically satirical treatment of the political process itself, suggesting that this process is not at all what it appears to be. Per this film, politics is not a matter of candidates discussing issues and offering themselves as effective representatives of the voters. Instead, it is a matter of secret deals and clandestine maneuvers, with the spoils of electoral office (even the presidency itself) going to those who execute these maneuvers most effectively. This message is also reinforced by the film's unique style. Narrated in a nonlinear fashion and featuring a number of odd-angled shots and a great deal of strange-sounding dialogue, the film has a disorienting, surreal feel that reinforces its suggestion of a fundamental strangeness and confusion in the political process.

Among other things, *The Manchurian Candidate* makes McCarthyism seem particularly strange and dishonest, and Frankenheimer has said that the critique of McCarthyism is the aspect of the film of which he is most proud. It thus stood as one of the first major Hollywood films openly to critique McCarthyism, which had previously been taken on only in marginal films or in indirect ways. However, at least one important early science fiction film, Robert Wise's *The Day the Earth Stood Still* (1951), was a plea for global peace and understanding that openly rejected the paranoid terms of Cold War anticommunism and the Cold War arms race. Here, the Christ-like alien Klaatu (Michael Rennie) comes to earth (supported by the powerful superrobot Gort) on a mission of peace. The climate on earth being what it is, Klaatu is greeted with suspicion and violence. He is, in fact, shot and killed by the U.S. military, though Gort is able to resurrect him so that he can deliver a stern warning to earth's leaders. Having convened a gathering of the world's leading intellectuals (and thus circumventing the world's political leaders), Klaatu announces that earth's arpidly accelerating arms race must be brought to and end. "It is no concern of ours how you run your own planet," he assures them, "But if you threaten to extend your violence, this earth of yours will be reduced to a burned-out cinder. Your choice is simple: join us and live in peace, or pursue your present course and face obliteration." Klaatu and Gort then reenter their flying saucer and fly away into space, ending the film with this ultimatum hanging in the air.

The Day the Earth Stood Still is a courageous film that went directly against many prevailing ideas of its time, while also demonstrating the capacity of science fiction film to be thoughtful and serious, as well as entertaining. In addition to its obvious condemnation of the arms race, one of the most important political statements in *The Day the Earth Stood Still* involves its extremely positive representation of intellectuals and scientists, especially one Professor Barnhardt (Sam Jaffe), who is characterized as a figure of courage, wisdom, and compassion. Barnhardt serves as a transparent stand-in for Albert Einstein, a controversial figure during the Cold War: not only was he both a foreigner and a Jew (World War II had discredited, but had not eliminated, American anti-Semitism), but he was also an international celebrity who openly used his prominence to agitate for peace. Meanwhile, the casting of Jaffe in the role made Barnhardt even more controversial as a character. The anticommunist purges that swept Hollywood in the late 1940s and early 1950s were at their very height, and Jaffe was among those who were suspected of having communist sympathies. Indeed, Jaffe's appearance in *The Day the Earth Stood Still* would be his last in an American film for seven years due to the blacklist.

This film demonstrated very early in the Cold War, the capacity of science fiction for political critique, especially critique of the xenophobic mentality of the Cold War arms race. Unfortunately, few films followed in its footsteps, though a notable late exception that serves very much as a companion piece to *The Day the Earth Stood Still* is James Cameron's *The Abyss* (1989). Indeed, Cameron's film, which appeared near the end of the Cold War joins Wise's film to bracket the Cold War period with alien-invasion tales designed to critique the arms race.

In *The Abyss*, an American nuclear submarine crashes into an underwater outcropping of rock and then slides over a cliff and sinks into a deep pit at the bottom of the ocean. The crew of a submersible oil-drilling rig (Deepcore 2), commanded by Virgil "Bud" Brigman (Ed Harris), is then called in to try to salvage the sub, aided by a team of Navy Seals. In the process, Brigman, descends into a deep trench while trying to disarm a nuclear bomb that has fallen into the trench. He is nearly killed in the effort but is rescued by a strange, luminous, angel-like alien that takes him aboard its huge ship, resting on the floor of the trench. Using their technological ability to manipulate water, the aliens create a room in which Bud can breathe. They begin to communicate with him by creating a video wall that displays a series of images, making it clear that they have been observing earth for some time. They then allow Bud to watch television news reports as they use their technology to create huge walls of water that approach coastal areas around the world. Just as the walls of water are about to crash down on the helpless people below them, the aliens stop the water short and allow it to recede harmlessly into the ocean. But they have made clear that they have great destructive power should they so wish. They convey to Bud that this display is meant as a warning for earth's military powers to cease their confrontational Cold War tactics, else the aliens will be forced to intercede. This time, however, the aliens have decided to give humanity one more chance, because they have also observed a great deal that is good in the race, as epitomized by Bud's willingness to sacrifice himself to disarm the bomb, saving his colleagues, and by the tenderness they have seen between Bud and Lindsey as she talked him down during the descent into the trench.

The Abyss include a number of sentimental elements, including the restoration of the relationship between Brigman and his former wife, Lindsey (Mary Elizabeth Mastrantonio). Nevertheless, it makes important points about the Cold War arms race, even if these points may have been a bit clichéd by 1989. The tension between the Navy Seals and the civilian crew of the oil rig also seems a bit familiar. It is particularly reminiscent of a similar military vs. civilian confrontation in Christian Nyby's *The Thing from Another World* (1951), one of the prototypical alien-invasion narratives of the 1950s. Here, opposed groups of scientists and military men encounter an alien ship (and an alien) in the arctic, an isolated setting that serves much the same function as the deep-sea setting of *The Abyss*.

However, the alien in *The Thing from Another World* is a vicious killer, set on the destruction of the humans it encounters, while the highly evolved aliens of *The Abyss* only want to save humans from themselves. Further, while *The Thing* presents its military men as sensible and strong, the scientists who oppose them are excessively devoted to logic and thus cut off from their own humanity. Moreover, the chief scientist, Dr. Arthur Carrington (Robert Cornthwaite), even wears a Russian-style hat, suggesting that his blind devotion to the scientific method aligns him with the cold rationality of communism.

In *The Abyss* it is the military men who are excessively devoted to their own narrow point of view, while the oil riggers who oppose them are aligned with genuine humanity. In short, as a Cold War film, *The Abyss* is much more in the antiwar spirit of *The Day the Earth Stood Still* than the militaristic spirit of *The Thing*, which urges vigilance against enemies, rather than understanding. On the other hand, the sentimentalism of *The Abyss* takes it well beyond *The Day the Earth Stood Still* to reassure its audiences that human beings can often be noble and kind and that the race is thus well worth saving.

This point is especially clear in the special edition of the film (available on DVD), which delivers a message entirely missing from the original theatrical version. Here, the aliens make it clear that they have the power to destroy humanity altogether but that their observations of Bud's love for Lindsey and of his willingness to sacrifice himself for her and his fellow oil riggers have convinced them that there is enough good in the human race that they might still be saved. Of course, there is also an implied warning (again reminiscent of *The Day the Earth Stood Still*) that the aliens might still find it advisable to destroy the human race if they do not heed this warning. Thus, in both *The Day the Earth Stood Still* and *The Abyss* humanity is threatened with destruction at alien hands as a way of warning against the potential destruction that humans might visit upon themselves as a result of the Cold War arms race.

In the post–Cold War years of the 1990s, alien-invasion films became less paranoid and more fun, as in Roland Emmerich's *Independence Day* (1996), a feel-good narrative about the ultimate ability of good old American courage and ingenuity to meet and defeat any possible alien threat. By this time, however, the emphasis had perhaps shifted more to the other major subgenre of Cold War science fiction film, the post-apocalyptic narrative. However, the most prominent post-apocalyptic narratives of the late and post–Cold War years were the *Terminator* trilogy and the *Matrix* trilogy, each of which envisioned an apocalypse brought about not by sinister communist enemies but by rebellious machines created through our own over-reliance on technology.

During the peak Cold War years, however, post-apocalyptic films were transparently related to the anxieties of the period, often in quite interesting and telling ways. Many of these films were patently silly, as in Roger Corman's *The Day the World Ended* (1955). This film features a hackneyed plot, stock characters, and a really cheesy-looking monster but it is still notable as one of the few films of the 1950s that actually showed the effects of radiation on humans, however unrealistic its depiction of those effects might have been. It thus differs from the most popular post-holocaust film of the 1950s, Stanley Kramer's *On the Beach* (1959), which shows no such effects. In this film, set in 1964 and based on Nevil Shute's 1957 Australian novel of the same title, a global nuclear war has apparently destroyed all human life everywhere on earth, except Australia, which has been spared because of its remote location. Unfortunately, the clouds of deadly radiation that cover the rest of the globe are headed for Australia as well, so the Australians themselves have only a few months before what seems to be inevitable death.

To an extent, *On the Beach* is more human drama than science fiction, detailing as it does the attempts of the various characters to cope with their impending dooms. Meanwhile, the film is entirely sanitized. There are no corpses, no radiation burns, not even property damage. While we do see shots of post-holocaust San Francisco and San Diego, the cities are entirely undamaged. The only change is that all the people seem to have disappeared. As such, the film's antiarms race message is a bit muted, though still clear.

Other post-holocaust films of the long 1950s were even more indirect in their representation of nuclear war and its aftermath. For example, in Edward Bernds's *World without End* (1956), the nuclear holocaust is projected hundreds of years into the future, and the film itself is set hundreds of years after that, when radiation levels have essentially returned to normal. Many aspects of *World without End* seem derived from H. G. Wells's classic 1895 novel, *The Time Machine*, which would be adapted more directly to film a few years later in George Pal's *The Time Machine* (1960). Indeed, *World without End* and Pal's film have at least one obvious intertextual link: Pal's time traveler is played by Rod Taylor, who had played one of the astronauts in *World without End*. The film version of *The Time Machine* is a reasonably faithful adaptation of Wells's novel and therefore seems to have little to do with the genre of the post-nuclear holocaust film. On the other hand, Pal (who had produced many of the leading science fiction films of the previous decade) does at one point have his time traveler (who begins his journey on New Year's Eve, 1899) stop off in 1966, where he is nearly killed in a nuclear assault on London. Therefore, when he subsequently travels into the far future (he ends up in the year 802,701, just as in Wells's book), the depiction of the dystopian environment of that future is given a post-holocaust cast.

By 1962, science fiction films began to deal a bit more directly (and less optimistically) with nuclear holocaust, though a film such as Ray Milland's *Panic in Year Zero* still resembles *On the Beach* in its failure to represent the actual effects of nuclear war on human victims. Indeed, graphic on-screen depictions of the actual effects of nuclear war were rare until the mid-1980s, when a spate of such films appeared, including *The Day After* (1983), *Testament* (1983), and *Threads* (1984), the latter a British entry. In the meantime, the nuclear holocaust films of the long 1950s were topped off, in 1963 and 1964, by an important series of what might be called pre-holocaust films. No doubt influenced by the perceived close call of the 1962 Cuban missile crisis, each of these films in its own way deals, not with the aftermath of a nuclear holocaust, but with a proposed scenario that might be envisioned as leading to such a holocaust. Actually, John Frankenheimer's *Seven Days in May* (1964, written by *Twilight Zone* maven Rod Serling) deals only indirectly with the prospect of nuclear holocaust. In this taut political thriller, Air Force General James Mattoon Scott (Burt Lancaster), the chairman of the Joint Chiefs of Staff, leads an effort of the U.S. military to take control of the federal government to prevent President Jordan Lyman (Fredric March) from pursuing a course of détente with the Soviets. Fortunately, Scott's aide, Colonel Martin "Jiggs" Casey (Kirk Douglas), learns of the plot and tips off the president, who is thereby able (just barely) to avert the coup.

Seven Days in May deals with nuclear holocaust in the sense that Scott justifies his coup attempt on the basis of his conviction that the Soviets—once the Americans are weakened by a policy of disarmament—are bound to launch a sneak nuclear attack on the United States. Lyman, on the other hand, counters with the theory that the coup itself might lead the Soviets to attempt a preemptive strike in order to defend themselves from the threat posed by an American regime headed by a zealot such as Scott. Meanwhile, the fanatic Scott is unambiguously identified as the villain of the piece, so that the film is quite clear in its critique of the hawkish military mentality that he represents. It is also clear in its suggestion that overzealous attempts to defend American democracy from outside foes might themselves lead to the downfall of the democracy that these attempts are supposedly designed to prevent. Scott, however, is more a symptom of a larger phenomenon than a cause. Thus, Lyman explains that the real enemy is not Scott and his supporters, but "an age, the nuclear age. It happens to have killed man's faith in his ability to influence what happens to him." It is this feeling of helplessness that makes the general population vulnerable to a demagogue like Scott, whom Lyman, in this sense, explicitly compares to Senator Joseph McCarthy.

Seven Days in May thus joins Frankenheimer's earlier *The Manchurian Candidate* (1962), which lampoons McCarthy even more directly, as two of

American film's central explorations of the mentality of the Cold War. Meanwhile, Sidney Lumet's tense thriller *Fail-Safe* (1964) explores the dangers of the Cold War arms race in a different way. Here, it is not crazed ideologues, but overly complex machinery that gets out of hand, sending American nuclear bombers toward Moscow by accident. The elaborate security measures that are built into the system make it impossible to recall the bombers and, in the end, Moscow is bombed, despite the best efforts of the President (Henry Fonda) and the American military to avert the bombing. Moreover, as a gesture of good faith, the president orders New York bombed as well, thus preventing Soviet retaliation, which might have led to the total destruction of both the United States and the Soviet Union.

The primary message of *Fail-Safe* is that our current course of developing more and more sophisticated defense systems will almost certainly lead to a catastrophe of this sort, even if human beings do not intentionally initiate nuclear war. Meanwhile, the film anticipates later films such as the *Terminator* and *Matrix* sequences by addressing a general anxiety over the growing importance of machines in American life. In particular, it expresses the widespread fear that we are becoming the servants of our technology, rather than the other way around. At the same time, the film, scripted by formerly blacklisted screenwriter Walter Bernstein, also criticizes the militant anticommunist hysteria that informed American attitudes during the Cold War. For one thing, the Soviets, and especially the Soviet premier, are presented in an extremely positive light, responding rationally and humanely to the crisis. But the same cannot be said for one of the major American characters, the civilian political scientist Professor Groeteschele (Walter Matthau), who serves as a top advisor to the Pentagon. Groeteschele, though a civilian, is an ideological counterpart to General Scott of *Seven Days in May*. A virulent anticommunist, Groeteschele urges the Pentagon to take advantage of the accidental bombing of Moscow to launch an all-out first-strike assault, destroying the evil Soviets once and for all. Luckily, cooler heads prevail, and no one takes his advice, though he is still at work at the end of the film, urging authorities to make no attempt to rescue human survivors of the bombing of New York and to concentrate instead on the recovery of corporate records, which are vital to the economy.

Groeteschele's attitudes are thus linked to corporate capitalism, though he himself admits that he learned his ruthless attitudes from the German Nazis. This background makes him a counterpart to the title character of the brilliant *Dr. Strangelove* (1963), which, more than any other single film captured the lunacy of the Cold War mentality, while at the same time suggesting that certain American attitudes in the Cold War might have been inherited from the Nazis. *Dr. Strangelove*, in its parodic focus on the comic absurdity of the arms race, also signals a turn to more satirical strategies in dealing with the tensions of the Cold War. Based (loosely) on the novel *Red Alert* (1958) by Peter George, *Dr. Strangelove* goes well beyond the basically serious novel in its absurdist satire of the ideology of the Cold War arms race. *Dr. Strangelove* became a cult favorite of the 1960s youth movement and was one of the classics of American culture of the 1960s, even though, strictly speaking, it is a British film, produced at London's Hawk Studios. In fact, the film is so representative that historian Margot Henriksen entitled her own 1997 study of the ideology of Cold War America *Dr. Strangelove's America.*

The premise of the film is simple: both the United States and the Soviet Union are so caught up in the arms race that they pursue insane courses that make nuclear holocaust almost inevitable. Indeed, the film's crisis is triggered by literal insanity, that of General Jack D. Ripper (played with appropriately grim lunacy by Sterling Hayden), commander of Burpelson Air Force Base and of a wing of the Strategic Air Command's fleet of B-52 nuclear bombers. Unhinged by his extreme anticommunist paranoia (which leads him to believe that communist conspiracies are seeking to "sap and impurify all of our precious bodily fluids" through techniques such as fluoridation of water), Ripper orders his bombers to attack the Soviet Union, thereby triggering the labyrinthine security procedures that make it almost impossible to recall such an order.

Most of the film involves the efforts of the American government to recall the attack and thus avert the inevitable Russian retaliation. Much of it is set in the memorable war room, where President Merkin Muffley (played by Peter Sellers, who also plays Dr. Strangelove and Group Captain Lionel Mandrake, a British exchange officer serving as Ripper's aide) convenes a meeting of his chief strategic advisors in an attempt to deal with the crisis. Chief among these advisors are General Buck Turgidson (played by George C. Scott and so named for both his phallic exploits and his penchant for inflated rhetorical posturing) and the zanily sinister Strangelove, whose continuing loyalty to his former Nazi bosses becomes increasingly obvious in the course of the film. When all attempts to avert the attack seem to be failing, Turgidson suggests an all-out assault while the United States still has the element of surprise on its side. Muffley, however, opts to warn the Russians, apologetically explaining the situation to Soviet Premier Dimitri Kissov in terms that make launching a nuclear strike seem like nothing more than a sort of social faux pas. The Americans then learn to their horror that the Russians, as a deterrent to precisely such attacks, have installed a Doomsday Machine that will be automatically triggered by any nuclear blast over the Soviet Union, enveloping the planet in a cloud of radioactive dust and destroying all life.

Ripper, the only man who knows the code that can cancel the attack order, commits suicide to avoid revealing it. Fortunately, however, Mandrake manages to deduce the code, but before he can deliver it to the president, he is taken captive by Army Colonel "Bat" Guano (Keenan Wynn), who suspects that Mandrake, as a foreigner, is a commie "prevert." Finally, after a comic scene in which he has to convince Guano to break open a Coke machine (despite concerns of potential retribution from the Coca Cola Company) to get change to use a pay phone, Mandrake calls the president and gives him the information so the attack can be averted. In the meantime, one of the bombers, commanded by Major J. T. "King" Kong (Slim Pickens), has been damaged by antiaircraft missiles and is unable to receive the command to avert the attack. The crew struggles to keep the plane aloft and manages to reach a potential target, only to find that the damage from the missile has also caused the bomb doors to jam. Kong crawls down into the bomb bay and manages to open the doors and release the weapon, dropping out of the plane astride the bomb and, in one of the most memorable scenes in modern film, riding it bronco-style, waving his cowboy hat and whooping it up as the bomb falls to earth.

The screen then goes white as the bomb hits the ground, which might have been the best ending, dramatically, for the film. However, Kubrick tacks on an additional scene that makes some important thematic points. In the scene, Strangelove, while involved in a comic wrestling match with his bionic right arm that seems intent on shooting upward in a Nazi salute, concocts a plan for preserving civilization by founding colonies at the bottom of mine shafts, safe from the radioactive cloud. This plan is a burlesque of virtually all of the post-holocaust fictions of the long 1950s, revealing the fantasy elements that lie behind so many of them. For example, Strangelove suggests that, in order to facilitate repopulation of the earth, the new colonies should include ten women for every man and that, in order to encourage the men to do their reproductive duty, these women should be chosen for their "stimulating sexual characteristics." Meanwhile, Turgidson's gleeful reaction to this plan reveals the true nature of his personality. The scene ends as both the Americans and the Russian ambassador, called to the war room as part of the effort to avert the crisis, begin to get concerned about a possible "mine shaft gap," suggesting that the two sides have still failed to learn their lesson about the folly of such competition. The film then ends with a sequence of shots of nuclear explosions and mushroom clouds, with sentimental music (Vera Lynn's "We'll Meet Again") playing in the background.

In many ways, *Dr. Strangelove* is weak as a political film. It does nothing to examine the historical and political background of the Cold War, depicting it essentially as an ego contest between American madmen and Russian madmen. In the kind of association between violence and sexuality that is central to much of Kubrick's work, the film characterizes the Cold War as a phallic competition driven by erotic energies, with macho generals on both sides trying to establish their greater manhood by proving that they have the bigger and more effective weapons. Strangelove (so memorable in Sellers's portrayal, despite the fact that he is actually onscreen a surprisingly short time) may be the film's most potent political image. His crucial presence as the president's chief strategic advisor in the Cold War (emphasized through the titling of the film) tends to align the American position with that of the German Nazis, suggesting that Cold War America has followed in Hitler's footsteps in attempting to exterminate the Soviet Union and all it represents. If nothing else, this motif calls attention to the willingness of the United States to align itself with repressive right-wing regimes around the world in the effort to win support in the battle against communism. Still, the primary political orientation of the film is certainly not procommunist, or even anti-American, but antimilitary, with the Soviet military leaders being at least as insane as the Americans in their blind pursuit of nuclear superiority.

The explosions at the end of *Dr. Strangelove* presumably mean the end of human civilization, and perhaps human life, on earth. But, in another sense, they signal the end of an era in post-holocaust fiction and film. After *Dr. Strangelove*, it would become increasingly difficult to produce post-holocaust films (and, to an extent, novels) with a straight face. In particular, after Kubrick's definitive statement on the absurdity of the arms race, film could no longer effectively perform its established function of soothing and softening nuclear fear. Indeed, it might be argued that *Dr. Strangelove* itself was partly responsible for the dramatic downturn in enthusiasm for the arms race among the American population from 1964 onward. Meanwhile, American society became more and more concerned with the war in Vietnam and with the domestic politics of the civil rights and women's movements. The golden era of nuclear fear was at an end, though the Cold War (and the tensions that went along with it) would persist for another quarter of a century, infecting American attitudes about everything from literature to liberation, from cinema to sexuality, in ways that we have only just begun to understand.

Films related to nuclear fear continued to appear as well. *The Missiles of October* (1974), a made-for-television film directed by Anthony Page, is a dramatization of the inside workings of government during the Cuban Missile Crisis of October, 1962. Amid a large and illustrious cast of some of the best known American television actors of the 1970s, the film features William Devane as President John F. Kennedy, Martin Sheen as Attorney General Robert F. Kennedy, Ralph Bellamy as U.S., ambassador to the United Nations Adlai Stevenson, and Howard Da Silva as Soviet Premier Nikita Khrushchev. Based partly on Robert Kennedy's book *Thirteen Days: A Memoir of the Cuban Missile Crisis*, the book details the furious efforts of President Kennedy, his cabinet, and other administration insiders to avert nuclear war in the most tense moments of the entire Cold War. President Kennedy (not surprisingly) comes off especially well in the film (as do Robert Kennedy and Stevenson), while the American military, portrayed as hawkish and eager for combat, comes off rather poorly. Perhaps the most surprising part of the film is the positive portrayal of Khrushchev as a wise elder statesman, less polished than the sophisticated and well-educated Kennedy but very much the equal of Kennedy not only in ability but in his desire for peace, even when it puts him at odds with much of the Kremlin bureaucracy. The film is quite evenhanded in its overall portrayal of the crisis, avoiding the good vs. evil oppositions that were so typical of the rhetoric of the Cold War. Indeed, while the film does not take sides, it clearly leaves open the possibility of seeing the aggressive American attitude toward Cuba as the most important cause of the crisis. In any case, the film was first broadcast in December 1974, four months after the resignation of President Richard Nixon due to the Watergate scandal. In that sense, the film is almost nostalgic about the dark days of the Cuban Missile Crisis, seemingly looking back to a time when the United States had genuine and effective presidential leadership. Kennedy, here, is a Lincolnesque figure, grimly doing what he feels is right while carrying the weight of the world on his shoulders.

Despite its title, Roger Donaldson's *Thirteen Days* (2000), a theatrical film that covers much of the same material as *The Missiles of October*, is based not on Robert Kennedy's book but on the book *The Kennedy Tapes: Inside the White House During the Cuban Missile Crisis* (1998). Edited (with commentary) by historians Ernest May and Philip Zelikow, the book presents the transcripts of tapes that President Kennedy secretly made of meetings and conversations that occurred among his advisors during the 1962 crisis. In the film, John and Robert Kennedy (played by Bruce Greenwood and Steven Culp, respectively) are still major figures, but presidential advisor Ken O'Donnell (Kevin Costner) emerges as perhaps the central figure in the film, partly because he is the only character for whom we see the impact of the crisis on his private life. John Kennedy still provides effective leadership through the crucial period, though he may seem a bit more humanly fallible (and less nobly Lincolnesque) than in *The Missiles of October*.

As in the earlier film, *Thirteen Days* is quite evenhanded, depicting the crisis as the result of mistakes on both sides and its resolution as the results of the efforts of "good men" on both sides to avert disaster. The later film, however, focuses almost exclusively on the American side, with very brief appearances by Soviet leaders (Khrushchev does not actually appear in the film at all). *Thirteen Days* is more effectively dramatic (the earlier film can be a bit plodding at points), and nuclear war seems even closer than in *The Missiles of October*. In *Thirteen Days*, however, the American military comes off even worse, though much of the drama now has less to do with the battles between the Kennedy administration and the Soviets than with the struggles of the administration to reign in a Pentagon bureaucracy that seems bent on war. General Curtis LeMay (Kevin Conway), the air force chief of staff, comes off as a particularly sinister figure, maneuvering at several points to move the military toward war, even if it means having to go around the president.

Among other things, the hawkishness of the American military as depicted in *Thirteen Days* (based, we should recall, on real historical records) provides a chilling retrospective suggestion that it was the Pentagon, rather than the White House, that was responsible for the subsequent buildup of American military activity in Vietnam, especially after the assassination of President Kennedy just over a year after the Cuban crisis. This aspect of the film even provides possible ominous hints (reinforced through the presence of Costner, the star of Oliver Stone's *JFK*) that Kennedy might have been killed as the result of a conspiracy (involving the military and the CIA) that grew out of his conflicts with the military over policy in both Cuba and Vietnam. Of course, such hints of conspiracy had, by the time of *Thirteen Days*, become a staple of American film. Often, however, the conspiracies depicted in American film were associated with the media rather than the government. It is certainly the case that the media have played a larger and larger role in American politics over the past century. The Hollywood film industry, of course, is a part of the media, so it should come as no surprise that the role of the media has often been a focus of American political films. This role has often been depicted as negative, and Hollywood itself has frequently come in for criticism in such films, though television has generally been identified as the main culprit in the corruption of the American political process in films about politics and the media. The next chapter discusses such films in detail.

CHAPTER 5

As Seen on Television: Politics and the Media in American Film

Alan J. Pakula's *All the President's Men* (1976) dramatizes the investigation of the Watergate scandal by *Washington Post* reporters Bob Woodward (Robert Redford) and Carl Bernstein (Dustin Hoffman). In so doing, it documents one of the best examples in all of American history of the impact of the media on American politics. In the film (as they had in reality) Woodward and Bernstein tenaciously work to uncover the truth about the June 1972 burglary of the Democratic Party's offices in Washington's Watergate Hotel, eventually uncovering crucial evidence of White House involvement not only in this break-in, but also in a variety of other questionable operations, including official attempts to hide the truth of those operations from the press and the public. As a result of these investigations, sitting president Richard Nixon, recently reelected by a landslide margin, is forced to resign from office.

All the President's Men looks back, via its title, to the novel and film versions of *All the King's Men*, suggesting corruption and abuse of power in the Nixon White House that resemble those of the fictional Willy Stark (who himself was based on real-world politician Huey Long). The Pakula film, however, is constructed as a taut political thriller, much in the mode of near-contemporary works such as Pakula's *The Parallax View* (1974), Francis Ford Coppola's *The Conversation* (1974), and Sydney Pollack's *Three Days of the Condor* (1975). All of these films show the influence of the Watergate investigations that produced a paranoid sense that the world was a far more dangerous and sinister place than most people had previously suspected, with powerful forces (including agencies of the U.S. government) at work in a variety of complex conspiracies. *All the President's*

Men, however, differs from the other films in that it is based on a true story and one the outcome of which was well known. To its credit, however, it maintains suspense throughout, even for audiences quite familiar with the story on which it was based.

All the President's Men, based on Woodward and Bernstein's 1974 book of the same title, was an effective enough film to win four Academy Awards, as well as four other nominations (including the categories of Best Director and Best Picture). It tells the story of how the two reporters, initially puzzled by a number of odd details about the Watergate break-in (which was carried out in order to plant wire-taps and photograph confidential documents in the Democratic offices), decide to pursue the seemingly small story. As they begin their investigation, they discover that information about the break-in or the burglars (mostly Cuban Americans) is suspiciously hard to uncover. It is almost, they conclude, as if the various potential sources they interview have all been coached to be nonresponsive to their questions. Indeed, their investigation meets with increasing resistance on a number of fronts, but they continue nevertheless, gaining much-needed support from *Post* executive editor Ben Bradlee (Jason Robards). Gradually, helped along at key points by hints from the mysterious figure of "Deep Throat" (played by Hal Holbrook), Woodward and Bernstein begin to assemble a more and more coherent (and ominous) picture from the bits and pieces of evidence they are able to acquire. This picture suggests a massive web of official conspiracy (with extensive involvement on the part of the CIA, FBI, and other agencies) of which the Watergate break-in and subsequent cover-up were only a part. As they uncover more and more sensitive information, there are suggestions that the two reporters might themselves be in danger of assassination, but they persevere, following the trail all the way to the White House, revealing, among other things, the existence of the now-famous tape recordings that would be crucial to Nixon's ultimate decision to resign from office in order to avoid impeachment and removal.

Not surprisingly, given the source, *All the President's Men* is told very much from the perspective of Woodward and Bernstein, focusing much more on their activities than on the machinations of the Nixon White House (Oliver Stone's *Nixon* would eventually dramatize much of the same story from the perspective of the White House). As such, *All the President's Men* is probably the most detailed documentation in all of American film of the work of investigative reporters. Moreover, though it may be a film more about reporting than politics, it also suggests that investigative reporting can be an integral part of the political process, demonstrating a crucial role for the media as a watchdog over the operations of a government that cannot necessarily be trusted to follow the rules or behave in the best interests of the general population.

In its positive portrayal of newspaper reporters as the righteous foes of corrupt politicians, *All the President's Men* participates in a long tradition in American film. Early films such as Lewis Milestone's *The Front Page* (1931) and Howard Hawks's remake *His Girl Friday* (1940) established newspaper reporters as central icons of American film, often standing as figures of rough-hewn rectitude in direct contrast to the oily unscrupulousness of crooked politicians. Newspaper reporters and editors have remained relatively positive characters in American film ever since, though Orson Welles's legendary *Citizen Kane* complicated the good reporter-bad politician dichotomy as early as 1941 with its focus on a character who is both a newspaper magnate and a politician.

Often found at the top of lists of "all-time great films," *Citizen Kane* is undoubtedly the most important film by a man widely regarded as America's most important film director. Michael Denning argues in his book *The Cultural Front* (Verso, 1996) that Welles is "the American Brecht, the single most important Popular Front artist in theater, radio, and film, both politically and aesthetically. … Welles is our Shakespeare" (pp. 362–63). And Denning is not alone in his admiration for Welles's work. For example, Thomas Schatz, in *Boom and Bust* (Scribner's, 1997), calls *Citizen Kane* "easily the most innovative and controversial picture in prewar Hollywood," noting also the unusual extent to which the film bears the creative stamp of its director (p. 90). Welles's innovative use of a variety of narrative strategies and of imaginative camera angles and techniques such as deep-focus cinematography (in which both the foreground and the background are entirely in focus) make *Citizen Kane* one of the most technically influential films in Hollywood history. His use of newspaper magnate William Randolph Hearst as the obvious model for his protagonist also provides a framework within which Welles addressed a number of important social and political issues, creating considerable controversy but also gaining considerable attention for his message.

Citizen Kane is the fictional biography of Charles Foster Kane, "the greatest newspaper tycoon of this or any other generation," with Welles delivering a dazzling performance in the lead role. It begins in the aftermath of Kane's death, with a cut to newsreel footage covering the highlights of Kane's career. The remainder of the film is structured around the efforts of Jerry Thompson (William Alland), a reporter for a picture magazine, to gather information for a retrospective story on Kane's life. In particular, Thompson seeks an innovative angle from which to address the story, hoping to find it through discovery of the meaning of Kane's dying word, "Rosebud." Thompson interviews a number of Kane's former acquaintances, including nightclub singer Susan Alexander Kane, the magnate's second wife (played by Dorothy Comingore); Mr. Bernstein, one of the principal managers of Kane's business enterprises (played by Everett

Sloane); and Jedediah Leland, Kane's longtime friend and sometime employee (played by Joseph Cotton). Thompson also uncovers considerable details about Kane's early life from reading the manuscript of a diary left by Wall Street banker Walter Payton Thatcher (played by George Coulouris).

Kane's rise to wealth and fame begins in his childhood in Colorado, when his formerly impoverished mother inherits some land on which immensely rich deposits of gold are discovered. But this sudden realization of the American dream comes with decidedly negative side effects. In particular, Kane's mother sends him to New York to live as a rich boy under the tutelage of Thatcher and thus presumably to have a better life away from his abusive father. Kane grows up with all of his material needs more than met, attending the best schools and learning the ways of the rich. He also grows up without affection or tenderness and will continue to have difficulty throughout his life, regarding other people as anything other than either competitors or possessions. At age twenty-five, he gains official control of his already huge financial empire, formerly held in trust by Thatcher, whom Kane resents and despises. Kane shows little concern for most of his holdings, but does take a strong interest in the New York *Inquirer*, a small newspaper he finds that he owns. He takes personal control of the paper and builds it into a major force in the New York media, aided by Bernstein and Leland. Kane becomes a more and more prominent figure as his media empire expands across the country, crusading against trusts and governmental corruption. However, he also shows a certain ruthlessness, and there are hints that he may (as Hearst has been accused of doing) have virtually orchestrated the Spanish-American War as a media event to give his papers something sensational to cover.

Kane marries Emily Norton (Ruth Warrick), niece of a U.S. president, and begins a political career of his own, campaigning for governor of New York in 1916 as a "fighting liberal" opposed to the corrupt political machine of Boss Jim Gettys (Ray Collins). The campaign goes well, and Kane seems destined for political success until he meets and begins an affair with young Alexander, finding her down-to-earth humanity irresistible and her apparent attraction to him for himself rather than his wealth. But the affair is discovered and exposed by Gettys, ending both Kane's gubernatorial bid and his marriage. Kane then marries Alexander and sets about attempting to make her into a successful opera star, thereby presumably validating his attraction for her. He spends huge sums of money, going so far as to build a new multimillion-dollar opera house in New York for Alexander to perform in. But she simply lacks the talent, and Kane's public support of her career becomes an object of derision.

After a momentary setback in which the Depression seriously damages his fortune, Kane continues to build his wealth but begins to retreat from the limelight, constructing "Xanadu," an elaborate private retreat in Florida, and stocking it with "the loot of the world." He and Alexander retreat to Xanadu while the estate is still under construction, but he spends little time with her there, leaving her to her own devices that largely consist of working jigsaw puzzles. These puzzles, like the earlier newsreels, function as one of the film's numerous self-referential images. Alexander eventually leaves, concluding that Kane is incapable of love and that he is growing to resent her role in his life. Kane, in a bravura scene, then goes berserk and wrecks her room, in the process finding and pocketing a child's snow globe that reminds him of his Colorado childhood. He keeps the globe with him until his death, living his last years in almost total isolation while watching his empire decline around him. By the time Thompson comes to Xanadu as part of his research, the never-completed palace is already beginning to decay. Thompson learns relatively little while he is there, but we the viewers learn the secret of "Rosebud" when we see workmen, clearing the estate of rubble, toss an old child's sled bearing that name into the furnace.

This last scene adds a touch of pathos, but in general Welles presents Kane's story in a mode free of sentimentality, though he does humanize the central character, thus producing a certain amount of sympathy for a man who himself has little sympathy for anyone else. But Kane's story is not merely a personal one. It comments in important ways on the rise of the modern American media and on the dehumanizing and alienating consequences of capitalism, whatever its material benefits. Indeed, Kane is an allegorical figure of modern American society, a fact apprehended in Welles's use during filming of working titles such as "American" and "John Citizen, U.S.A." Among other things, Welles's portrayal of Kane has an antifascist slant (In one shot, Kane is shown rubbing elbows with Hitler), producing a warning that the tendencies of the American media and American capitalism might, if left unchecked, lead in the direction of fascism. The film thus makes an important political statement even if it is now best remembered for its technical innovations.

By the 1950s, the representation of media in American film began to shift its emphasis from newspapers to television, which has typically been depicted as a corrupting force in American politics (and society) ever since. Television in general has almost invariably been treated negatively in American film since the new medium first arose as an important challenge to the power (and income) of the American film industry. Much of the early criticism of television in film had to do with expressions of contempt for the overt commercialism of the new media, suggesting that the artistic integrity of television programming was inherently damaged by the intrusion of commercial advertising. Thus, Frank Tashlin's *Will Success Spoil Rock Hunter?* (1957) treats television advertising as an object of humor, spoofing early television commercials as ridiculous and tawdry. On the other hand, the satire here is applied with a particularly light touch, perhaps because the critique in this film of the commodification of sexuality as a marketing tool might also be taken to apply to Hollywood.

Much more serious (and political) as a critique of television is Elia Kazan's *A Face in the Crowd*, also released in 1957. Kazan's film begins in the Tomahawk County Jail in Pickett, Arkansas, where a Sarah Lawrence–educated local radio reporter, Marcia Jeffries (Patricia Neal), comes to interview the prisoners for her program, "A Face in the Crowd," which features interviews with ordinary people on the street. In the jail, she encounters a seemingly bitter prisoner by the name of Larry Rhodes (Andy Griffith), whom she dubs "Lonesome." Rhodes turns out to be a colorful character—and just happens to have a guitar; he overcomes his bitterness and agrees to perform on Jeffries's program when he is offered an early release from jail in return. Rhodes is an immediate hit with his folksy blues singing, billed as representing the viewpoint of "outcasts, hoboes, and nobodies." Jeffries convinces him to become a regular performer on her station, and he quickly becomes a local celebrity.

Rhodes soon graduates to a television program in Memphis after negotiating a shrewd deal with a station there. He is again a great success, and his career as a media star is launched. Rhodes is, from the start, a savvy performer, who knows very well how to parlay his apparent naiveté into media success. He soon has his own network television show in New York, on which he hawks a patent medicine that supposedly increases sexual potency, in the grand tradition of the American con (and American capitalism). As his popularity soars, Rhodes begins to exert considerable personal influence around the country, eventually becoming involved in politics. He becomes a consultant to Senator Worthington Fuller (Marshall Neilan), a potential right-wing presidential candidate who hopes to learn to use the new medium of television (of which Rhodes is obviously a master) to further his presidential ambitions. The sinister General Haynesworth (Percy Waram), Fuller's behind-the-scenes backer, explains the need to master the new medium by noting that the masses of people are dupes who need to be "guided" by elite thinkers like themselves. And television is the perfect tool for such "guidance." As Haynesworth puts it, "Let us not forget that in TV we have the greatest instrument for mass persuasion in the history of the world."

Rhodes hopes for a cabinet post in the new administration should his man be elected, but he is clearly out of his element in the world of high-powered politics. He becomes increasingly alienated, bitter, and cynical about his own success. Jeffries, who accompanies him on his rise to fame, is very much aware of his growing megalomania and of his tendency to chase other women, such as the adoring young Arkansas majorette Betty Lou

Fleckum (Lee Remick), whom Rhodes marries, then displays semi-nude on his program as a sort of trophy. It is Jeffries who eventually destroys the phenomenon that she helped to create, by leaving a microphone open when Rhodes thinks it is off, thereby inducing him unknowingly to broadcast his true contempt for his audience. In the end, he is left only with his beloved self-invented applause machine to keep him company and respond to his talents.

Rhodes is reminiscent of any number of figures from American cultural history, and might be taken as a sort of amalgam of figures such as Will Rogers, Walter Winchell, Woody Guthrie, and Elvis Presley—with an extra dash of nastiness thrown in for good measure. In the world of film, he anticipates such characters as Bob Roberts, though he lacks Roberts's political savvy. Director Kazan later claimed that *A Face in the Crowd* "anticipated Ronald Reagan" in its vision of the political power of the entertainment media, while screenwriter Budd Schulberg once claimed that the characterization of Rhodes was in part a comment on Joseph McCarthy's use of the media in his own rise to power. Rhodes is, from one point of view, a man of the people who is corrupted by big business interests, but it is also the case that Rhodes is a shrewdly amoral character who, from the very beginning, knows what he wants and is willing to do anything to get it. In this sense, he may be a prototype of the right-wing demagogue. He is, however, no Guthrie or Presley, and his singing, which is more like yelling, is pretty awful. The dramatic success of the obnoxious Rhodes is never very believable, and Schulberg and Kazan surely underestimate both, the ability of American popular culture to produce genuinely seductive images and the taste of the American people (questionable though it may be). Indeed, through its portrayal of the success of his folksy populism, the film shows an elitist contempt for mass taste that mirrors Rhodes's own.

American cinema in the highly political decade of the 1960s is remarkably free of films devoted to examinations of the role of the media in politics. However, Haskell Wexler's remarkable *Medium Cool* (1969) ends the decade with a highly political exploration of American society's fascination with violence and the complicity of the media in that fascination. It focuses on television news reporter/cameraman John Cassellis (Robert Forster) as he travels about Chicago, accompanied by his soundman, Gus (Peter Bonerz), in search of stories that will interest a television audience that seems interested only in the sensational and the violent. Initially, Cassellis is a hollow man, devoid of feeling for the people and material he covers, interested only in getting a good piece of film. His cynicism and lack of human emotion are established in the opening scene as he calmly films the victim of a car crash, calling an ambulance only after he completes filming. Later, we see him involved in a dalliance with a beautiful young woman, Ruth (Marianna Hill), for whom he clearly feels little but sexual attraction. Then he meets Eileen Horton (Verna Bloom), a young woman freshly arrived in Chicago from the hills of West Virginia. Cassellis's relationship with Eileen and her young son, Harold (Harold Blankenship), seems to bring a certain amount of authentic humanity into his formerly superficial life. He also begins to realize the political irresponsibility of his former attitude toward his work, but this new turn is short-lived.

Medium Cool is set in Chicago just before and during the 1968 Democratic National Convention. With the recent assassinations of Martin Luther King and Robert Kennedy as background, the film builds toward the Chicago police riots that erupted during the convention. It particularly notes the way in which the antiestablishment demonstrators who gathered in Chicago for the convention relied upon media coverage to keep official violence in check, only to find that the presence of the media seemed to spur the police to even greater levels of brutality. Combining documentary footage with a fictional narrative, much of the film has a highly authentic look, enhanced by actual police harassment of Wexler and his crew while they were filming and by several scenes in which the frame between the scene and the camera crew is broken.

Medium Cool, whose director is himself a legendary cinematographer (and was the lead cinematographer on this film), is extremely important for its innovative visual style, but this style is also part of the film's message in that it contributes to a blurring of the boundaries between fiction and reality that the film sees as a crucial by-product of the media saturation of modern American life. In addition, the film contains a sort of catalog of the oppositional political concerns of the 1960s. Because it was central to the Chicago police riots, the antiwar movement is a constant presence in the film. The film also contrasts the tenement in which Eileen and Harold live with the wealth that exists elsewhere in Chicago, while Cassellis's initially exploitative relationships with women bring in the women's movement, as does a flashback scene in West Virginia in which Harold's father warns him against letting uppity women take over things. There are also several significant scenes that emphasize the civil-rights movement, including one important sequence in which Cassellis and Gus nervously travel into a black ghetto in search of material on black radicals.

Ultimately, however, the major focus of the film is the media and its failure to support the lofty idealistic goals of the political movements of the 1960s. As the convention begins, with Cassellis inside the hall covering the event, Harold disappears into the violence-filled streets. Eileen searches frantically for him in scenes filmed amid the unrest in Chicago at the time, including shots of the Chicago police, reinforced by the National Guard, moving in on the actual crowds through which Eileen moves. She is eventually joined by Cassellis, but the film then abruptly ends as the car in which they are driving crashes, killing Eileen and seriously injuring Cassellis. This crash seems pointless at first, except perhaps to provide a rather gratuitous echo of the film's beginning, or perhaps as an allusion to the French film *Week End* (1967), one of many references in the film to the work of Jean-Luc Godard, whom Wexler greatly admired. But the camera then pulls back to reveal a movie cameraman filming the accident, then slowly turning his camera on the audience of the film. The implication is clear: this cataclysmic ending, however seemingly gratuitous, is precisely the sort of ending demanded by American audiences in their lust for violence. This media-fed lust has also fueled the viciousness of the Chicago police riots, a phenomenon that points toward potentially even more dire consequences in the future.

This critique of the contribution of the media to the popular American fascination with violence (and the damaging effect of this fascination on the political process) is even more powerful in Robert Altman's *Nashville* (1975), perhaps the central American film about that topic. *Nashville*, widely considered one of the most important American films of the 1970s (one of the peak decades for American film), is an impressive satire that uses a critical examination of Nashville's country music industry to comment on the violence, greed, apathy, and rampant commodification that Altman sees as characteristic of American society as a whole, during the 1970s. The film focuses on the activities of twenty-four different major characters, most of them involved in the music business, carefully weaving their separate stories into a coherent fabric. It is essentially a slice of Nashville life, following the various characters during several days of relatively normal activity toward the film's conclusion, in which most of them come together during a free concert being held in Nashville's Centennial Park. This concert is held to promote the presidential campaign of third-party candidate Hal Phillip Walker, a populist with no coherent political philosophy other than dissatisfaction with the status quo—a dissatisfaction of which the recent Watergate scandal provides a crucial background, though it is never explicitly mentioned in the film. In this concert, politics and popular culture smoothly merge, suggesting the highly commodified nature of both in modern America.

As a result of this structure that surprisingly effective, *Nashville* is really more a series of character sketches than a narrative. Many of the characters are successful country music performers, some of whom can be related to actual country stars, though it is probably better to see them as representing types rather than specific individuals. These country stars include the cynical, corrupt, and self-promoting Haven Hamilton (Henry Gibson); the frail, earnest Barbara Jean (Ronee Blakley); the ambitious and back-biting Connie White (Karen Black); and the black man made good, Tommy Brown (Timothy Brown). There are also would-be stars, including

Albuquerque (Barbara Harris), who has some talent, but cannot seem to get a chance to use it, and Sueleen Gay (Gwen Welles), who has no talent whatsoever and is eventually reduced to stripping before an audience of leering businessmen (played largely by members of the actual Nashville Chamber of Commerce) in order to get a forum in which to sing. (Her reduction to the status of a commodity in this scene, however, is little different from the commodification of the film's more talented performers by the demands of the music industry.) Altman also indicates the way in which, by the mid-1970s, the Nashville music industry was already extending its scope beyond traditional country music. He thus includes Tom, Bill, and Mary, a trio of pop-folk singers, who are recording in Nashville. The three form a romantic triangle as well, with Tom (Keith Carradine) regularly bedding Mary (Christina Raines), who is the wife of Bill (Allan Nicholls). Tom seduces every other woman he can get his hands on as well, including Opal (Geraldine Chaplin), an absurd British radio journalist who has come to report on the Nashville scene for the BBC, and Linnea Reese (Lily Tomlin), an otherwise virtuous suburban wife and would-be gospel singer.

The principal narrative thread that holds most of the individual stories together involves the efforts of political consultants John Triplette (Michael Murphy) and Linnea's husband, Delbert Reese (Ned Beatty), to recruit various performers for Walker's Centennial Park concert. They have considerable success and manage to recruit even such major stars as Hamilton and Barbara Jean, though none of the performers have any real commitment to Walker's candidacy. Instead, Hamilton sees the concert as an opportunity for self-promotion, while Barbara Jean's unscrupulous manager-husband, Barnett (Allen Garfield), sees it as a chance for his wife to reestablish her stardom after a recent nervous breakdown. The concert is performed on the steps of one of Nashville's most bizarre landmarks, the Parthenon, a full-scale and completely restored reproduction of the Parthenon of Athens. Hamilton and Barbara Jean open the concert beneath a huge American flag, only to be interrupted when Kenny Fraiser (David Hayward), a mysterious figure who has floated through the entire film, emerges from the audience and shoots both performers, apparently killing Barbara Jean. The two victims are rushed off the stage, and momentary chaos ensues. Tellingly, however, the concert goes on without missing a beat. Albuquerque, seizing her opportunity, grabs the mike and launches into a bluesy rendition of the film's theme song, "It Don't Worry Me." The performance is highly successful. She is soon joined by a gospel choir that is already on stage for the concert, while the audience claps and sings along, demonstrating the "waning of affect" that cultural critic Fredric Jameson sees as principal characteristic of postmodern society in his book *Postmodernism, or, The Cultural Logic of Late Capitalism*

(Duke University Press, 1991). They are, in fact, almost entirely unaffected by the shootings, which have become common events in America by the mid-1970s. Albuquerque turns out to be a better singer than Barbara Jean, anyway, so the crowd need not worry about being entertained.

Fraiser's motivation in the shooting is never specified, though it can be taken as an expression of frustration that there seems to be no legitimate outlet for political action in the society he sees around him. Meanwhile, the shooting is explicitly compared with the assassination of John F. Kennedy (who has been mentioned repeatedly earlier in the film). Grabbing the microphone, the wounded Hamilton reminds his frightened audience that "This isn't Dallas. It's Nashville. You show 'em what we're made of. They can't do this to us in Nashville." However, that Nashville does in fact "keep a goin'" (echoing the lyrics of one of Hamilton's songs) is clearly meant not as praise for Nashville but as a criticism of the shallowness of the mid-1970s American society that the city represents in the film. Meanwhile, the centrality of Albuquerque's virtuoso performance to the subsequent reaction (or lack thereof) to the shootings can be taken as a critique of American individualism—in which admiration for Albuquerque's personal performance distracts the audience from politics, while the ease with which she replaces Barbara Jean in the hearts of the audience suggests that American individuals are really just interchangeable commodities, none of them truly valued as distinct human beings.

The simulated Parthenon, sporting a huge American flag as decoration, provides the perfect setting for the culminating scene in *Nashville.* For one thing, it recalls the way in which American democracy was self-consciously linked in its formative years to ancient Greek precedents, as signaled by the classic Greek architecture that informs so many of the public buildings and monuments in Washington, D.C. Yet Nashville's Parthenon is, like the American culture it symbolically represents in the film, stylistically impressive but spiritually hollow. It presents a shiny, pristine white exterior, presumably mimicking the real Parthenon at the height of its glory, but also suggesting an Americanized and commodified version of the monument, cleaned up, improved, and stripped of any religious significance it might have had in ancient Athens and made instead into a sort of tourist attraction—and a statement of the economic clout of the city of Nashville, the self-proclaimed "Athens of the South." Meanwhile, the interior of Nashville's Parthenon abandons any attempt to reproduce its Greek predecessor but instead functions as an art museum—focusing on American art. The impressive structure thus stands as an emblem of the ability of American culture to co-opt predecessor cultures for its own use—just as the modern American culture industry has co-opted country music, transforming it from a working-class expression of folk values into a high-profit capitalist enterprise.

Nashville is a compelling film whose documentary quality enhances the effectiveness of its social critique. Meanwhile, the film's air of realism is enhanced by the fact that it includes so many actual musical performances by its actors, who in general both wrote and performed their own songs. Some of the songs are highly successful, and Carradine's "I'm Easy" became a major hit and won an Oscar for best original song. However, many in Nashville found the film unrealistic and were understandably upset by Altman's characterizations of the country music industry, which are at times exaggerated for satirical purposes. However, the target of the satire in *Nashville* is not country music, but the destruction of country music by the country music industry. It is a film not about the tawdriness of Southern culture, but about the ways in which modern American capitalism has conscripted country music, removing it from its authentic folk roots and making it just another thoroughly commodified capitalist enterprise. Subsequent events in the history of country music that is now virtually indistinguishable from mainstream pop music except that its practitioners occasionally wear cowboy hats have proved Altman's point. In terms of profits, the Nashville music industry now flourishes as never before. But there is little connection between the rough-hewn old-style country music of pioneers such as Hank Williams or the Carter Family (whose music maintains genuine folk roots) and the high-tech electric blues of Travis Tritt and Wynonna or the slickly produced pop megahits of Faith Hill and Shania Twain.

Altman's follow-up to *Nashville* was *Buffalo Bill and the Indians, or Sitting Bull's History Lesson* (1976), another film that explores the impact of the media and popular culture on the national identity of modern America. Released in July 1976, in the midst of the celebration of the bicentennial of the Declaration of Independence, *Buffalo Bill and the Indians* is one of the most radical assaults on the mythology of America in all of American film. Focusing on the show "Buffalo Bill's Wild West," an extravagant staging of the mythology of the American West that was one of America's most successful show-business phenomena before the advent of the film industry, the film demonstrates the element of theater and spectacle that was central to the mythologization not only of the West, but of America as a whole. Buffalo Bill is presented in the film as pompous, preening, and self-absorbed, so obsessed with his own image that he is beginning to lose the ability to distinguish between reality and his own intentionally fabricated images. Bill, played at just the right pitch by Paul Newman, is a drunk who has only one drink a day (in a huge schooner) and a womanizer who consorts only with opera singers, thus enhancing the air of theatricality that already surrounds him. Even Bill's famous long hair is fake, as is, one suspects, much of the patriotic rhetoric with which he seeks to present himself as the quintessential American hero—as a sort of allegorical representative of the American national identity. Given his allegorical status, the implications of Bill's fabricated image are huge. As one of his admirers suggests, "It's a man like that made this country what it is today."

Set in 1885, when Buffalo Bill's Wild West, founded in 1883, was just hitting its stride, the film devotes a great deal of its time to scenes from the show, which is rousing entertainment, but which also represents an extremely staged and stylized version of the West, despite its claims to historical authenticity. As the film begins, the famous Sioux chief, Sitting Bull (Frank Kaquitts), is about to join the show, as he in fact did for a period during 1885 and 1886. Much of the film is structured around an opposition between Buffalo Bill, as charlatan and simulacrum, and Sitting Bull, a genuine hero, whose quiet dignity stands in sharp contrast to the superficial showmanship of Buffalo Bill. By extension, the traditional culture of the Sioux is suggested as an authentic alternative to the fabricated and commodified culture of modern America. Sitting Bull, as it turns out, has joined the show not in quest of wealth or fame, but as an attempt to help his people, of whom only a little over one hundred remain after recent massacres at the hands of the American military. For one thing, he hopes to use his income from the show to provide blankets and other needed supplies to his people. For another, he hopes to parlay his participation in the show into an audience with U.S. president Grover Cleveland (Pat McCormick), to whom he hopes to plead the case of his people.

Not surprisingly, tensions immediately flare between Bill and Sitting Bull, who objects to the show's falsification of history and in particular to Bill's plan to restage the massacre of General Custer and his men at Little Big Horn as a case of cowardly betrayal on the part of the Sioux. Sitting Bull, instead, suggests an authentic restaging of a massacre of the inhabitants of a peaceful Sioux village by the U.S. Cavalry. Moreover, as if Bill did not have enough problems, writer Ned Buntline (Burt Lancaster), whose dime novels were primarily responsible for creating the myth of Buffalo Bill in the first place, shows up at the camp and refuses to leave when Bill, not wishing to be reminded of the origins of his myth, tries to get rid of him. Buntline plays a marginal, but crucial role in the film, providing commentary that indicates the manufactured nature of Bill's celebrity and, by extension, American celebrity as whole. As he tells Bill, when he finally agrees to leave, late in the film, "It was the thrill of my life to have invented you."

Finally, Bill agrees to let Sitting Bull participate in the show by simply riding his pony alone about the arena, assuming that such a no-frills performance will lead audiences to jeer and humiliate the proud chief. Instead, Sitting Bull's regal presence wins the day, and the crowd cheers him wildly, confounding Bill, who looks on. Sitting Bull then turns out to be prescient as well, as President Cleveland, in the midst of a honeymoon trip, arrives with his new bride and asks for a command performance of the show. But the president is a pompous buffoon with a tendency to spouting empty platitudes of the kind favored by Bill. Cleveland refuses even to hear Sitting Bull's request, rejecting it as impossible to meet, even without knowing what it is.

Soon afterward, word comes that Sitting Bull has been found dead. (In reality, Sitting Bull was assassinated in 1890, several years after leaving the show.) That night, Bill sees a vision of the chief and tries to explain and justify himself to the apparition; clearly, there is a level at which Bill understands the complete inauthenticity of his image and everything it represents. Nevertheless, the show goes on. The next day, Bill adds a new routine in which he easily defeats Sitting Bull, now played by his former interpreter, William Halsey (Will Sampson), in hand-to-hand combat. The crowd cheers wildly at this allegorization of genocide, and the film ends with a close-up of Bill/Newman, with blue eyes shining and perfect teeth gleaming, a perfect vision of the star as con man.

Buffalo Bill and the Indians was largely shunned by audiences and bashed by critics. Daniel O'Brien's description of it in his book *Robert Altman: Hollywood Survivor* (Continuum, 1995) as "a dull disappointment, a failed attempt to add a note of subversion to the patriotic celebrations of America's Bicentennial year" is a typical critical judgment (pp. 69–70). It is, however, a riotously funny and highly entertaining piece that nevertheless makes a number of crucial points about the mythologization of the American past and the founding of the American national identity on the Madison Avenue-like conversion of genocide into heroism. The choice of Buffalo Bill and his show as the focal point for this message was perfect, though many audiences in 1976 were probably unaware of the extent to which Bill, in his heyday, really did come to be known as the embodiment of the American national identity. Moreover, Bill's image referred not just to the past, but to the future, setting the stage for the conquest of the West in the nineteenth century to serve as the paradigm for American imperialist expansion around the globe in the twentieth century.

If *Nashville* and *Buffalo Bill and the Indians* stand as bitter indictments of the American culture industry as a whole, John Schlesinger's *The Day of the Locust* (1975) is one of the nastiest film critiques ever produced of the film industry itself. Schlesinger's film participates in a long line of films about Hollywood, looking back to such films as Preston Sturges's *Sullivan's Travels* (1942), Billy Wilder's *Sunset Boulevard* (1950), and Vincente Minnelli's *The Bad and the Beautiful* (1952), while looking forward to such films as Altman's *The Player* (1992). However, while all of these films may critique the venality and banality of the Hollywood film industry, all ultimately show a certain affection for it. *The Day of the Locust*, on the other hand, is much more uncompromising in its condemnation of the Hollywood dream factory as a corrosive presence in American society. The film, an adaptation of Nathanael West's 1939 novel of the same title, continues the novels bitter critique of Hollywood, at the same time bringing to life the strange cast of characters through which West (drawing upon his own experience as a Hollywood screenwriter in the late 1930s) enacted his vision of the Hollywood as the quintessence of American consumer culture, in all of its bogus glory. Set, significantly, against the background of the Depression, both film and book depict Hollywood as a factory for the production of prefabricated dreams and thus as a central means through which the desires of the American public can be manipulated by unscrupulous magnates. Importantly, however, the thoroughly commodified nature of these dreams implies that the desires associated with them can never be fulfilled with any level of satisfaction. Thus, *The Day of the Locust* depicts Hollywood as a giant dumping ground upon which broken dreams can be discarded to make way for the ever newer dreams constantly being turned out by the American Culture Industry.

The film stars William Atherton as artist Tod Hackett, an aspiring Yale-educated painter who has been brought to Hollywood to work as a set and costume designer for a film studio. While there, he falls in love with Faye Greener (Karen Black), a beautiful but untalented would-be starlet who has thus far been able to find work only as an extra. Faye is both a product and a victim of the Hollywood dream factory. A walking object of commodified desire, she is unable to experience any genuine emotions but instead treats every situation in her life as if it were a scene in a movie. The venal Faye encourages but evades Tod's attentions and instead goes to live, as a purely "business arrangement," with Homer Simpson (Donald Sutherland), a former bookkeeper from the Midwest who has retired early to California for his health. Faye, disappointed by her own lack of success in the film industry, takes out her frustrations on Simpson and treats him with great cruelty, inviting potential rivals (including a cowboy from Arizona and a young Mexican) to live in Simpson's garage. Eventually, she leaves Simpson after a drunken party at which her admirers fight over her. The various segments of the plot converge in a final apocalyptic scene during which a crowd gathered for a movie première turns to bloody mob violence after the distraught Simpson goes berserk and murders Adore (Jackie Earle Haley), a child film star of ambiguous gender, who has been taunting him. Simpson is then set upon by the crowd that begins mindlessly to attack and destroy everything in sight. Tod vainly attempts to save Simpson, then is overwhelmed by a sense that the scene is an enactment of a painting he has been working on through much of the film. In the aftermath of the riot, Tod decides to leave Hollywood.

The Day of the Locust indicts not only the film industry, but all of Los Angeles, as a land of duplicity and inauthenticity. Both are, in fact, part of a nightmare realm dominated by images of commodified sex and violence and inhabited by grotesquely dehumanized victims of the American dream factory. Moreover, this characterization becomes not a bizarre deviation from the norm of American life but the ultimate expression of it. Indeed, *The Day of the Locust* depicts Hollywood as the epitome of an American capitalist system that generates desire through the presentation of beautiful images, then drives individuals to violence and despair when they discover that these desires can never be realized.

Sidney Lumet's *Network* (1976) continued the mid-1970s critique of popular culture, turning its lens on television. *Network* is a scathing and viciously cynical commentary on the debased and thoroughly commodified nature of American culture in the postmodern era of late capitalism. Anticipating the tabloidization of the news that has become an increasingly obvious feature of American television programming in the 1990s, the film focuses on the willingness of a television network to stoop to any level of exploitation in the interest of higher ratings. At the same time, it conducts a thorough critique of the global capitalist system of which this unscrupulous network is merely a symptom.

The film begins as long-time network news anchor Howard Beale (Peter Finch) is fired from the United Broadcasting System (UBS) because of falling ratings. He then goes on the air, announces his "retirement," and informs his audience that he plans to commit suicide on the air during his last broadcast, one week thence. Network officials are horrified, but he is given a chance to go back on the air the next night to issue a more dignified farewell. Instead, he announces that he just "ran out of bullshit" and decided to start being honest with his audience for a change. To the surprise of network executives, this approach seems to be a great success with the viewing audience, and ratings begin to rise. Beale is allowed to stay on the air as a regular commentator, railing against the sad state of American civilization and adopting the slogan that becomes a national catch-phrase, "I'm as mad as hell, and I'm not going to take it any more!"

Ratings soar, especially after programming executive Diana Christensen (Faye Dunaway) takes over the production of the news show, converting it into increasingly tawdry entertainment. Max Schumacher (William Holden), president of the news division of UBS and a long-time friend of Beale (who has by now clearly become insane), protests this exploitation of Beale and the general commodification of the news. As a result, Schumacher is fired, and UBS continues to cash in on Beale's increasingly mad ravings, which become the top-rated act on television. Then Beale goes too far and rails against a deal in which the parent company of UBS is about to be acquired by Saudi Arabian oil interests, injecting badly needed capital into the company. He declares the deal a threat to American democracy and urges his audience to write to the White House in protest.

Beale is then called on the carpet by Arthur Jensen (Ned Beatty), chairman of the board of the parent corporation. Jensen, in thundering tones, lectures Beale on the new world of global capitalism, which he describes as the "multinational dominion of dollars" in which "there is no America. There is no democracy. There is only IBM and ITT and AT&T, and Dupont, Dow, Union Carbide, and Exxon." "The world," he tells Beale, "is a business," in which only profit matters and in which nations and ideologies are irrelevant. The deranged Beale treats Jensen's diatribe as a sort of message from God, then goes back on the air preaching the gospel of global capitalism. Audiences find his arguments that we are now in a postnational and postindividualist age depressing, and ratings plummet. When Jensen insists that Beale be left on the air to deliver this message regardless of ratings, ruthless UBS chief Frank Hackett (Robert Duvall) conspires with Christensen to have Beale assassinated on the air by members of the Ecumenical Liberation Army (ELA), an ultraleftist terrorist group that UBS has already appropriated, turning their terrorist activities into a weekly television series.

In addition to this main plot, the film also features the obligatory romantic subplot, though its presentation of the romance between Christensen and Schumacher hardly conforms to the conventions of Hollywood romance. Despite their professional disagreements, Schumacher, aging and in search of one last burst of passion before he recedes into old age, falls in love with the cold-blooded Christensen, who for her part seems incapable of real passion. Predictably, their relationship soon collapses, and Schumacher returns to his wife, but not before he delivers an assessment of Christensen that is also an indictment of the late capitalist culture of which she is a product. Again recalling Jameson's notion of the waning of affect, while referring to the fragmentation of experience that is another key element of Jameson's description of life in the postmodern era, Schumacher tells Christensen, "You're television incarnate. Indifferent to suffering, insensitive to joy. All of life is reduced to the common rubble of banality. … You even shatter the sensations of time and space into split seconds and instant replays."

In fact, there are many ways in which *Network*'s indictment of global capitalist society provides a striking anticipation of the more theoretically coherent discussions of late capitalism and postmodernism in the work of Jameson, though the UBS appropriation of the ELA and of communist Laureen Hobbs (Marlene Warfield) cynically suggests that the ability of capitalism to conscript any and all opposition for its own purposes goes beyond even that attributed to it by Jameson, who considers socialism the one point of view that cannot be appropriated by capitalism. Meanwhile, one could argue that the film inadvertently illustrated the appropriative power of capitalism by itself becoming an important part of

American culture in the mid-1970s. *Network* is a powerful critique of the dehumanizing consequences of late capitalism and of the complicity of the media and popular culture in that phenomenon. Yet the film was produced by a large corporation (MGM) and was a major critical and commercial hit, winning four Oscars and being nominated for six others. It thus, demonstrated the ability of capitalism to turn a profit even from the criticism of capitalism—just as Beale's initial rants against the system caused his ratings to soar.

Network is a fine film, but it nevertheless illustrates the tendency of American film to comment on television and its effects in decidedly unsubtle ways. No doubt, much of this lack of subtlety is meant as an intentional reference to the lack of subtlety in television itself. However, one of the most effective films about the impact of television and the media on the American consciousness, Hal Ashby's *Being There* (1979), is a notable exception to this trend. *Being There* is, in fact, an extremely subtle and enigmatic film, one that poses far more questions than it answers, refusing to supply the simple, sound-bite answers that the film itself associates with the mediatization of America.

In the film, Peter Sellers plays Chance, a middle-aged, simple-minded gardener who works on the estate of a rich employer, the "Old Man." He may, in fact, be the employer's son (probably illegitimate), though that information is never supplied. Instead, all we know is that Chance has lived his whole life on the enclosed grounds of the estate and has never, in fact, left the grounds. Chance has never learned to read or write (and may in fact lack the intelligence to do so), so all of his knowledge of the outside world comes from television, which he watches incessantly, but indiscriminately, flipping at random among children's cartoons, movies, game shows, commercials, concerts, and news programs, viewing all with an equal enthusiasm and superficiality. Soon after the film begins, the employer dies, and lawyers arrive to close up the house. Chance is thus ejected into the outside world, issuing forth in a daze, into the shabby urban neighborhood that surrounds the estate.

Because Chance has worked primarily as a gardener on the estate, the resonances of the story of the fall from the Garden of Eden are fairly clear here, though his suggestive name suggests a variety of other allegorical readings as well. Among other things, his sojourn into the outer world seems marked by an amazing sequence of good luck that eventually finds him ensconced in the palatial estate of aging (and dying) tycoon Benjamin Rand (Melvyn Douglas). Having no genuine social skills, Chance merely responds to prompts in a manner programmed by his viewing of television. However, his pithy remarks (which can always be interpreted by his interlocutors in a manner flattering to themselves) are consistently mistaken for laconic profundity, while his tendency to see everything through the optic of his experience as a gardener is taken for metaphorical insight into society and the human condition.

Chance quickly becomes a trusted associate of old Rand and a much-desired object of sexual fascination on the part of Rand's lonely wife, Eve (Shirley MacLaine), who attempts (with Rand's blessing) to lure Chance into a sexual liaison, much as the original Eve had tempted the original Adam from his innocence. Chance, however, cannot be tempted, apparently because his arrested intellectual and emotional development has left him trapped in a childhood world devoid of sexual desire. (There are even hints that his genitals have never physically advanced past a childish state.) Through the well-connected Rand, Chance meets the president of the United States (played by Jack Warner), who is much impressed by Chance's earthy wisdom. Soon Chance becomes a darling of the media, a guest on television talk shows, and even the heir apparent to the presidency. As the film ends, a group of political cronies, acting as Rand's pallbearers, discuss Chance's suitability as a presidential candidate while carrying the coffin to be entombed. Chance himself wanders away from the burial and ends the film walking, Christ like, across the waters of a lake.

This ending allows for multiple interpretations, but it perhaps most obviously comments on the way in which the political power brokers, along with the media, hope to convert Chance into a superhuman figure, largely in order to further their own ambitions for political power or simply to attract audiences. That a public hero can be manufactured in such a calculated way is telling, as is the fact that Chance, in particular, would be chosen for this role. There is no implication whatsoever that Chance's simple-mindedness conceals a deeper form of wisdom. His stupidity and vacuity are clearly genuine. He is essentially an empty vessel, a blank slate that makes him a perfect candidate for public office: with no ideas or opinions of his own, he is less likely to get into trouble or to conflict with the image produced for him by his backers.

In many ways, Chance is reminiscent of figures from the literary past, such as Flaubert's Emma Bovary, whose response to reality is mediated by her engrossed reading of romantic novels. However, Chance is an actual idiot who literally cannot tell the difference between television and reality, as is evidenced in a scene in which he attempts to do away with a gang of would-be muggers by simply turning them off with his remote control. Madame Bovary's confusion is much more subtle. Moreover, Emma's unrealistic and romantic attitudes lead to her downfall, while Chance's profound disengagement from reality makes him a rousing success, suggesting that reality itself has by now been so pervaded by the processed vision of television that his inability to distinguish between reality and television is, in a way, an advantage. Meanwhile, the way in which the media and the general public respond to his empty platitudes provides a damning commentary on what it takes to succeed as a public figure in a media-dominated America.

The most problematic (and perhaps tantalizing) aspect of *Being There* is its appeal to mythological precedents, such as the fall from the Garden of Eden or Christ's walking on water, motifs that cry out for allegorical readings while providing no clear allegorical referents. Indeed, amid the thoroughly routinized and rationalized environment of late capitalism, such allegorical gestures cannot really function. Instead, such fragmentary supernatural references function as bits and pieces of historical memory of a time when it was possible for such magical motifs to function more fully. *Being There* implies that, in the contemporary world of America, magic has been replaced by the media, with television now playing the role once played by religion and the supernatural. Chance, meanwhile, plays the conventional role of the holy fool, with television serving as his God.

One of the most effective recent critiques of television culture is Robert Redford's *Quiz Show* (1994). Though this film does not deal directly with politicians and the electoral process, it is a highly political film that comments, in important ways, on the relationship between television and American society. The film appropriately begins with the theme music of "Mack the Knife," a song from Bertolt Brecht's *Threepenny Opera*, a play that characterizes capitalism as a form of legalized crime. *Quiz Show* then pursues this capitalism-as-crime theme by exploring the famous television quiz show scandals of the 1950s, in the process narrating not only the destruction of American values by capitalist greed, but the complicity of the media, especially television, in this destruction. Indeed, the film's central message seems to be that television has corrupted American values not only by offering easy opportunities for the unscrupulous, but by creating a population of viewers who are inured to deceit.

Focusing on the NBC game show, "Twenty-One," the film begins as Herbert Stempel (John Turturro), a geeky Jew from Queens, is in the midst of a long winning streak on the show. But Stempel, who "has a face for radio," is too uncharismatic for television, so the show's ratings begin to slip. The show's sponsor then conspires with the producers to ensure that Stempel will be defeated, eventually convincing Stempel to lose intentionally by holding out the promise of future appearances on television. Stempel's anointed replacement is Charles Van Doren (Ralph Fiennes), a handsome upper-class WASP, who is far more presentable on television. A Columbia University literature professor, Van Doren, as a member of one of American's most prominent intellectual families, also has a perfect pedigree.

Although he is reluctant at first, Van Doren eventually agrees to cooperate in the fixing of the show, rehearsing beforehand with the producers to ensure that he will be able to answer the questions that arise on the program. He wins large sums of money, becomes an immediate media star, and is surrounding by adoring admirers. Stempel becomes a lonely, bitter, and forgotten man. When his complaints are ignored by the network, he reports the fixing of the show to the district attorney's office. A subsequent grand jury investigation produces no results, except that Richard Goodwin (Rob Morrow), a young investigator for a congressional oversight committee, gets word of the potential scandal and decides to check into it. Goodwin, on whose book about the scandal, the screenplay is based, has impeccable credentials. He graduated first in his class at Harvard law school and clerked with Supreme Court Justice Felix Frankfurter, but, as a Jew from a relatively modest background in Brookline, Massachusetts, he cannot match the aristocratic pedigree of Van Doren, whose father is a respected Columbia professor and whose family hangs out with the likes of Edmund Wilson, James Thurber, and Lionel Trilling.

Goodwin is at first a bit dazzled by his introduction to America's intellectual elite; he also takes a real liking to Van Doren, complicating matters even more. Nevertheless, Goodwin doggedly pursues his investigation, and his efforts provide most of the narrative thrust of the film, which becomes a sort of detective drama. Eventually, Goodwin accumulates enough evidence to force congressional hearings at which the scandal is revealed, and Van Doren confesses his role in the conspiracy. To Goodwin's disgust, however, the investigation merely implicates individuals such as Van Doren and the producers of "Twenty-One," while never even attempting to determine the involvement of the sponsors or the network, whose president turns out to be a golfing buddy of the congressman who chairs the committee. As Goodwin remarks in disgust, leaving the hearing room, "I thought we were gonna get television. The truth is, television is gonna get us."

This ominous warning is central to the message of the film that seeks to indict not just the quiz show scandal of the 1950s, but the media as a whole as the culprit in a general decline of American values into cynicism and greed from the 1950s forward. If even someone like Van Doren can be seduced by the gold and glamour of television, then there seems to be little chance to resist its inexorable colonization of the American mind. On the other hand, the fact that these scandals occurred so early in the television age tends to suggest that this tendency predates television and should more properly be located in the phenomenon of capitalism, television thus being merely a particularly effective tool with which capitalism can do its unscrupulous work.

Nevertheless, a film such as Barry Levinson's *Wag the Dog* (1997), set forty years later than *Quiz Show*, clearly implies that television has become a more and more corrosive force in American society in the intervening years. Levinson's film also makes clear the ways in which the influence of television has, by the 1990s, invaded the political process. At the same time, it also blurs the boundary between film and television (as historical reality had already done) by featuring a Hollywood film producer who helps to develop images for television. *Wag the Dog* is, at first glance, an exaggerated satire of the manipulation of the media in American political campaigns. On closer examination, however, it may be disturbingly realistic.

In the film, the president of the United States is in the midst of a reelection campaign when a teenage "Firefly Girl" (something like a slightly older version of a Girl Scout) accuses him of sexually assaulting her in the Oval Office. His handlers must then come up with a way to divert media attention away from the burgeoning sex scandal, at least for the eleven days remaining until the election—while the president himself basically just tries to keep a low profile. Realizing they need extra help for a job this big, the president's campaign team, headed by Winifred Ames (Anne Heche), decides to call in "fixer" Conrad Brean (Robert De Niro), an expert at dealing with precisely such crises. Brean, citing as his inspiration the Reagan administration's 1983 invasion of Grenada within twenty-four hours of the bombing deaths of 240 U.S. marines in Beirut, decides that only a war could provide a diversion big enough for their needs. However, the times being what they are, he sees no need for a real war. Instead, he hires Hollywood producer Stanley Motss (Dustin Hoffman) to orchestrate a fake war. After all, Brean points out to Motss as he sells him the idea, "war is show business" and people respond far more to the images and slogans of a war than to the war itself.

Motss whips up a few key scenes (complete with patriotic musical accompaniment) to feed to the media to convince them that the United States is now fighting a war in Albania (chosen largely for its obscurity). In the key scene, a young woman (Kirsten Dunst) is shown fleeing a burning village, carrying a kitten in her arms—with the village, the flames, and even the kitten provided via computer-generated images. The strategy initially works, as the media begins to focus on the war rather than the sex scandal. In response, the president's opponent is able to get—within days— information from the CIA to the effect that the war has already ended. Needing to extend the diversion a few days more, Motss and Brean come up with the idea that a lone, heroic soldier has been left behind enemy lines, then focus their media blitz on the supposed attempts to rescue the soldier. Afraid that they might actually have to produce him for the media, they tab Sergeant William Schumann (Woody Harrelson) for the role, choosing him from the Pentagon's personnel files largely because his surname allows them to generate a media campaign around his last name, nicknaming him "Old Shoe" and noting that he has been left behind like that item. Unfortunately, they find out only later that Schumann is a dangerous psychotic who has spent the last twelve years in a military prison for raping a nun.

One misfortune leads to another. Brean, Motss, and Ames board a small plane with Schumann to take him to Washington, only to have the plane crash in a rural area. Schumann is then shot and killed by an irate storekeeper after he attempts to assault the man's daughter. But never fear, a quick spin to the media campaign converts Schumann into a fallen hero killed in battle, generating a wave of sympathy that sweeps the president back into office in the election. Then Motss, enraged that the president's own lame media campaign (consistently of little more than repetition of the cliché "Don't Change Horses in Midstream") is given credit for his reelection, decides to go public so he can get credit for what he has done. However, before he can do so, Motss is found dead (supposedly from natural causes), with the obvious implication that he has been killed by the president's operatives.

This chilling ending provides a closing reminder that the highly amusing escapades we have just seen have a decidedly dark side. For one thing, the film delivers a disturbing message about the intervention of the media in the political process. At one point, Ames expresses contempt for television and is asked what she has against the medium. Her reply, that it has "destroyed the political process," can be taken as the central statement of the film, and events since 1997 have only served to reinforce the point. Indeed, while *Wag the Dog* is something of a farce, real-world events since its release make it appear closer and closer to reality. This is especially the case after the 2003 U.S. invasion of Iraq, based on inaccurate (possibly falsified) intelligence about the existence of weapons of mass destruction in Iraq. This invasion, like the whole "war on terrorism" of which it was supposed to be a part, was as much a media campaign as a military one, and fears of a global terrorism crisis (promoted by extensive media hype, especially on the Fox News network) were central to the success of George W. Bush's own "Don't Change Horses in Midstream" reelection campaign in 2004. Throw in the fact that the supposed U.S. invasion of Albania in *Wag the Dog* is justified on the basis of the claim that the country has long been a harbor for terrorists, and the film begins to appear more and more prophetic.

Wag the Dog participated in a flurry of concern about the intervention of the media in politics in the late 1990s, fueled at least in part by the rather lurid around-the-clock coverage of the Bill Clinton–Monica Lewinsky sex scandal, coverage that turned a minor indiscretion into a perceived national crisis and caused Clinton to be impeached by the House of Representatives, though he was not convicted in the Senate or forced from office. In this sense, *Wag the Dog* looks back to *Network* that grew at least in part out of the Watergate scandal, though the film that perhaps best epitomizes late 1990s skepticism about the media is Costa-Gavras's *Mad City* (1997). Here, dim-witted, out-of-work security guard Sam Baily (John Travolta) stumbles into a situation in which he finds himself holding a museum director and a visiting elementary-school class hostage inside a small California natural-history museum. Television reporter Max Brackett (Dustin Hoffman) happens to be in the museum restroom at the time and decides to try to parlay his presence on the scene into a resurrection of his flagging career. However, events spiral out of Brackett's control as the hostage situation becomes a major media spectacle, spurred by polling numbers that suggest that Baily has become a "poster child for the disenfranchised" whose plight encapsulates the frustrations of the American working class.

Eventually, however, the public turns against Baily, especially after a museum guard wounded in the early moments of the crisis suddenly and unexpectedly dies from his wounds. The media, of course, follows suit, producing increasingly negative coverage of Baily in reaction to new nega-tive polling numbers—which of course produces even more negative numbers. Ultimately (and almost inevitably), the crisis ends in tragedy. All the hostages are released safely, but Baily, realizing that his life has been ruined, blows himself to bits with dynamite. Brackett, however, seems to be the only media figure emotionally affected by the death; the others, includ-ing network anchor Kevin Hollander (Alan Alda), merely circle like soul-less sharks, smelling a spectacular, high-ratings end to the story.

Mad City is an extremely bitter indictment of the television news media as a amoral enterprise willing to do anything and everything (including the manipulation or even fabrication of news stories) in search of higher ratings, regardless of who gets hurt. In this sense, it is something of a companion piece to *Network*, though it is less dramatically effective than this important predecessor and earlier Costa-Gavras political films such as *Z* (1969) or *Missing* (1982). On the other hand, the relative lack of success of *Mad City*, despite its stellar cast and director and the relevance of its topic, may itself be taken as a telling commentary on its contemporary world. Audiences jaded by saturation coverage in the media of such topics as the O. J. Simpson trial and the Clinton-Lewinsky affair have come to expect little more from the media than what we see in *Mad City*. The film lacks dramatic impact because it tells us nothing we do not already know—and have all too often come to accept as natural and inevitable in our media-dominated age.

Of all the media critiques produced in the 1990s, Oliver Stone's *Natural Born Killers* (1994) may be the finest film and the most powerful political statement. It may, in fact, be the director's masterpiece, despite the fact that it triggered a firestorm of negative criticism especially among those who saw it as precisely the sort of gory media spectacle that it was meant to criticize. Here, Stone pulls out all the stops, employing all the resources of American popular culture to produce a scathing indictment of that culture. This is a high-risk effort, and the film was excoriated as debased, obscene, and immoral, especially from right-wing Republicans and conservative Christians. It was, for example, singled out by Bob Dole in his 1996 presidential campaign as an example of the negative influence of Hollywood films because of its celebration of grotesque violence. But Dole, who at the same time endorsed the equally violent films of fellow-Republican Arnold Schwarzenegger as wholesome entertainment, admitted that he had not actually seen *Natural Born Killers*, thus epitomizing the extent to which the film's critics so often spoke out of ignorance. The film does indeed include a great deal of horrifying violence, but (unlike the films of Schwarzenegger) it does not endorse violence as a solution to life's problems. In *Natural Born Killers*, the horror is directed at the violence and at the celebration of violence in American popular culture, a celebration of which the film is powerfully critical.

Natural Born Killers focuses on young lovers Mickey and Mallory Knox (Woody Harrelson and Juliette Lewis) as they work their way across the American Southwest (down the suggestively numbered Highway 666) on a three-week crime and murder spree. In this sense, the film is the culmination of a cinematic tradition that includes such predecessors as *You Only Live Once* (1939), *They Live by Night* (1948), *Bonnie and Clyde* (1967), *Badlands* (1973), and *Kalifornia* (1993). It was also followed by such films as Gregg Araki's *The Doom Generation* (1995), which treats much of the same material as *Natural Born Killers*, but with a darkly comic twist. In a very real sense, *Natural Born Killers* is a sort of self-critical summa of American popular culture as a whole. The film is composed of a dizzying array of fragments, quick-cutting MTV-style from color to black and white, from film to video, and among different film stocks, creating a highly disorienting look and feel that greatly enhances the thematic content. This visual fragmentation, of course, mirrors the fragmentation of contemporary American culture. Further it is supplemented by generic fragmentation; the film is essentially constructed from bits and pieces of parodies of various popular genres, including not only crime and police films but Westerns, sitcoms, cartoons, television commercials, and tabloid journalism. Scenes from a variety of earlier films and television shows often literally play in the background of scenes in *Natural Born Killers*, thus identifying the film's predecessors, while also indicating that contemporary American reality exists only within the context of media images.

The film makes especially good use of popular music, employing a sound track that brilliantly enhances the impact of various scenes. The haunting apocalyptic ballads of Leonard Cohen are particularly effective in this sense. One of the major strategies employed in the sound track involves a careful mixture of contemporary violent rock and rap music with traditional saccharine products from earlier years (such as Patsy Cline's "Back in Baby's Arms"), clearly suggesting that these various musical forms arise from similar impulses in American culture, despite their apparent differences. The film makes similar suggestions through its allusions to 1950s television programs that idealize American life (such as *Leave It to Beaver* and *I Love Lucy*). In particular, such idealized sitcoms are skewered in one of the film's most striking set pieces, the presentation of the initial meeting and courtship of Mickey and Mallory via a parodic television sitcom (entitled "I Love Mallory," complete with laugh tracks), in which the two young people meet, fall in love, then murder her grossly abusive father (Rodney Dangerfield) and wimpy mother (Edie McClurg) before setting off on their crime spree.

Crucial to this spree is the extensive media coverage it attracts, making cult heroes of the murderous Mickey and Mallory. In particular, notorious television tabloid journalist Wayne Gale (Robert Downey, Jr.) makes Mickey and Mallory the focal point of his program, "American Maniacs," which specializes in mass murders and other sensational crimes. Jack Scagnetti (Tom Sizemore), the police detective who devotes himself to the pursuit of the couple, is a media star (and murderer); one of the most controversial aspects of the film is its tendency to suggest that the dark impulses that drive Mickey and Mallory are so endemic in American society that they also underlie the activities of the police and prison officials who serve as the film's representatives of official authority.

Eventually, Mickey and Mallory are captured and incarcerated, at which point *Natural Born Killers* becomes a prison film, depicting conditions in the prison, run by deranged warden Dwight McClusky (Tommy Lee Jones) as an especially brutal form of the viciousness that pervades all of American society. McClusky, in fact, plots with Scagnetti to murder Mickey and Mallory in prison, feeling that their demonic presence is somehow stirring the other inmates to violence. Meanwhile, Gale brings his camera crew to the prison for an exclusive live interview with Mickey, to be conducted and broadcast immediately following the Super Bowl.

In the midst of the interview, a riot erupts in the prison. Mickey over-powers his captors and takes Gale and a prison guard hostage. They go to Mallory's cell, where Scagnetti is attempting to rape her before killing her. Scagnetti is killed instead, and the couple, with the aid of the other inmates, manages to escape from the prison (on live television), still holding Gale as a hostage. McClusky, overtaken by the prisoners he has tormented for so long, is torn to pieces. (Stone was forced to remove a scene of the prisoners displaying McClusky's head on a spike, one of many cuts required to reduce the film's rating from NC-17 to R.) Free in the woods, Mickey and Mallory make a final statement for Gale's camera, then turn the camera on their hostage, videotaping as they blow him to bits with shotguns. The film then cuts to a brilliant final scene in which Mickey and a pregnant Mallory drive in a camper van with their two children, thus further linking the murderous pair with ordinary middle Americans, suggesting that they are a product of, not an aberration from, the mainstream ideology of contemporary America.

That the critique in *Natural Born Killers* of the violent tendencies of American society is brilliant did not stop it from being widely ignored or misunderstood. The film, of course, was engaged in a difficult project, and other cinematic critiques of American violence—such as Norman Jewison's *Rollerball* (1975) or Paul Verhoeven's *Starship Troopers* (1997)—have similarly been received as specimens of precisely the sort of violent cultural spectacles they were meant to condemn. This phenomenon can be attributed to the fact that audiences both expect and want to see spectacles of violence—and other escapist entertainments from the tedium of everyday life—when they view films. Such desires and expectations make serious explorations of political issues in film extremely difficult, especially when these issues involve precisely the kind of tedium (such as working-class life) that film audiences hope to escape. The exploration of such issues is made even more difficult by a general aversion to any serious discussion of class issues in American culture. Nevertheless, some films have addressed such issues, and sometimes in very effective ways. These films are discussed in the next chapter.

CHAPTER 6

Working on the Chain Gang: Labor and Class in American Film

C lass, race, and gender are widely acknowledged to be the three major categories of social division in American society. Of these, the category of class has received by far the least attention in American culture, perhaps because the realities of class difference contradict most strongly the American national narrative of equal opportunity and equal justice. After all, while the American capitalist system has often taken advantage of race and gender differences to further the exploitation of the poor and powerless by the rich and powerful, that system does not fundamentally require discrimination on the basis of race and gender in order to function. Class differences, on the other hand, are a necessary and integral part of capitalism, which cannot function without them. Therefore, demands for class equality represent a far more serious threat to the basic organization of American society than do campaigns for equality on the basis of race and gender.

In a similar way, the American working class has been significantly underrepresented in American culture as a whole, including film. Through much of its history, in fact, the Hollywood film industry has been centrally engaged in the production of dream images designed to provide pleasant diversions from the grueling realities of working-class life. Relatively few films have focused on the day-to-day lives of working people (including their time spent laboring on the job); even fewer have focused on attempts of workers to resist exploitation, through trade unions or other means. Nevertheless, there are exceptions, some of them notable, to this trend. For example, early silent films, produced at a time when film itself was largely regarded as a somewhat disreputable entertainment for lower-class audiences, quite often focused on the tribulations of the working class. A number of subsequent films have focused on working-class characters, and even on labor union activity, though few have posed fundamental challenges to the inherent class-based inequities of the capitalist system.

Many early silent films depicted workers (especially those involved in activities such as strikes) as degenerate or demented subhuman fiends. But others were genuinely sympathetic to the plight of the working class and even radical in their support of collective action to improve that plight. Many of these films reacted to specific issues or events. For example, *A Martyr to His Cause* (1911), made by workers with funds supplied by the American Federation of Labor, was designed to garner public support for the case of John McNamara, secretary-treasurer of the International Association of Bridge and Structural Iron Workers Union (BSIW), who was charged (along with his younger brother, James) in the October 1, 1910, bombing of the downtown printing plant of the *Los Angeles Times* (a notoriously antilabor paper). The subsequent trial, in which famed attorney Clarence Darrow was brought in by labor leader Samuel Gompers to defend the brothers, became one of the most important in U.S. labor history, though it ended abruptly when Darrow convinced the brothers to plead guilty.

The film seeks to create a sympathetic (and sentimental) image of John McNamara by showing various scenes from his life that portray him as an ordinary, decent citizen who loves his family and works hard to make a better life for them. As such, it plays to relatively conservative values in its portrayal of McNamara as a solid citizen, but it is nevertheless radical in its defense of union activity and in its presentation of the legal system as part of a criminal antilabor conspiracy. As Steven Ross notes in his book *Working-Class Hollywood: Silent Film and the Shaping of Class in America* (Princeton University Press, 1998), the film was a good example of the strategy of worker-filmmakers of "wrapping explicit political messages in the popular garb of narrative melodramas filled with romance and action" (p. 92).

Similar strategies were employed in Frank Wolfe's *From Dusk to Dawn* (1913), one of the most sophisticated (and successful) films about working-class subjects made in Hollywood in the first two decades of this century. Made with the cooperation of the Socialist Party in Los Angeles, the film's plotline centers on a romance between two working-class characters, iron molder Dan Grayson and laundress Carlena Wayne. But this romance develops against a background of labor activism and leftist politics. Some of the film's most powerful images involve scenes of poverty in the squalid urban slums in which workers much live, combined with scenes of the stifling and unsafe conditions under which they must work. These scenes are made all the more powerful by their accuracy, many of them having been taken from actual documentary footage. Employing a technique frequently used by writers such as Émile Zola (and used earlier in film by D. W. Griffith), Wolfe also enhances the power of his images of the hardships and poverty of workers by cutting back and forth between these images and scenes of the luxury enjoyed by the decadent rich who have gained their wealth through exploitation of the poor workers.

One of the more radical works of the early political cinema is the film *Why?* (1913), an uncompromising look at the corruption and decadence of the upper classes, with a suggestion of a workers' revolution as the inevitable response. Indeed, the seeming celebration of violent rebellion in *Why?* caused an outcry of protest from critics and potential censors, who argued that the new medium needed to be reined in before it led to an actual rebellion. *Why?*, of course, was unusual in its seeming call for revolutionary violence, and political film in America, especially after the rise of Hollywood, would ultimately prove to be more of a vehicle for bourgeois reform than for proletarian revolution.

Other pre–World War I pro-labor films included *What Is to Be Done* (1914, inspired by the then-recent Ludlow Massacre) and *The Jungle* (1914, based on Upton Sinclair's well-known novel about conditions in the meatpacking industry). With the advent of World War I and the subsequent Red Scare, radical pro-labor films virtually disappeared from the American screen from 1914 to 1921, when they experienced something of a revival. This revival included the release of an expanded and updated version of *The Jungle* by the Labor Film Service in 1922. This service also produced *The Contrast* (1921), which deals with a West Virginia coal strike and would prove to be the biggest success of the films produced by the service, though it often had to be shown in secret because of official efforts to suppress it as inflammatory. Other examples of the resurgence of working-class cinema in the 1920s include *The New Disciple* (1921), *Labor's Reward* (1925), and *The Passaic Textile Strike* (1926).

Genuinely radical films virtually disappeared from the cinematic landscape of America in the Depression decade of the 1930s. Granted, many of the "social-problem" films of the 1930s address issues related to class, but they tend to do so in indirect or allegorical ways, while avoiding any hints of support for socialism or radical labor activism. Even a film like Charlie Chaplin's *Modern Times* (1936), which treats class issues quite openly, does so via the sugar-coating of charming comedy. *Modern Times* is one of the classic landmarks of American film, partly because it brought Chaplin and the Little Tramp into the sound era and partly because of its crucial commentary on the place of technology within the modern world as a whole. In some ways, *Modern Times* is a dystopian work that describes the potential horrors of mechanization and industrialization in a mode reminiscent of earlier films such as Fritz Lang's *Metropolis* (1926), while suggesting the political oppression that might accompany growing technologization in a mode that anticipates later works such as George Orwell's dystopian novel *Nineteen Eighty-Four* (1949). Yet Chaplin's Tramp, carried over from the earlier silent films, remains his lovable self, and *Modern Times* conducts its social critique in a charmingly comic mode that is entirely lacking in most dystopian works. Moreover, Chaplin's film is quite specifically set in the midst of the Depression of the 1930s and thus has a direct contemporary topicality that sets it apart from most dystopian satire, which may involve a critique of contemporary society but which typically does so through a mode of defamiliarization achieved through settings in times or places distant from those being commented upon.

Modern Times begins with a symbolic shot of a giant clock face, followed by suggestive parallel shots of a herd of sheep and a stream of workers going into a modern factory to begin their shift. The film then continues as the Tramp works on an automated factory assembly line, surrounded by huge, menacing machinery while he repetitively tightens nuts in a mechanical fashion that threatens to reduce even the Tramp, that ultimately human figure, to a machine. Some of the film's most striking scenes occur during these early moments as the Tramp struggles to keep up with the ever-increasing speed of the conveyors on the line. One of the film's most comic, but also most telling, comments on the dangers of technology occurs when the Tramp is used to test the new "Bellows Feeding Machine," which is designed automatically to supply workers with food while they stay at work on the line, thus eliminating the need for lunch breaks. Predictably, the machine goes berserk, pummeling the Tramp and leaving him covered with food. These early scenes are also important because of their introduction of sound. It is significant that the first recorded human voice to appear in a Chaplin film is the voice of the plant's president giving commands over an Orwellian telescreen through which he, Big Brother-like, can keep the entire plant under surveillance. Throughout the film, mechanically reproduced human voices are associated with oppressive authority, while the Tramp continues speechless, his status as a silent-film character lost in a sound film further establishing his alienation within modern society.

In another strikingly self-reflexive moment, the Tramp falls onto the conveyor and is drawn into the plant machinery, winding through a series of gears in a manner that is unmistakably similar to film being threaded through a projector, suggesting Chaplin's own sense that, as a filmmaker, he was being overwhelmed by a modern technology that, among other things, forced him to begin using sound in order to survive in the film business. The Tramp emerges from the gears apparently deranged, then runs amok in the plant and finally has to be taken away in an ambulance. He then undergoes one misadventure after another, including a later arrest when he is mistakenly identified as the communist leader of a working-class street demonstration.

Eventually, the Tramp meets up with a young woman identified merely as the Gamin (Paulette Goddard), and the two, both outcasts from mainstream society, strike up a relationship. In one telling sequence, the Tramp lands a position as a night watchman in a department store. He invites the Gamin to join him inside during his shift, and the two frolic among the abundant commodities that stock the store awaiting purchase by well-to-do customers, in powerful contrast to the poverty that reigns on the streets outside. Their night in the store includes, among other things, a famous scene of Chaplinesque physical comedy in which the Tramp roller-skates blindfolded in the toy department, repeatedly veering dangerously near the edge of a balcony where the safety railing has been removed for repairs. When some hungry workers break into the store looking for food, the Tramp joins them. He is discovered the next morning sleeping off his revels and is again sent to jail.

After repeated jail terms, the Tramp lands a job as a singing waiter. Predictably, he is a comic disaster as a waiter, though he fares better as a singer. Unable to remember his lines, he sings a nonsense song, "Titina," simply making up gibberish as he goes along, accompanied by a hilarious comic dance. The Tramp's first words on film are thus sung, not spoken, and they make no sense, suggesting that his virtues as a performer do not lie in verbal communication. Just as things are looking up, juvenile authorities show up to take the Gamin back to the orphanage from where she escaped, and the two have to make an abrupt escape. The film ends the next morning as they walk together, smiling happily despite their recent disappointments, down the middle of a road that extends out of sight into the distance.

This apparent romance ending does not resolve any of the social and economic problems that arise in the film, and there is evidence that Chaplin changed the ending to avoid making an explicit statement about the need to take political action to resolve those problems. On the other hand, the ending, as it stands, suggests that these problems are not easily solved, especially by lone individuals like the Tramp. Meanwhile, the ending may be richer than it appears, as much a parody of a romance resolution as a resolution proper. The Tramp and the Gamin walk off together not into the sunset, per convention, but into the sunrise, suggesting that they are going not into the future but against the grain of history, into the past, where they, as silent-film characters, properly belong.

John Ford's *The Grapes of Wrath* (1940), another classic work, also treats class issues frankly, though it substantially dilutes the radical political message of John Steinbeck's similarly titled 1939 novel, on which it was based. The film was highly successful, despite its potentially controversial political content. It was nominated for Academy Awards in almost every major category (including best picture, best screenplay, and best actor, for Henry Fonda), winning the award for best director and best supporting actress (Jane Darwell). While the film clearly mutes the political message of the novel (which is at times genuinely radical), it is actually a relatively faithful adaptation of the book. There are, however, notable exceptions, including the excision of the book's controversial ending, a scene of solidarity among the poor in which the Joad daughter, Rosasharn, whose baby has just died, offers her breast to a starving man so he can derive sustenance from her milk that would otherwise go to waste. Still, the film remains a powerful portrayal of the sufferings of the poor in Depression-era America, complete with an acknowledgment that this suffering is exacerbated by the greed of the rich. The film, like the book, begins as Tom Joad (played by Fonda) returns from a prison sentence unjustly received when he killed a man in self-defense, setting the stage for a thorough indictment of the current social and economic system that runs throughout the book. On the way back to the family farm in Oklahoma, Tom runs into the Christ like Jim Casy (John Carradine), an ex-preacher who will serve as a sort of mentor for Tom with his trenchant observations about morality, society, and life in general. When Tom arrives at the farm, he finds that his family is preparing to move to California in search of work, having been driven off their land not by drought, but by the large farming corporations that are gradually taking over the area and instituting large-scale mechanized farming methods. When the Joads finally arrive (after a long and difficult journey) at the promised land of California, they find that, contrary to what they had been led to believe, jobs there are quite scarce. Indeed, ruthless fruit and vegetable growers have propagated a false vision of California as a land of plenty in order to lure an excess of workers to the area so that wages can remain low as desperate migrants compete for scarce jobs. Meanwhile, the legal system and the media are mobilized to protect the growers and to keep the pickers in a position of weakness, defeating their efforts to achieve justice.

The Grapes of Wrath presents a dreary picture of the lives of the Joads and their fellow migrant farmers. But the film, like the book, does occasionally suggest that there is hope for a better future. One of the central messages of Steinbeck's novel involves the potential power of collective action to improve the lives of exploited workers, and at least some of this message is preserved in the film. For example, the film reproduces the book's presentation of the government-sponsored Weedpatch Camp as a sort of utopian enclave, where the poor band together under their own leadership, make their own rules, and live together in peace and harmony. The camp is nothing more than an example of working socialism, and the fact that the camp is sponsored by the U.S. government potentially makes it even more subversive as an image, suggesting a call for centralized government planning and management of resources, perhaps along the lines of the Soviet Union. The camp is even administered by a central committee, the Soviet undertones of which seem clear.

The film's ending, in which Ma Joad (played by Darwell) envisions a better future when the perseverance of the poor will at last pay off, is also hopeful, if less striking than the ending of the book. Similarly, the film contains some suggestions of the value of working-class collective action, though the film shows less faith in the masses and more faith in strong individual leaders than does the book. The film's most famous scene of working-class perseverance (and one of the most famous scenes in American film history) occurs as Tom bids goodbye to his mother before leaving to go on the run from the forces of the law that have already murdered Casy. Tom vows to devote himself to the fight for justice, telling Ma Joad that, while she may never again see him in the flesh, he will be symbolically present wherever there is injustice or resistance to it. "I'll be there," he tells her. "Wherever there's a fight so hungry people can eat, ... whenever there's a cop beating a guy, I'll be there." The first volume of Ford's "poor folks" trilogy (which continued with *How Green Was My Valley* and *Tobacco Road*, both released in 1941), *The Grapes of Wrath* is by far the best and most important film of the three, both for its deft use of imagery and narrative and for its genuine class-based sympathy for those who have suffered from the abuses of capitalism in one of its darkest hours. Because of the need to maintain a united front against the menace of fascism, the entry of United States into World War II at the end of 1941 effectively brought an end to radical critiques of the capitalist system in America for the duration of the war. Meanwhile, the Cold War political climate after the war made it virtually impossible to produce any such critiques of capitalism until the 1960s, at least within the official Hollywood system. One notable exception to this trend, however, was *Salt of the Earth* (1954), though this was an independent film made entirely outside (and directly in opposition to) the Hollywood film industry. *Salt of the Earth* was also largely suppressed and kept out of circulation at the time.

Otherwise, virtually no films contained a sympathetic representation of working-class experience during the 1940s and 1950s. Perhaps the most important exception to this trend was the sequence of boxing pictures that—beginning with Rouben Mamoulian's *Golden Boy* (1939) and extending through such films as Robert Rossen's *Body and Soul* (1947), Mark Robeson's *Champion* (1949), and Robert Wise's *The Set-Up* (1949)— allegorically figured boxers as working-class characters exploited by the industry in which they work, dominated by corrupt promoters, gamblers, and managers. Such films figure the fight game as a microcosm of capitalism in which individuals battle ruthlessly for financial gain, while those who do the real work are constantly exploited by those who do little more than put up working capital.

One of the most radical expressions of support for collective working-class action ever produced within the Hollywood system is Stanley Kubrick's *Spartacus* (1960), though this film cloaks its class-based political commentary in allegory, using ancient Roman slaves as stand-ins for modern American workers. *Spartacus* is based on a 1951 novel by leftist writer Howard Fast, written mostly while Fast was in prison for his leftist political beliefs. The screenplay for the film was written by blacklisted screenwriter Dalton Trumbo, making it one of the first films significantly to defy the blacklist, in that sense following hard on the heels of Otto Preminger's *Exodus*, for which Trumbo was also given screenwriting credit. Actually, Trumbo was originally hired to write the script under the pseudonym "Sam Jackson" (after Fast had proved unable to come up with a suitable script of his own), but (partly because of the release of *Exodus*) conditions had changed enough by the release of the film to allow Trumbo to be credited under his own name. Trumbo had significant disagreements with Kubrick during the making of the film (as Kubrick's screenwriters typically did), but the ultimate result is a magnificent example of epic filmmaking, a gorgeous cinematic spectacle in which a cast of big-time movie stars enacts a story replete with significant. It followed in the footsteps of the near-legendary *Ben-Hur* (1959), another historical epic to which it has often been compared, though in fact, it eclipses *Ben-Hur* because of the greater importance of its message.

Both the film and Fast's novel are based on a real historical event, the famous rebellion, ending in 71 B.C., in which the gladiator Spartacus led a rebel army composed of slaves and other gladiators in a two-year war against the power of Rome. While ultimately unsuccessful, this rebellion would long stand as a source of inspiration for the Left, as when the communist rebels who nearly took control of the German government under the leadership of Rosa Luxemburg and Karl Liebknecht in 1919 referred to themselves as "Spartacists." Moreover, like the novel, the film clearly suggests parallels between Roman slavery and American slavery, while also indicating parallels between the Roman exploitation of slave labor and the exploitation of proletarians in modern capitalist America.

Nevertheless, *Spartacus* is not really a radical film. For one thing, it was an extremely expensive film that had to seek a mass audience in order to recover the cost of the film. In its attempt to attract and please such an audience, it mutes its political message, while making a number of concessions to the conventions of Hollywood cinema. Spartacus himself (played by Kirk Douglas, who was also the film's executive producer) espouses a personal ideology that sounds suspiciously similar to Jeffersonian democracy, while the film pays an excessive amount of attention to Hollywood motifs such as Spartacus's romance with the former slave Varinia (Jean Simmons). In addition, the film sometimes seems to get carried away with its own status as a gorgeous spectacle. But the very splendor of the film makes it unique among left-leaning works of the American cinema that have seldom had access to the budgets required to produce such a grand epic.

The film begins as Spartacus and other slaves work in the mines of Libya, providing a potential link to modern proletarian culture, in which miners are often central figures. Spartacus at this point, is a virtual beast, brutalized throughout his life, and much of the first hour of the film details his coming to awareness that his plight is shared by others with whom he might make common cause. Spartacus's rebelliousness leads him to be sentenced to death, a fate from which he is saved when he is purchased by Lentulus Batiatus (Peter Ustinov) for training as a gladiator. The film details this training in considerable detail. In a particularly key scene, Spartacus is offered Varinia as a sexual favor, with the expectation that he will brutally rape her. He declines, feeling that the two of them are being mated like animals and understanding that she is a slave like himself. The two begin to develop a bond. Then, a group of Romans, including powerful Roman patrician Marcus Licinius Crassus (Laurence Olivier), arrives at the training camp and asks to be entertained by some gladiatorial fights to the death. Chosen to participate in one contest, Spartacus is rendered helpless by his opponent, an Ethiopian. However, the Ehtiopian refuses to kill Spartacus and instead rushes the Roman onlookers, whereupon he is killed. His body is hung up as a warning to the other gladiators, while his death also serves as an important lesson in solidarity for Spartacus. Meanwhile, Crassus purchases Varinia and sends her away to Rome.

When the trainer Marcellus (Charles McGraw) taunts Spartacus concerning Varinia, Spartacus becomes furious and kills him, triggering a full-scale revolt among the gladiators. Soon, Spartacus leads the gladiators into the surrounding countryside, freeing slaves as they go and thus building a burgeoning army that grows along with Spartacus's stature as a leader. Varinia is among the first slaves liberated by the rebels, joining Spartacus as his wife and soon becoming pregnant. They camp on Mount Vesuvius for military training, then conceive a plan to march across Italy to the port city of Brundisium, where they hope to bribe pirates to take them away from the peninsula and out of the immediate reach of Roman power. Meanwhile, back in Rome, the Senate debates a response to the revolt, which becomes the center of a power struggle between Crassus and Gracchus (Charles Laughton), who counters Crassus's haughty patricianism with a belief that real political power resides in the masses of common people. Among other things, the scenes in the Roman Senate suggest political maneuvering, in-fighting, and corruption of a kind that can be taken as a commentary on American politics at the end of the 1950s.

By this time, the class-based oppositions of the film are clear. Spartacus and the freed slaves represent working-class rectitude, while the Roman upper classes suggest the decadence and dishonesty of the rich and privileged. Meanwhile, Spartacus's army begins its march, winning a series of surprising victories over the Roman armies that are sent to stop them. As the slave army nears Brundisium, Gracchus attempts to arrange for their safe passage with the pirates, hoping to get them out of Italy and thereby remove any opportunity for Crassus to make political capital out of their defeat. Crassus outmaneuvers him, however, and arranges for the pirates to betray the rebels, while two Roman armies converge on Brundisium. Spartacus has no choice but to turn North and march on Rome in a desperate last-ditch fight for freedom by freeing the slaves there.

Crassus, now the first consul of Rome and commander-in-chief of the Roman armies, meets the advancing slave army with a vastly superior force, defeating them in a decisive battle that destroys Spartacus's army once and for all. Crassus searches among the dead and the prisoners, hoping to identify Spartacus. In the process, he locates Varinia and her newborn infant son lying alive amid the carnage. He sends the two of them back to his house in Rome. Finally, he offers a reprieve from crucifixion for all of the prisoners if they will identify Spartacus. In order to save his fellows, Spartacus comes forward and cries, "I am Spartacus!" But then another voice cries out the same, and eventually (in one of the signature scenes of American film) all of the prisoners proclaim themselves to be Spartacus, serving the double function of defeating Crassus's desires and making the point that, in a very real sense, they all *are* Spartacus, the symbol of their collective effort. Frustrated, Crassus orders them all crucified, saving a few for gladiatorial contests; soon the Appian Way is lined with the bodies of 6,000 crucified rebels hanging on crosses.

Spartacus is crucified as well (though the historical Spartacus was apparently killed in battle), following a last emotional scene in which he kills the young former slave Antoninus (Tony Curtis) in a gladiatorial battle to save Antoninus from the agony of being crucified. Antoninus dies in his arms. Meanwhile, Gracchus, continuing his opposition to Crassus, arranges for Batiatus to rescue Varinia and her son. Using the power invested in him as a senator, Gracchus grants articles of freedom to Varinia and the infant, then bribes Batiatus to take them away to safety. Gracchus then prepares to commit suicide, knowing that Crassus's soldiers will soon be coming for him. On the way out of Rome, Varinia sees Spartacus hanging on the cross, still alive. She can do little but bid him a tearful farewell and wish him a hasty death, but she is at least able to show him his son and to announce that his son is free.

Despite its leftist origins and vaguely leftist message, *Spartacus* obeyed the conventions of Hollywood film well enough to win six Academy Award nominations and four Academy Awards, though it failed to be nominated for best picture. The film was rereleased in a significantly abridged form in 1967 but restored to its original length in 1991. Indeed, one scene cut from the original, in which Crassus makes homoerotic suggestions to Antoninus, then his slave, was added in the 1991 restoration.

With *Spartacus* as an exception that was muted by its own Hollywood style and that could even then be produced only because of its allegorical cloaking, radical working-class commentary was virtually absent from American film from the suppression of *Salt of the Earth* in 1954 to the late 1970s, though it should be noted that *Salt of the Earth* itself saw something of a resurrection in showings on college campuses in the 1960s. At that, however, *Salt of the Earth* puts a great deal of emphasis on gender and ethnicity, two favorite concerns of the oppositional political movements of the 1960s, and it was probably because of these concerns, rather than its emphasis on class and on the importance of union representation, that the film appealed to youthful audiences in that decade.

Hal Ashby's *Bound for Glory* (1976) represented something of a return to the spirit of *The Grapes of Wrath*, by which it was clearly influenced. As such, it shares many of the working-class concerns of *The Grapes of Wrath*, though its historical distance from its own 1930s setting diminished any controversy over its politics when it was released. Ashby's film narrates the rise of folk singer Woody Guthrie (played by David Carradine), beginning in 1936 in the dying dust-bowl town of Pampa, Texas, and ending as he heads for New York and fame. In between, the film, loosely based on Guthrie's 1943 memoir of the same title, presents a cross-section of America during the Depression, as Guthrie leaves his wife and children behind in Texas to head for California in search of work. Along the way, the film presents some fine landscapes, contributing to cinematographer Haskell Wexler's winning of an Academy Award for the film. Guthrie finds that agricultural work in California is poorly paid and hard to come by. He does get his start in show business, singing on a local radio program that stars country singer Ozark Bule (Ronny Cox). Bule also introduces Guthrie to the plight of California's migrant farm workers, whom he is helping to form a union to resist the brutal exploitation they have been suffering at the hands of large farming interests. Guthrie's political consciousness is quickly galvanized by the plight of the farm workers, and he becomes involved in the union effort as well. This new political commitment is sometimes an obstacle to Guthrie's burgeoning singing career, as he continually resists the pressure to make his music more commercial and less political. But his faith in and devotion to common working people is also central to what makes his music special as an expression of the point of view of the poor and disenfranchised. As the film ends, Guthrie decides to forego lucrative commercial opportunities in Los Angeles and instead goes back on the road, heading for New York, where there are, after all, "people and unions" and thus an audience for his music.

Perhaps because of the influence of *The Grapes of Wrath*, the film version of *Bound for Glory* puts more emphasis on the plight of the California farm workers than does Guthrie's memoir, which spreads its emphasis over his wanderings around the country, meeting all sorts of poor people who help to inspire his radical politics and to whom his music will ultimately give a voice. Meanwhile, it is clearly the evolution of Guthrie's music that provides the real crux of the film. At that, the film focuses on Guthrie's best-known songs, including the title track and the classic "This Land Is Your Land," leaving out some of his more radical music, such as those contained on the album *Ballads of Sacco and Vanzetti*, recorded somewhat later than the period covered by the film or the memoir, just after World War II. The film also pays far too much attention to Guthrie's personal relationships, such as his troubled marriage to his wife, Mary (Melinda Dillon), and his courtship of a rich woman, Pauline (Gail Strickland). Such experiences are not, of course, what makes Guthrie worthy of our attention, but they are the typical stuff of Hollywood film, and director Ashby may have felt that such material would humanize Guthrie and increase the interest of audiences accustomed to films that focus on personal relationships. Still, the film as a work of political cinema would surely have profited by paying more attention to Guthrie's music and politics and less to his personal life.

Paul Schrader's *Blue Collar* (1978) is unusual among American films in the extent to which it focuses on working-class experience, especially in the actual workplace. It also suggests that members of the working class are often exploited by powerful forces in a society that does not appreciate their contributions to it. Unfortunately, the film continues what was by then a well-established Hollywood trend by identifying the labor union that represents the workers as the most important of the forces that exploit them. It thus promulgates the insidious false impression that workers would be far better off without union representation at all. Moreover, by focusing on auto workers, the film clearly aims its indictment of unions at the United Auto Workers (UAW), though the union of the film is called the "AAW." *Blue Collar* thus labels as corrupt and ineffectual what was (and still is) one of the best-run and most successful labor unions in America.

In the film, Zeke Brown (Richard Pryor), Jerry Bartowski (Harvey Keitel), and Smokey James (Yaphet Kotto) are three buddies who work at the Checker Cab plant in Detroit. All are plagued by money troubles, and all are frustrated by the refusal of their union to represent them adequately. They thus conceive a plan to break into the safe at union headquarters, thus solving their financial woes while at the same time striking back at the union for its lack of attention to their needs. They manage to carry out the crime but come away with little cash. They do, however, wind up with an incriminating ledger that records illegal loans of union funds to various individuals in Las Vegas and elsewhere. They then decide to use the information in this book to blackmail the union.

Predictably, the three soon find that they are in it over their heads. The union quickly discovers their identities, putting them all in mortal danger. Brown decides to accept a job from the union as the shop steward at their plant, both for his own protection and out of a belief that he can really change things. James, on the other hand, is murdered in a fake industrial accident. Bartowski, seeing no alternative, decides to talk to John Burrows (Cliff De Young), an FBI agent who is investigating corruption in the union. As the film ends, Brown and Bartowski are at each other's throats, each accusing the other of selling out. A voiceover then reminds us of James's earlier statement that the powers-that-be will do anything necessary to foster dissension within the working class. But, however powerful the potential implications of this final statement about the importance of working-class solidarity, *Blue Collar* fails adequately to explore the issues toward which it gestures. In his book *Film and the Working Class: The Feature Film in British and American Society* (Routledge, 1989), Peter Stead describes it as "a film that could have achieved greatness but which settled for routine entertainment" (p. 225).

Working-class concerns returned to center stage in American cinema with the immense success of Martin Ritt's *Norma Rae* (1979), a box office hit that won two Academy Awards and was nominated for two others. It is thus one of the most prominent films about organized labor in the history of American cinema, probably exceeded only in this sense by the antiunion *On the Waterfront*. *Norma Rae*, though, is avowedly pro-union. The film appropriately focuses on the Carolina textile industry, which has been the focal point of some of the most bitter labor struggles in American history— and which was involved in such a dispute (at the J. P. Stevens mills in Roanoke Rapids, North Carolina) at the time the film was made. Its sympathies are quite strongly with the textile workers and their attempt to organize, and the film is important for its focus on the title character (played by Sally Field and based on real-life union activist Crystal Lee), thus calling attention to the centrality of women workers in this struggle. On the other hand, *Norma Rae* has a tendency to descend into romantic cliché and to portray its oppositions in terms of good vs. evil rather than genuine class struggle.

The film is as much a story of Norma Rae's personal development as of the union movement in the textile mills, and much of the plot involves her growing sense of herself as a mature, responsible, and independent individual. The agent of her transformation is a Jewish northern union organizer,

Reuben (Ron Leibman), who comes to town to rally the workers. He encounters considerable opposition but eventually succeeds, largely because Norma Rae sees the value of what he is doing and comes strongly to his aid. Norma Rae's work with Reuben causes her husband, Sonny (Beau Bridges), to become jealous. In the end, however, Sonny and Norma Rae are reconciled, the textile mill is unionized, and the company, which eventually attempts to drive out the union through terror tactics, is forced to give in to many of the union's demands. Norma Rae remains a leader of the local workers, and Reuben moves on to the next town where workers are being exploited due to their lack of collective representation.

In addition to the central focus on gender, *Norma Rae* is strong in its treatment of race—particularly in its recognition of the importance of solidarity between black and white workers, while the company attempts to split the workers along racial lines. The contemporary topicality of the film gives it an extra force as well. Finally, while the ultimate focus on the protagonist's private life and feelings weakens *Norma Rae* as a political film, this strategy obviously allowed the film to appeal to American audiences and thus to spread its pro-labor message more widely.

Norma Rae can be considered the founding text in the subgenre of "women's labor" films that marginally includes such films about female office workers as Colin Higgins's *Nine to Five* (1980) and Mike Nichols's *Working Girl* (1988). It also includes poor-woman-makes-good flicks such as the Julia Roberts vehicles *Pretty Woman* (1990) and *Erin Brockovich* (2000), though the emphasis in such films is typically far more on individual courage and ability than on concerted class action. Further, the female protagonists of such films often require the help of a strong male in order to succeed. Even worse, they sometimes identify female "success" as landing a rich man.

Much more in the spirit of *Norma Rae* (partly because it involves labor unions) is Nichols's *Silkwood* (1983), though *Silkwood* contains an extra element of political commentary because it also participates in the genre of antinuclear energy films, of which James Bridges's *The China Syndrome* (1979) is probably the best example. Based on a true story, *Silkwood* details the efforts of Karen Silkwood (Meryl Streep) to blow the whistle on the shoddy methods being practiced at the Kerr-McGee nuclear fuel processing plant in Oklahoma in the early 1970s. Silkwood becomes increasingly concerned that the plant is not employing adequate safety measures to protect the workers in this highly hazardous industry. She and the other workers are repeatedly exposed to radiation in the course of her work, while the company continually assures them that the radiation levels they have experienced are within acceptable limits. Meanwhile, Silkwood also discovers that the company is cutting other corners as well, such as altering inspection X-rays of welds in fuel rods, thus possibly allowing the production of faulty rods that could lead to a disastrous nuclear accident. However, *Silkwood* extends its critique beyond Kerr-McGee or the nuclear industry in its implied criticism of corporate America as an impersonal machine bent on making profits, whatever the human cost.

While the union that represents the Kerr-McGee workers attempts to improve the conditions in the plant, the company works to decertify the union, thus paving the way to even shoddier treatment. Silkwood responds by becoming a union activist, working both to preserve the union as the official representative of the workers and to encourage the union to take stronger measures to demand safer working conditions. Eventually, the union arranges for Silkwood to meet with a reporter from the *New York Times* so she can present the evidence she has gathered concerning the company's shoddy practices. On the way to the meeting, she is killed in a suspicious automobile accident the cause of which was never determined and about which the film refuses to speculate, though it is clear from the film that the Kerr-McGee Corporation would certainly not be above murder.

Niki Caro's *North Country* (2005) is another work somewhat in the tradition of *Norma Rae*, though the emphasis here is more on gender than on class. In addition, the central character, mine worker Josie Aimes (Charlize Theron), is much more of an individual protagonist than a representative of her fellow workers, though her resistance to her treatment by the Minnesota mining company that employs her does ultimately benefit all of the women who work in the mine. Aimes is based on Lois Jensen, an employee of the Eveleth Iron Mine in northern Minnesota who filed a suit over the habitual sexual harassment she suffered while working in the mine; this suit eventually became the first successful sexual harassment class action lawsuit in American legal history. In the film, Aimes triumphs over adversity through her successful lawsuit, eventually even winning the support of some of the men in the mine. There is little indication, however, that this new solidarity represents any kind of genuine working-class action.

Class is very much the issue, however, in John Sayles's *Matewan* (1987), one of the very few truly radical pro-labor films in American cinema. Although made on a small budget, *Matewan* is one of the finest films ever made about American labor. Beautifully shot by cinematographer Haskell Wexler, *Matewan* is a work in the tradition of the proletarian culture of the 1930s, reflecting the spirit of that culture far more accurately than did *The Grapes of Wrath*, which grew more directly out of that culture. Based on the bitter and bloody labor battles that tore through the West Virginia coal fields in the early 1920s, the film focuses on a conflict between the Stone Mountain Coal Company and the coal miners who work for the company in the mines near Matewan, West Virginia. This dispute is clearly presented in terms of class struggle, as the protagonist, the union organizer, ex-Wobbly, and admitted "red" Joe Kenehan (Chris Cooper), urges the miners to transcend their other differences so they can present a united front against their common class enemy. There are two kinds of people in the world, he tells them, those who work, and those who do not but feed off of those who do. In the end, the conflict turns to violence, as the company sends in hired killers to terrorize the miners, only to find that the miners, supported by local police chief Sid Hatfield (David Strathairn) are willing and able to meet force with force.

As the film begins, in 1920, the Stone Mountain Coal Company announces a cut in the tonnage rate paid to miners for coal. Already angered by the poor working conditions in the local mines, the miners, who have been struggling for some time to organize in the face of violent company opposition, declare a strike. The United Mine Workers Union sends Kenehan to Matewan to help the miners conduct the strike effectively. Although naturally suspicious of outsiders, the miners soon accept his help, and he wins an early victory when he convinces the Italian and African American workers who have been brought in to break the strike to go out as well. He also convinces the original strikers to welcome these new allies, overcoming their racial and ethnic prejudices in the interest of class solidarity. This solidarity is a major theme of the film, as African Americans such as "Few Clothes" Johnson (James Earl Ray) and Italians such as Fausto (Joe Grifasi) become main figures in the strike, while the families of the African Americans, Italians, and longtime West Virginians learn to regard each other as allies rather than enemies.

Nevertheless, the miners face formidable opposition from a coal company that is determined to deny them the right to organize. The company sends two hired thugs from the Baldwin-Felts agency to spearhead the effort to break the strike. These men, Hickey and Griggs (Kevin Tighe and Gordon Clapp), are virtual personifications of evil and would appear exaggerated and cartoon-like were it not for the historical fact that such agents, widely deployed against strikes in the early twentieth century, were in fact willing to stoop to any level of crime in their effort to destroy unions. In fact, Sayles has noted in an interview that he had "tone those guys down" relative to the historical record in order to make them believable at all to modern audiences.

Kenehan consistently urges the strikers to employ nonviolent methods, but the company and their hired thugs make it increasingly difficult to stick to such methods. After most of the strikers are evicted from their company-owned housing, they set up a camp in the woods. This camp is then repeatedly attacked by armed gangs hired by the company. In the meantime, individual strikers are harassed, intimidated, and even murdered. Meanwhile, Hickey and Griggs, aided by C. E. Lively (Bob Gunton), a strike leader who is actually a spy for the company, concoct a plot to discredit Kenehan by claiming he is a company agent. As a result, Kenehan is almost killed by the strikers, but he is saved when fifteen-year-old miner (and fledgling Baptist preacher) Danny Radnor (Will Oldham) discovers the plot and cleverly signals it to the miners in one of his sermons.

The strikers stand firm and even manage to spread their strike throughout Mingo County. Desperate, the coal company sends a larger force of Baldwin-Felts agents to Matewan in an undisguised mission to kill the leaders of the strike. Hatfield faces off against more than a dozen hired killers, ordering them out of town. A gun battle ensues, but, to the surprise of the hired guns, the miners appear to support Hatfield. As a result, the Baldwin-Felts men are routed. Most of them, in fact, are killed, including Hickey, who is blown away by Danny's mother, Elma Radnor (Mary McDonnell), the boardinghouse manager Hickey and Griggs have been terrorizing throughout the film.

The miners thus score a victory in this first all-out battle of the West Virginia coal field wars, though Kenehan and several others are killed. Meanwhile, the narrator (an aged Danny looking back from the perspective of the 1980s) informs us that Hatfield was later gunned down by Baldwin-Felts agents. It is clear, though few details are given in the film, that the miners will not win the war that has begun in Matewan. Indeed, as dramatized in Denise Giardina's novel *Storming Heaven* (published in 1987, the same year *Matewan* was released), this war culminated in the Battle of Blair Mountain, a crucial historical event in which thousands of Appalachian coal miners, in the summer of 1921, took up arms to oppose the increasingly brutal and corrupt practices (including the murder of Hatfield) through which they were being exploited by the mining companies and oppressed by the allies of the companies who were running the local governments of the area. In the battle, the miners were defeated by a combined force of sheriff's deputies, company thugs, and the U.S. Army, sent in by President Coolidge to help quell the rebellion and prevent it from spreading among the poor and oppressed of other areas of the country.

If *Matewan* views class issues from the bottom up, Oliver Stone's *Wall Street*, released in the same year, views them from the top down. In particular, *Wall Street* is the definitive film commentary on the culture of greed among the wealthy in 1980s America. Director Stone, the son of a stockbroker, presents the world of Wall Street as one of ruthless competition in which unscrupulous predators compete in a no-holds-barred battle for supremacy for money and power, without regard for the lives and finances of the small investors, honest brokers, and company employees whose lives and finances may be ruined along the way. *Wall Street* is, in fact, a sort of morality play, complete with allegorical characters who represent particular forces and positions within the capitalist phenomena being described.

The protagonist of the film is Bud Fox (played by Charlie Sheen), a struggling young broker dazzled by the world of high finance and hoping to get the big break that will move him to the next level of wealth and power. Like his namesake in the animal world, Fox is both predator and prey, willing to break the rules in pursuit of success, but still troubled by the basic sense of fairness and decency that has been implanted in him by his virtuous working-class father, Carl (played by Martin Sheen, Charlie's real-life father), a machinist and union representative for Bluestar Airlines. Carl's influence for the good is balanced by Bud's admiration for big-time Wall Street shark Gordon Gekko, played by Michael Douglas in a performance that won him an Academy Award for best actor.

The basic plot of the film is simple and in many ways strikingly parallel to that of Stone's earlier Vietnam War film, *Platoon* (1986), which also stars Charlie Sheen as a naif in a brutal world. However, *Wall Street* presents a vivid depiction of the complex workings of high finance that is both convincing and understandable. It also involves numerous complications and a certain amount of suspense as the various characters perform high-stakes financial maneuvers. The persistent Bud manages, early in the film, to get Gekko's attention and to become Gekko's protegé, bringing him immediate rewards, including a job promotion, a spectacular new apartment, and an impressive new girlfirend, the beautiful decorator Darien Taylor (played by Daryl Hannah). But director Stone is careful to make it clear that Bud's newfound success is potentially transitory, as easily lost as won. Taylor, for example, is essentially on loan to Bud from Gekko, with whom she is also secretly having an affair. Just as ambitious as Bud, she leaves him as soon as he breaks off his association with Gekko. This breakup, meanwhile, is fairly predictable, given the kernel of decency that remains in Bud's character.

Gekko is the embodiment of greed, and indeed one of the film's most memorable set pieces is Gekko's "greed is good" speech, delivered at a stockholders' meeting of Teldar Paper, a company he is attempting to take over with the help of Bud. But Gekko takes over companies not to run them, but to destroy them. He is a specialist in acquiring companies through insider trading, then liquidating them, dismantling the companies he acquires and selling off the pieces, generally to the great detriment of the companies' employees. When Gekko tries to use this strategy on Bluestar, Bud decides he has had enough. He bands together with his father and representatives of the company's other employees and concocts a strategy that saves the airline from Gekko's clutches, causing Gekko to lose a fortune on the deal. This takeover is hardly radical, however. Rather than leaving the airline in the control of its workers, this strategy actually leaves the company in the hands of Gekko's arch-enemy, the virtuous (and much richer) British billionaire, Sir Larry Wildman (Terence Stamp), a builder and saver of struggling companies. As the film ends, Bluestar is "saved," but Bud is arrested for his earlier unscrupulous dealings (whether in support of Gekko or in opposition to him is unclear). He will apparently go to jail, though Bud cooperates with authorities, wearing a wire to get incriminating evidence against Gekko, who will presumably go to jail as well.

Stone's film is clearly meant to be an indictment of the entire capitalist system, with its ideology of profit at all and any cost. Its indictment of the ruthless machinations of this system is at times powerful and effective. Gekko, on the other hand, is an especially rapacious case, apparently because of feelings of inferiority engendered by his own working-class background, which leaves him with a drive to prove that he is not just as good as, but better than the Ivy-League types who comprise most of his peers in his new role as wealthy financier. It is here that the film's figuration of class is particularly problematic, though it is almost a cliché in American film, as when the working-class background of aspiring politician Peter Burton in *True Colors* (1991) drives him to be especially ruthless and ambitious. Despite the presentation of Carl Fox and other representatives of the working class as admirable figures, the characterizations of both Bud and Gekko seem to suggest that working-class individuals fare better when they stay in their place, doing their jobs in workmanlike fashion and leaving high finance for those who, like Wildman, are born with wealth and can thus handle it with dignity and grace.

Sayles followed *Matewan* with another story of the exploitation of the working class in 1988 with *Eight Men Out*, a baseball film that follows somewhat in the tradition of the boxing films of the 1940s in using competitive sports as an allegory for capitalism. *Eight Men Out* narrates the 1919 "Black Sox" scandal, when eight members of the Chicago White Sox were charged with conspiring with gamblers to lose the World Series intentionally. The film does a good job of telling the story and includes some very effective scenes from the actual games of the Series, which the White Sox ultimately lost to the Cincinnati Reds, five games to three. It also brings many of the individual players to life as they struggle with the moral dilemma of participation in the fix. Ultimately, however, *Eight Men Out* is most important for its exploration of the roots of the scandal in the exploitative practices of White Sox owner Charles Comiskey (Clifton James), who makes huge profits from the team but pays the players so poorly that they become fair game for unscrupulous gamblers who offer them a chance at easy money by throwing the Series.

Eight Men Out is a fine baseball film that doubles as an effective commentary on the exploitation of labor by capital, nicely summed up the lament of one of the players during the trial that he and the other players are facing possible jail sentences, while Comiskey and the gamblers are in the back room dividing up the profits that the players have earned through their labor and talent. Meanwhile, the film explodes the myth that baseball and America were both pure and innocent before the scandal, and that the corrupt Black Sox players somehow destroyed this innocence. In *Eight Men Out*, the scandal was a product of corruption, rather than a cause of it, while the players were victims of this corruption, not the instigators. Meanwhile, Sayles has stated that he was influenced by the Watergate scandal in his depiction of the Black Sox controversy. The film also has a particular contemporary relevance as a potential rejoinder to negative fan reaction to recent attempts by baseball players to resist exploitation by owners through collective union actions.

Another variation on the working-class film that appeared in 1988 was Robert Redford's *The Milagro Beanfield War*, based on John Nichols's novel of the same title. The film definitely mutes the leftist political stance of the original novel, but it is still quite clear in its depiction of the negative impact of capitalist modernization on the small New Mexico town of Milagro, whose poor inhabitants find themselves the victims of considerable economic exploitation at the hands of rich capitalists. The film also makes it clear that the local and state governments support these capitalists, presumably in the interest of economic growth for the region. However, the local citizenry rebels against their exploitation by these powerful interests, especially after the development of a new recreation area threatens to destroy their farmlands. Their efforts have implications that reach all the way to the state capital, where the governor orders that the development of the Miracle Valley Recreation Area be put on hold, given that it seems to be causing more trouble than it is worth. In the end, the people of Milagro celebrate their victory, at least for the time being.

The brief flurry in the production of films representing working-class points of view in the late 1980s can perhaps be attributed to the antilabor (and pro-business) policies of the Reagan administration that called attention to the realities of class inequality in America. That so few such films have been produced since that time can be attributed to a number of factors, including the relative health of the American economy during the Clinton administration of the 1990s and the relatively repressive climate that has discouraged dissent and critique of the American capitalist system during the Patriot Act era of the years after September 11, 2001. Meanwhile, even the relatively few films that have critiqued corporate culture since the late 1980s—such as Michael Mann's *The Insider* (1999)—have not focused on class and have not challenged capitalism itself, but only what are presented as capitalism's bad apples, such as the tobacco industry.

It is also the case that, in the years since the late 1980s, the working-class portion of the American capitalist system has been gradually displaced from the United States into China and the former Third World. Many of the issues of exploitation and class inequality formerly addressed in films such as *The Grapes of Wrath* have now gained complexity, becoming international. In this sense, films about class and labor essentially merge with films about issues related to globalization, and some of the most interesting and important political films of recent years have moved precisely in this direction.

One of the best of such films is a British-German production, Fernando Meirelles's *The Constant Gardener* (2005), an exposé of the corrupt and exploitative practices of the international pharmaceutical industry, focusing on horrifying practices such as the testing of drugs on unsuspecting populations in Africa. Among American films, one might single out Stephen Gaghan's *Syriana* (2005), a complex film that essentially does the same for the international oil industry that Steven Soderbergh's *Traffic* (2000), which had been scripted by Gaghan, did for the international drug trade. In fact, this comparison is more than apt: *Syriana* suggests that the oil industry (often with official government support) is informed by dishonesty, intrigue, and a murderous greed that would be very much at home in the drug trade.

Of course, the most overt example of international politics is warfare, and it is certainly the case that war films represent one of the richest families of American films with political implications. The controversial war in Vietnam, in which American troops were extensively engaged in the 1960s and 1970s, has triggered a particularly interesting body of films, many of which explicitly or implicitly critique the political ramifications of the war. The next chapter discusses films about the Vietnam War and its impact on American politics and society.

CHAPTER 7

Apocalypse Then: The Vietnam War in American Film

The American experience in Vietnam that included three decades of entanglement and one decade of all-out war remains one of the most traumatic single experiences in the history of the United States, rivaled only by the Civil War in its impact on the national psyche. The Vietnam War has also been a central concern of American film since the 1970s, and an entire subgenre of films dealing with the war and related issues have evolved since that time. Major Vietnam War films such as Francis Ford Coppola's *Apocalypse Now* (1979), Oliver Stone's *Platoon* (1986), and Stanley Kubrick's *Full Metal Jacket* (1987) deal directly with the American experience of combat in Vietnam and are among the best-known works of modern cinema. However, numerous other films have addressed the war in a variety of different ways, making for a surprisingly diverse set of thematically related works.

Hollywood was hesitant openly to criticize the war in Vietnam while American troops were still engaged there, though numerous films—perhaps most notably Dennis Hopper's *Easy Rider* (1969)—captured the spirit of a 1960s counterculture that was centrally informed by opposition to the war. Meanwhile, several films about war that are not about the Vietnam War itself were received as Vietnam War films because they were released during the American involvement in Vietnam and because many of their statements about war seemed highly relevant to the ongoing conflict in Vietnam. This was especially the case at the beginning of the 1970s, when the fighting in Vietnam was at its peak. For example, Joseph Heller's novel *Catch-22* (1961), an absurdist black comedy about the American invasion of Italy in World War II, gained a following throughout the 1960s among readers who read it as a satire of a militarist mindset that remained highly relevant in the Vietnam era. The novel was then adapted to film (under the direction of Mike Nichols) in 1970, and enjoyed considered success with audiences who clearly read it as a comment on the folly of the American military misadventure in southeast Asia. Similarly, Dalton Trumbo's classic 1939 antiwar novel *Johnny Got His Gun* (set in World War I) gained a renewed readership in the light of the Vietnam experience and was adapted to film by Trumbo himself in 1971.

By far the most important of the films in this category is Robert Altman's *M*A*S*H* (1970). Written by Ring Lardner, Jr. (like Trumbo a member of the Hollywood Ten), *M*A*S*H* became a signature film of the anti-Vietnam War movement. Lardner won an Academy Award for his adaptation of the screenplay from the 1968 novel by Richard Hooker. The film also made its director a major player in Hollywood and inspired a similarly titled television series that ran from 1972 to 1983 becoming one of the most important (and beloved) series in American television history. Although set in the Korean War, the film's mockery of war as an absurd exercise in futility appealed in particularly direct ways to a generation of young people galvanized into political action by opposition to the war in Vietnam. Further, the irreverence shown toward authority by its major characters, who continually flaunt military discipline and get away with it, provided vicarious pleasure for viewers who had grown increasingly suspicious of authority.

M*A*S*H has no real plot, but is simply a series of episodes detailing daily life in the 4077th M.A.S.H. unit (Mobile Army Surgical Hospital), operating only three miles from the front during the Korean War. Many of the surgical scenes are powerfully realistic, making a strong statement about the inglorious carnage of war. But the prevailing mood is anarchic comedy, beginning with the opening scene in which Captain Hawkeye Pierce (Donald Sutherland), newly arrived in Korea, steals a jeep to drive out to his unit, taking with him another new surgeon, Captain Duke Forrest (Tom Skerritt). The two are soon joined by heart surgeon Captain Trapper John McIntyre (Elliott Gould), and the three of them proceed to wreak havoc on the base with their antiauthoritarian antics. Of course, all are highly skilled surgeons, which is one reason their behavior is tolerated, though it is also the case that their commanding officer, Colonel Henry Blake (Roger Bowen), is preoccupied with other matters, such as seducing nurses. Their principal opposition comes from their fellow surgeon, Major Frank Burns (Robert Duvall), a sanctimonious religious fanatic, and head nurse Major Margaret Houlihan (Sally Kellerman), a career army nurse who is obsessed with regular army discipline.

Burns and Houlihan, of course, function primarily as butts for the film's humor. They are certainly no match for Pierce, McIntyre, and their supporters, who outsmart and make fools of them at every turn. In one episode, a microphone is placed under Houlihan's bed so that her love-making with the holier-than-thou Burns (who has a wife and kids back home) can be broadcast over the camp's public address system. In the aftermath, Burns is driven to distraction and taken away in a straightjacket. Houlihan, now saddled with the nickname "Hot Lips," remains behind to continue the fight and to be tormented by Pierce and his allies until she finally gives in by the end of the film and joins the fun. Pierce and McIntyre are at their antiauthoritarian best on an outing in Tokyo, where they are called so that McIntyre can perform surgery on the son of a congressman, but where they spend most of their time in various extracurricular activities. Confronted by a stodgy colonel who disapproves of their antics, they get him off their backs by drugging him and then photographing him in various compromising positions in a geisha house. Other major episodes include an elaborate mock suicide and funeral for the camp dentist, "Pain-less Pole" Waldowski (John Schuck), who decides that he wants to die after concluding that he is gay, despite his reputation as a womanizer with immense phallic endowments. The ceremony is concluded, however, when Waldowski is resurrected by the good offices of nurse Lieutenant "Dish" Schneider (Jo Ann Pflug) and returns to his former self. In the final major episode, the unit fields a football team for a challenge match against General Hammond (G. Wood) and his unit. Hammond fields a team laced with professional footballers, but the M.A.S.H. unit responds by acquiring a ringer of its own, in the person of ex-49er Oliver "Spearchucker" Jones (Fred Williamson). The medical unit also employs certain special skills, such as incapacitating the opponents' star player with drugs, and the upshot is that they win the game (and their extensive bets) on a trick play as the gun sounds to end the contest.

In the final scene, Pierce and Forrest complete their tours of duty and are ordered home, departing by again absconding with the same jeep in which they arrived. The film then ends as the camp's public address announcer, who has broadcast descriptions of various World War II movies being shown on the base throughout the film, describes the film we have just seen, thus announcing an explicit dialogue between *M*A*S*H* and more conventional war films. But this dialogue is implicit throughout, and the film is clearly intended as an interrogation not only of war and war films, but of the elements of American society (especially American popular culture, with its core of violence) that might make this society particularly prone to involvement in warfare. In this sense, the film is a direct, and potentially subversive investigation of the background of the U.S. involve-ment in Vietnam. Of course, the conflicts in Korea and Vietnam were both offshoots of the Cold War in which American military force was brought to bear to prevent the spread of communism, but *M*A*S*H* does not really address the specific ideologies involved in either conflict. In any case, the film's politics, like much of the oppositional politics of the 1960s, are hardly procommunist, but thoroughly bourgeois, celebrating the victories of rebellious individuals over a bureaucracy-ridden authority.

Others films made during the conflict in Vietnam can be taken as antiwar statements, even though they are not specifically about Vietnam (or even modern warfare). Probably the most important group of such films included a series of revisionary Westerns that were released during the Vietnam War and that could be interpreted allegorically as a comment on the war in Vietnam, generally by using the genocidal destruction of Native Americans and their culture an allegorical replacement for the havoc being wrought at the time by American forces in Vietnam. Such anti-Vietnam War Westerns include *The Professionals* (1966); *The Wild Bunch* (1969), *Little Big Man* (1970), *Soldier Blue* (1970), *Two Mules for Sister Sara* (1970), and *Ulzana's Raid* (1972). Collectively, these films suggest that the Vietnam War was enabled by a tendency in the American national psyche toward violence and hatred of the Other that has been present throughout the history of the United States.

The first major film directly based on the war in Vietnam was actually a strong pro-war film, the John Wayne vehicle *The Green Berets* (1968), an overt piece of right-wing propaganda in favor of the American war effort. This film (also codirected by Wayne) spares no effort to depict the Vietnamese communists as vicious, bloodthirsty murderers, bent on destroying the lives of the Vietnamese people. The Americans, on the other hand, are depicted as saviors of the Vietnamese people, who have come to Vietnam to liberate the country from the efforts of an international communist conspiracy to enslave the people there. *The Green Berets* draws upon every imaginable sentimental cliché to emphasize the evil of the Vietnamese communists, including a focus on a poor Vietnamese orphan boy, seen burying his beloved puppy after the dog is killed in an attack by the evil communists. To make matters worse, the kindly GI who befriends the boy is killed in a trap set by the nefarious Viet Cong, leaving the poor boy all alone in the world. But, as the film ends, American colonel Mike Kirby (Wayne) assures the boy that he will be taken care of because the boy, after all, "is what this war is all about."

The Green Berets depicts the war in Vietnam as a simple, good vs. evil struggle of good-guy Americans against bad-guy Vietnamese communists. There is essentially no mention of the fact that so many Americans saw the war differently, other than a bizarre suggestion early on that the American press has (for some unstipulated reason) chosen not to report the true extent of the evil of the Vietnamese communists, who have (according to this film) maliciously tortured and murdered every public official, teacher, and professor in the entire country of South Vietnam—and "kidnapped a like number," though it is unclear how anyone would be left to be kidnapped if they had all already been killed. *The Green Berets* also assures audiences of an impending American victory, both because the Americans have better weaponry (especially air power) and because American fighting men like the Green Berets themselves are far superior to the cowardly Viet Cong troops (and their decadent leader, a general shown living in high style in a former French colonial mansion, sipping wine and seducing young women).

Films made about Vietnam after the end of the war had to come to grips with the fact that this American victory did not occur. Virtually all such films, perhaps with the advantage of hindsight, are antiwar films—and often in ways that suggest the insanity and futility of wars in general. In this sense, the Vietnam War films represent a major sea change in American cinema. There had been antiwar films before, as when Lewis Milestone's *All Quiet on the Western Front* (1930) and Arthur Hiller's *The Americanization of Emily* (1964) deflated the glorification of World War I and World War II, respectively. But most American war films had, in fact, glorified war, with the huge body of World War II films (many made during the war and specifically designed to promote the war effort) leading the way.

Even in the case of Vietnam, antiwar films specifically about the combat there did not begin to appear until the American involvement there was over. One of the first of these was Sidney J. Furie's *The Boys in Company C* (1978), which follows a group of U.S. Marines through basic training and a tour of duty in Vietnam in 1968, the year the war began to turn against the Americans once and for all. As such, it is a sort of forerunner of *Full Metal Jacket*; it even features R. Lee Ermey as the drill instructor during their training. Furie's film helped to establish many of the standard cinematic images of Vietnam, including the futility of the American war effort and the corruption of America's South Vietnamese allies. And, if the film's critique of the politics behind the American mishandling of the war now seems almost clichéd, it is important to remember that *The Boys in Company C* was one of the first films to present such a critique.

Furie followed in 1984 with another Vietnam War film, the poorly received *Purple Hearts*, though by this time several films about Vietnam had appeared. Another early Vietnam War film was Ted Post's *Go Tell the Spartans*, also released in 1978. Although lacking the budget and hype of later and better-known films such as *Apocalypse Now, Platoon*, or *Full Metal Jacket, Go Tell the Spartans* is actually a fairly good film that illuminates certain aspects of the war that many of its better known cousins do not. In particular, *Go Tell the Spartans* is set in 1964 when Americans were supposedly serving in Vietnam only as advisors to the South Vietnamese government forces. Yet it suggests that, even at this early date, anyone who bothered to look could see that the Americans had no business in Vietnam and that their involvement there would probably be a disaster.

Go Tell the Spartans features Burt Lancaster as Major Asa Barker, the salty commander of a group of American military advisors in South Vietnam. Barker seems already to realize that the American presence in Vietnam is ridiculous, as can be seen from his tendency to ignore instructions from his superiors and to file fabricated intelligence reports because he knows the information will be useless, anyway. Early in the film, he is ordered to check out the abandoned hamlet of Muc Wa, site of an old French outpost. He ignores the order and files a false report, a fact of which his superior, General Hamitz (Dolph Sweet) is perfectly aware. Hamitz then orders Barker to send American advisors, along with a detachment of South Vietnamese regular army and militia, to occupy Muc Wa, even though Barker argues that this action could not possibly have any effect except to stir up trouble. But, given a direct and specific order of this kind, he has no choice but to obey, so he sends the force. "Cowboy" (Evan Kim), a fanatical hater of communists, commands the South Vietnamese troops, though he is only a sergeant. The American forces, who are clearly in charge, are headed by Lieutenant Raymond Hamilton (Joe Unger), assisted by Sergeant Oleonowski (Jonathan Goldberg) and Corporal Stephen Courcey (Craig Wasson).

On the way to the outpost, they take a Viet Cong prisoner, whom Cowboy interrogates, then murders when he refuses to talk.

Otherwise, they arrive at the outpost without difficulty, noting the inscription on the gate of the old French cemetery, which, quoting the doomed Spartans at the disastrous battle of Thermopylae, translates to "Stranger, when you find us lying here, go tell the Spartans we obeyed their orders." Once they establish control of the outpost, they almost immediately find themselves under attack by the Viet Cong. Hamilton is killed, and Barker is forced to send his right-hand man, Captain Al Olivetti (Marc Singer), to assume command of the outpost. Eventually, Barker goes there by helicopter to evacuate the Americans. Courcey, however, refuses to leave and insists on staying with the South Vietnamese, for whom there is no room on the helicopter. Resigned, Barker stays as well, and together they attempt to lead the South Vietnamese to safety on foot. They are soon overwhelmed by the Viet Cong, and most, including Barker, are killed. Courcey survives and staggers homeward as the film ends with the year 1964 emblazoned on the screen as a reminder of the next decade of things to come.

Among other things, Cowboy's nickname indicates the close connection of this film to the genre of the Western, with Muc Wa playing the part of the frontier outpost and the Viet Cong playing the part of the Indians. This generic mix, echoing the earlier family of Vietnam-oriented Westerns that appeared around the beginning of the 1970s, potentially suggests a link between the genocidal extermination of Native Americans and the American assault on Vietnam. But this film makes little overt political commentary and settles mostly for a suggestion of the absurdity and hopelessness of the American involvement in support of a South Vietnamese government that is clearly unworthy of support. Cowboy's viciousness is only one characteristic of American's South Vietnamese allies in this film; they are also corrupt, undisciplined, and incompetent. Most of the American advisors are not much better, and it is quite clear that the American/South Vietnamese alliance, like the Spartans at Thermopylae, is doomed to destruction in the war.

Apocalypse Now was the first major American film about the Vietnam War. It was also one of the most anticipated films in the history of American cinema, especially as its release was continually delayed by now-legendary difficulties with the script, casting, and shooting. These difficulties themselves make an almost epic narrative that serves as a sort of allegory about the American experience in Vietnam, as detailed in the documentary film *Hearts of Darkness* (1991). Once it was finally released, *Apocalypse Now* was initially regarded by many as a disappointment. It was nominated for eight Academy Awards, including best picture and best director, but won only in the technical categories of best cinematography and best sound. Over time, however, the film has come to be widely regarded as a classic. For example, when the American Film Institute announced its list of the hundred greatest films of all time in 1998, *Apocalypse Now* came in at number twenty-eight on the list.

In an artistic sense, *Apocalypse Now* is probably the finest of the many films that have been made about the Vietnam War. Drawing upon Joseph Conrad's *Heart of Darkness* for its basic atmosphere and plot structure, the film is an impressive and intelligent work of cinematic art, using all of the visual and auditory resources of the medium to create a brooding atmosphere of insanity, terror, and darkness. Meanwhile, the connection to Conrad helps to initiate a number of other intertextual dialogues as well, with predecessor texts ranging from T. S. Eliot, to The Rolling Stones, to the whole genre of the American war movie. *Apocalypse Now* does little to represent the Vietnamese point of view or to explain the background of the conflict, but that is partly the point, suggesting as it does a lack of understanding that informed the entire American presence in Vietnam. The film depicts the American presence in Vietnam as entirely nonsensical, as an absurd exercise in metaphysical evil with little rational motivation behind it. It also effectively uses music and other images from American popular culture to suggest that this evil arises from something deep within American culture, asking viewers therefore to reexamine and reevaluate their commitment to the American way of life. As such the film probes not only into the dark heart of the Vietnamese jungle, but into the heart of darkness of the American soul as well.

The film begins with one of the most powerful opening sequences in all of American film, featuring apocalyptic images of explosive destruction, wrought by American helicopters as they bomb the Vietnamese jungle. Then, with the Doors' "The End" sounding hauntingly in the background, the scene shifts to a Saigon hotel room, where an experienced American military intelligence operative, Captain Willard (Martin Sheen), awaits his next assignment and hovers near the edge of insanity. This scene helps to set the tone of basic insanity that the film sees in the American involvement in Vietnam, a motif that takes an important turn when Willard's assignment finally comes. He is to travel deep into the jungle of Cambodia to locate and assassinate Colonel Walter E. Kurtz (Marlon Brando), a Green Beret officer who has supposedly gone insane and begun to use "unsound methods," including the murder of South Vietnamese army officers suspected of complicity with the enemy. From the beginning, Willard sees something suspect about the assignment. Insanity, after all, is the norm in Vietnam. Moreover, Willard thinks to himself, "Charging a man with murder in this place is like handing out speeding tickets at the Indy 500." Perhaps, then, the real danger of Kurtz is not that he violates American policy in Vietnam, but that he reveals the nature of that policy all too clearly.

To reach Kurtz, Willard is to go up the Nung River on a small navy patrol boat, manned by a crew that includes its Chief (Albert Hall); Chef (Frederic Forrest), a saucier from New Orleans; Lance (Sam Bottoms), a famous surfer from Southern California, and Mr. Clean (a young Laurence Fishburne), a teenage slum kid from the South Bronx. First, however, they must get into the river, the mouth of which is heavily guarded by enemy forces. This problem is solved with the aid of an air cavalry unit commanded by the memorable (and tellingly named) Lieutenant Colonel Kilgore (Robert Duvall), who has a passionate love for killing and for surfing. He combines the two as his helicopters assault an enemy-controlled village at the mouth of the river, blasting away at the terrified villagers as Wagner's "The Ride of the Valkyries" sounds from a loudspeaker mounted on Kilgore's helicopter. There is something definitely postmodern about this weird musical accompaniment, which converts the attack into sheer spectacle, but the choice of Wagner also potentially links the American assault to the genocidal legacy of German Nazism. Then, as the village is still being subdued, with the help of fighter planes dropping napalm (the smell of which Kilgore loves in the morning because to him it smells like victory), Kilgore tops matters off by ordering Lance and several other surfers in his unit to grab their boards and head out into the water to take advantage of the excellent surfing conditions.

The basic absurdity of this scene combines with the tragic impact of the attack on the people of the village to comprise one of the film's central comments on the nature of the American involvement in Vietnam. The bulk of the film then presents the trip up the river, as the boat moves deeper and deeper into the heart of the dark, menacing jungle, while Willard reads Kurtz's dossier and muses on the object of his quest. In this sense, *Apocalypse Now* parallels Conrad quite closely, providing important reminders of the close historical parallel between the European colonial conquest of Africa in the late nineteenth century and the imperialist assault on Vietnam by American troops a century later. Along the way, Willard and the other men on the boat encounter a variety of scenes that gradually reinforce the film's mood of strangeness and insanity. In one scene that makes a rather obvious statement about the violent and sexist nature of American popular culture, they stop at an American base where Playboy Playmates dance, using guns as obviously phallic props, on stage as part of a U.S.O. show. The show is a great hit, though the reaction of the men suggests a certain amount of misogynist hostility, as when Lance expresses his "approval" of the moves of one of the dancers by yelling, "You fucking bitch!" Eventually, the aroused men rush the stage, and the endangered Playmates have to flee by helicopter, no doubt leaving the soldiers to take out their sexual frustration (and aggression) on the Vietnamese. This comment on American popular culture is reinforced by the film's use of Western popular music and by frequent allusions to Disneyland, Charles Manson, and other icons of American culture, which is thus characterized as spectacularly violent and unreal, much like the war itself.

Later, in one of the film's most horrifying scenes, the boat encounters a Vietnamese sampan coming down the river. They stop the sampan and begin to search it. Then, when a woman on board makes a sudden move to conceal something on the sampan, the Americans open fire, apparently killing all of those on board. The concealed object turns out to be a puppy, and the sampan turns out to be an innocent civilian vessel. They then discover that one woman on the sampan is still alive, and Chief orders his men to take her on board the American boat so she can be taken for medical attention. Willard, unwilling to have his mission interrupted, coldly pulls his pistol and shoots the woman, obviating the need for medical care.

Eventually, they make their way through the various strange scenes that await them and reach Kurtz's compound, the strangest scene of all. Kurtz reigns, godlike, over what is apparently an ancient temple and religious site, accompanied by his loyal Montanyard troops, who apparently regard themselves as his children. Willard and Chef go ashore into the surreal scene, and are greeted by a manic American photojournalist (Dennis Hopper), who attempts to make them understand Kurtz, whom he obviously worships. Willard is taken captive and placed in a cage, where Kurtz later presents him with Chef's head, apparently in an attempt to break his spirit. Willard is later released and allowed free access to Kurtz's quarters.

Kurtz, filmed mostly in low light that both obscures Brando's obesity and emphasizes the dark, mysterious nature of Kurtz, explains his vision to Willard, while seeming to spend most of his time reading the poetry of T. S. Eliot, with its hints of cultural and metaphysical crisis. Willard is much impressed with Kurtz, but eventually kills him. In a grotesque scene in which the film's generally effective mythic symbolism is a bit overdone and heavy-handed, Willard hacks Kurtz to death with a machete, intercut with scenes of the symbolic slaughter of an ox by Kurtz's "children." Willard and Lance then make their way back to the boat and head back down the river, as echoes of Kurtz's whispered last words, "the horror, the horror," echo in the background.

The surreal look, sound, and feel of *Apocalypse Now* might be interpreted as a sort of realism, intended to convey the experience of Vietnam more accurately than any straightforward realistic account could ever do. It is also the case, however, that the film does not attempt conventional realism and so cannot be criticized if all of its events do not seem quite credible. The film, like most American films about Vietnam, focuses on the American experience, but it does at least give some suggestion of the impact of the American presence on the Vietnamese. However, some of the descriptions of the Vietnamese communists certainly border on a combination of Orientalist and Cold War stereotypes,. When Kurtz expresses his admiration for the ability of the Viet Cong to commit astonishing acts of brutality in the interest of their cause, he suggests a vision of coldly fanatical Oriental communists. However, he does indicate that the Viet Cong are human beings, "filled with love," and that it must require superhuman strength (which he greatly admires) for them to do some of the things they do. Nevertheless, he avoids the common sense explanation that the Viet Cong were not superhuman, but simply fought with greater resolve than the Americans because they were defending their homes, while the Americans had no idea what they were fighting for.

Apocalypse Now was rereleased in 2001 in an extended form as *Apocalypse Now Redux*, a "director's cut" version that differs from the original essentially in the restoration of scenes that had been deleted in order to decrease the length of the film. *Apocalypse Now Redux* is thus 53 minutes longer than the original, coming in at a whopping 3 hours, 13 minutes running time. Of the added scenes, the most significant is an extended sequence in which Willard and the boat crew stop off at a leftover French plantation, the owners of which have somehow been able to stave off attacks by the North Vietnamese, the Viet Cong, the South Vietnamese, and even the Americans in holding this vestige of French colonial rule in Indochina.

While at the plantation, the crew buries Mr. Clean, who had earlier been killed in fire from the jungle alongside the river. They also share an elaborate French meal with the denizens of the plantation, making it clear how out of touch with the realities of Vietnam the Frenchmen really are. However, this scene makes it clear that the Americans are equally out of touch, with one of the Frenchmen pointing out that, historically, the Viet Cong evolved out of the Viet Minh, the force led by Ho Chi Minh that opposed the Japanese occupiers of the area during World War II. In particular, he points out that the Viet Minh had substantial American support, meaning that, to a large extent, the Viet Cong are creatures of the Americans, who now seek to destroy them, but are finding that they are not so easy to destroy.

This sequence thus characterizes the entire American military intervention in Vietnam as a string of errors, miscalculations, and misperceptions. The air of confusion created within the film contributes to this message, though this strategy otherwise threatens to obscure the film's political implications. The politics of Oliver Stone's *Platoon* are only a bit more clear, despite its graphic realism. For one thing, the film's "grunts" are interested more in simple survival than in political questions. For another, though *Platoon* as a whole at least avoids demonizing the Vietnamese communists and acknowledges some of the racist atrocities committed by the American forces, it does very little to examine the underlying causes of the conflict. Indeed, the film is not really about the conflict between the Americans and the Vietnamese communists at all. Instead, it focuses on internal conflicts within the American platoon that is the central focus of the film, treating the enemy forces as simply another in a series of natural obstacles (heat, rain, disease, insects, snakes) that are encountered by the American forces in the jungles of Vietnam. In the process, the American presence in Vietnam seems to be criticized as much for its damage to the natural environment as to the Vietnamese people.

Platoon follows a single American infantry platoon in Vietnam through several months in late 1967 and early 1968. It begins as protagonist Chris Taylor (Charlie Sheen) and other new recruits arrive by plane to begin their tours of duty in Vietnam. In an ominous moment that sets the tone for much of the rest of the film, they disembark at an American airbase and are immediately confronted with the sight of body bags being arranged for shipment back to the states. Taylor, something of a stand-in for writer/ director Stone, is a rich kid who has dropped out of college and volunteered for service in Vietnam, partly as a way of rebelling against the bourgeois conformism of his parents, and partly as a sort of social protest against the unfair burden being borne by the poor in the conduct of the war. He finds, however, that the working-class soldiers in his platoon, many of them African Americans, are largely unimpressed by his gesture, which they see as both foolish and pointless, especially given the ongoing class differences that pervade American society. As one of black soldiers, King (Keith David), tells Taylor, "The poor are always being fucked over by the rich. Always have, always will."

This consciousness of class remains in the margins throughout *Platoon*, though the film is largely a simple story of good vs. evil. As the naïve Taylor struggles to learn to survive amid the tumultuous confusion of Vietnam, he also gradually becomes aware that the platoon is riven by a conflict between two of its sergeants. Sergeant Barnes (Tom Berenger) is a vicious killer, willing to go to any extreme or commit any atrocity to subdue the enemy. His quest to destroy the enemy is at one point explicitly compared to Ahab's quest for the white whale. On the other hand, Sergeant Elias (Willem Dafoe) retains a sense of humanity, decency, and compassion, both for his men and for the Vietnamese civilians who continually get caught up in the war. In opposition to Barnes's gung ho patriotism and racist hatred for the Vietnamese, Elias is philosophical about his growing feeling that the Americans are losing the war. "We've been kicking other people's asses for so long, I figure it's time we got ours kicked," he declares.

In one horrifying scene, the platoon invades a village and burns it to the ground. In the process, Barnes pointlessly murders a Vietnamese woman. Elias, who stops Barnes from committing further killings, declares his intention of filing a formal complaint against Barnes when they get back to the base. Soon afterward, Elias is shot by Barnes, then finished off by the enemy, falling to his knees and dying in a scene clearly designed to parallel his death to the crucifixion of Christ. Taylor, certain that Barnes is responsible for Elias's death, tries to convince the other men in Elias's squad to take revenge on Barnes, but Barnes faces them down and then beats up Taylor. Later, amid the confusion of a disastrous battle in which the platoon is virtually destroyed, Taylor comes upon a wounded Barnes and coldly kills him. Reinforcements eventually arrive to rescue Taylor and the other survivors. Now twice wounded, Taylor is shipped back to the States, unfortunately finishing the film with a lame voiceover in which he declares his intention of drawing upon his experience in Vietnam in order to seek "goodness and meaning" in the rest of his life. As Timothy Corrigan puts it in his book *A Cinema without Walls: Movies and Culture after Vietnam* (Rutgers University Press, 1991), this final statement produces a "blur" that "borders on nonsense" (p. 43).

Still, *Platoon* does an excellent job of portraying the hardship, confusion, and sheer terror that comprised the texture of day-to-day experience for American soldiers in Vietnam. It was greeted with considerable critical acclaim, largely because of the realism of its portrayal of this experience. Nominated for eight Academy Awards, the film won four, including those in the prestigious categories of best picture and best director. *Platoon* was eventually joined by *Born on the Fourth of July* (1989) and *Heaven and Earth* (1993) to complete Stone's important trilogy of films about Vietnam. In the meantime, it was almost immediately followed by Stanley Kubrick's *Full Metal Jacket*, which joins *Platoon* to provide the two central depictions of actual combat in Vietnam in American film.

Actually, though, *Full Metal Jacket* is less about the war than about certain aspects of the culture and ideology of America that enabled the war to occur. For one thing, the film features numerous allusions to previous American war films, especially those involving John Wayne, presented as the epitome of masculine posturing. Popular music is used to particularly good effect throughout the film, as mostly upbeat popular tunes sound in the background of gruesome and horrifying scenes of combat and destruction. The potential implication that American popular culture is entirely consonant with the American involvement in Vietnam is then further reinforced by the film's treatment of media coverage of the war. In one memorable scene, a newsreel crew films a Marine combat unit in Vietnam, while the men pose as if appearing in a movie, perhaps a Western. "We'll let the gooks play the Indians," one of them says, completing the link among American popular culture, the racist war in Vietnam, and the genocidal extermination of Native Americans.

The first forty-five minutes of *Full Metal Jacket* are devoted to the training undergone by a group of new marine recruits in preparation for their service in Vietnam. During this training, the men are subjected to extreme abuse at the hands of their sadistic, foul-mouthed drill instructor, Sergeant Hartman (R. Lee Ermey, in a memorable performance). This training is clearly designed to be dehumanizing, part of a process through which the men are intentionally transformed from human beings, who might have sympathy for the enemy, into unfeeling killing machines. During this training, a private (played by Matthew Modine) dubbed "Joker" by Hartman because of his wisecracks emerges as something of a leader among the men. Much of this segment of the film focuses on the particular difficulties suffered by Private Leonard Lawrence (Vincent D'Onofrio). Overweight and not too bright, Lawrence becomes a special target of Hartman, who dubs him "Gomer Pyle" and rides him mercilessly. Hartman even encourages the other trainees to be cruel to Lawrence as well, thus using Lawrence as a tool to stimulate ruthlessness in the others. On the last night of training, Lawrence literally becomes a killing machine, shooting and killing first Hartman, then himself.

The film then suddenly cuts to Vietnam, where the trainees are now Marines serving in the war. Joker is a reporter for *Stars and Stripes*, charged with the formidable task of putting a good face on the American war effort. Soon after this segment begins, the North Vietnamese and Viet Cong launch their Tet offensive in early 1968, turning the tide of the war against the Americans once and for all. Joker and his photographer, Rafterman (Kevyn Major Howard), are sent into the field in Hue City, where some of the most serious fighting is underway. Joker and Rafterman join a Marine unit that includes "Cowboy" (Arliss Howard), another of the trainees from the first segment of the film. They accompany Cowboy and his fellow Marines as they work their way through the ruined city, trying to clear it of snipers and other enemy troops. Indeed, all of the battle scenes in the film occur in this urban setting, making *Full Metal Jacket* rather unusual among Vietnam War films, which tend to focus on jungle warfare. This decision was motivated partly by historical reality, as Hue City (the capital of Vietnam prior to World War II) was, in fact, a crucial site of conflict in the Tet offensive. But it is also obviously motivated by the fact that the entire film was shot in England, where jungle settings are hard to come by, to say the least.

Despite this urban setting, the film still captures some of the especially terrifying nature of combat in Vietnam, which was so often waged against mysterious and unseen enemies. It also captures much of the cynicism that informed the efforts of the American soldiers in the war. In one scene, the men of the unit view two of their comrades, who have just been killed. "At least," says Rafterman, inanely, "they died for a good cause." Animal Mother (Adam Baldwin), the unit's most ruthless and effective killer, looks at Rafterman in disbelief. "What cause was that?" he asks. "Freedom?" responds Rafterman, tentatively. Animal Mother scoffs, "Flush out your headgear, new guy. You think we waste gooks for freedom? This is a slaughter."

Ultimately, Cowboy is also killed, though the mission is largely success-ful. Joker and Rafterman survive to report the story, while American troops from around the city stream back toward their base on the banks of the nearby river. In one final bizarre, but telling comment on the fundamental link between American popular culture and the American war effort in Vietnam, the men, in perfect unison, sing the Mickey Mouse Club theme song as they march along, rifles on their shoulders. The implication is clear. Third World opponents of American imperialism must face not only the formidable physical weaponry of the American military but also the even more formidable psychological weaponry of Disney and other bastions of American popular culture. In this sense, the film presents a powerful critique of American imperialism, though the effectiveness of this critique is ultimately limited by the failure to adequately explain the link between American culture and American imperialism. The film also presents no points of view other than the American masculine one, and it fails to document the true impact of American imperialism on the people of Vietnam and the Third World.

Both *Platoon* and *Full Metal Jacket* are clear in their critique of the American intervention in Vietnam, even if their politics are otherwise a bit muddled. Of the several Vietnam War films released in the late 1980s, the one that comes closest to expressing pro-war sentiments is John Irvin's *Hamburger Hill* (1987). Even this film suggests that the combat and casualties of Vietnam were pointless and meaningless, but it also suggests (bizarrely) that the very meaninglessness of the sacrifices made by the soldiers who fought in Vietnam lent an added nobility to their experience. Indeed, this film attributes a certain admirable nobility to war in general, though war is also presented as a grueling experience that only tough, macho men can understand and appreciate.

The film begins with a shot of the Vietnam War memorial, calling attention to the number of American deaths during the war, and it is clearly meant as a sort of homage to those who fought and died in Vietnam. It then moves fairly quickly into an extended sequence set in an American camp in Vietnam, basically designed to introduce viewers to the major characters. Then comes the main narrative, based on a real battle that involved an American assault on entrenched North Vietnamese forces on Dong Ap Bia, a small mountain in the jungle-covered region along the border between South Vietnam and Laos, also known as Hill 937. This hill, the taking of which involved one of the bloodiest battles of the entire Vietnam War, was dubbed Hamburger Hill by the soldiers who fought there, because of the high level of casualties incurred (70 American dead, 372 wounded). The battle was also highly controversial, and both Congress and the American press extensively questioned whether the strategic value of the hill was really worth the cost. Indeed, after fighting from May 10 to May 20, 1969, to take the hill, the Americans quietly abandoned it on June 7, apparently realizing there was no point to holding it.

The film focuses on a single American squad, led by Sergeant Frantz (Dylan McDermott), as they make one charge after another up the hill, but are continually repelled by Vietnamese forces—though at one point they are mistakenly attacked by American helicopters. The battle scenes are punctuated by sudden outbursts of some of the most shocking and graphic violence ever shown in American film to that time; these scenes are among the grimmest to appear on the screen since Kubrick's *Paths of Glory* (1957). By the time they take the hill, there are only three of them left, and their ultimate success in reaching the crest of the hill seems pointless. Indeed, throughout the film, the soldiers comfort themselves in the face of hellish conditions by declaring that the events they are experiencing "don't mean nothin'." This mantra then becomes a summary judgment about the entire battle for the hill. Yet the film seems to want to suggest that the very fact that there was no point to the fighting made it more honorable, more a sheer demonstration of toughness and machismo that only real men, tempered in battle, can appreciate. The film indicates that the honor of war is certainly something that the press cannot hope to understand—not to mention the antiwar protestors back home, who are at several points in the film portrayed as ignorant, heartless betrayers of the soldiers who are fighting in the war.

In its denigration of the antiwar effort, *Hamburger Hill* recalls the spirit of *The Green Berets* and certainly differs from most of its own contemporaries. It especially differs from the strong antiwar stance of *Platoon* and from the portrayal in Brian De Palma's *Casualties of War* (1989), of atrocities committed by American soldiers while in Vietnam. De Palma's film, which (like *Hamburger Hill*) is based on a real incident in the war, follows hard on the heels of *Platoon* and *Full Metal Jacket* to join the parade of films about the Vietnam War made by major American directors in the late 1980s. This incident, as reported in a 1969 article by Daniel Lang in *New Yorker* magazine, involved the abduction, rape, and murder of an innocent Vietnamese girl by a patrol of American soldiers. In so doing, it addresses many of the issues and concerns that have been central to films about the war, including the dehumanizing effect of the war on American soldiers, the brutal (and usually racist) treatment of the Vietnamese by their American invaders, and the element of sexual aggression that resides in all wars but seemed to become particularly obvious and brutal in this one. *Casualties of War* can thus be taken as a statement about the horrors of war in general, though it functions most specifically as a critique of the American presence in Vietnam, for which rape and murder are effective metaphors. On the other hand, the film, while presumably sympathetic to the plight of the raped Vietnamese girl, focuses primarily on the anguish of an American GI who refuses to participate in the rape. It does nothing to challenge the disturbing tendency of American Vietnam War films to treat Vietnamese women as little more than passive objects for male sexual desire—and aggression.

The patrol is commanded by Sergeant Meserve (Sean Penn), only twenty years old, but a grizzled veteran of Vietnam, slated to return home in less than a month. The other members of the patrol include the vicious racist Corporal Clark (Don Harvey) and three privates: the gullible Hatcher (John C. Reilly), the radio operator Diaz (John Leguizamo), and the innocent new recruit Eriksson (Michael J. Fox). Ordered out on a mission to look for Viet Cong tunnels, Meserve, frustrated by not being able to visit town (or a brothel) on his last leave, decides to take a detour to a village to abduct a girl for the sexual gratification of himself and his men. At first, Eriksson is convinced that Meserve is only kidding, but then watches in horror as Meserve and the others actually go to a village and abduct a girl.

They take the girl with them through the bush for several miles, treating her roughly on the way and obviously living out a fantasy of male power, a fantasy in which the film sometimes seems almost complicit. Eriksson and

Diaz privately agree between themselves that they will not participate in the serial rape of the girl, but Diaz gives in to the pressure applied by the others, leaving Eriksson as the only one who refuses. Meserve verbally abuses him and accuses him of being a homosexual, then sends him off to stand sentry duty. There, he hears the girl's screams as the other four callously rape her in sequence.

Later, Eriksson tries to comfort the girl, who speaks no English and is therefore unable to represent her position to Eriksson or to the audience. No subtitles or other devices are used. Eriksson, meanwhile, misses an opportunity to help her escape. Then, he goes along as the others take the girl, injured, traumatized, and seriously ill, along with them on a planned ambush of some Viet Cong forces spotted in the area. When she is unable to control her coughing, and thus threatens to give away their position, Clark, on Meserve's orders, brutally stabs her and leaves her for dead. She is nevertheless able to struggle to her feet and attempt to stagger away. The others see her and open fire, finishing her off in the midst of the battle with the Viet Cong.

When they get back to base, Eriksson reports the kidnapping, rape, and murder to a lieutenant and a captain, both of whom simply advise him to keep his mouth shut. That night, Clark attempts to murder Eriksson with a hand grenade, but fails. Eriksson finally tells his story to a sympathetic chaplain (Sam Robards), who helps him convince the army to conduct an official inquiry. The other four members of the patrol are convicted at a court martial and receive prison sentences ranging from eight years for Diaz to life for Clark, though Hatcher's conviction is later reversed on a technicality. Meserve, who spearheaded the entire crime, oddly receives only a twelve-year sentence. Eriksson returns to civilian life, still haunted by the memories of it all, still disturbed whenever he sees a young woman who looks Vietnamese.

Eriksson's experience points toward the lingering impact of the war on those who fought there—and on the United States as a nation. In fact, an entire family of Vietnam War films is devoted to an exploration of the postwar experiences of American soldiers who had served in Vietnam. Indeed, such films began to appear about the same time as the major body of films about the war itself—and were in fact more prominent until the flurry of Vietnam War films that appeared in the late 1980s. However, perhaps the best-known film that deals with the post-Vietnam experience, Michael Cimino's *The Deer Hunter* (1978), is a sweeping saga that attempts to follow the lives of its major characters before, during, and after the war. *The Deer Hunter* won much critical praise (and numerous awards) at the time of its release. However, while the film touches on a large number of important issues, it never really makes a clear statement about any of them. The film's biggest shortcoming is its Orientalist treatment of

Vietnam, depicted as an exotic land of debased pleasures, while the Vietnamese are depicted as crazed savages capable of unlimited cruelty and perversion. On the other hand, some have seen the film's specific focus on working-class Americans as a virtue, and it is certainly unusual among American films in this sense. In point of fact, however, *The Deer Hunter* treats the working class as unremittingly masculine (and white), while depicting working-class males mostly as drunken louts who get their pleasure primarily from drinking beer, killing animals, and beating up women.

The Deer Hunter begins in the steel mill town of Clairton, Pennsylvania, as three millworkers—Michael (Robert De Niro), Nick (Christopher Walken), and Steven (John Savage)—prepare to depart for military service in Vietnam. The film's first segment focuses on the day-to-day working-class culture of this community, beginning with scenes of camaraderie among the mill workers as they drink beer and play pool after the end of their shift. Then follows a long segment that shows the wedding ceremony and reception for Steven and his fiancée, Angela (Rutanya Alda). This segment again gestures toward a portrayal of the communal values of this working-class community of Slavic immigrants. Steven and Angela (who, we learn, is pregnant by another man) then go away for a brief honeymoon, while Mike and Nick, accompanied by friends Stan (John Cazale), John (George Dzundza), and Axel (Chuck Aspegren), go into the nearby mountains for one last hunting trip together. Mike, who approaches deer hunting with a sort of religious reverence, bags a buck, and the five friends return to town in a drunken revel, with the deer strapped on the hood of the car.

The film then suddenly cuts to a scene of battle in Vietnam. Mike, Nick, and Steven are all captured by the Viet Cong, who are depicted as brutal savages, taking great pleasure in devising exotic methods to torture and terrorize their prisoners. They especially enjoy forcing their prisoners to play Russian roulette, a technique that causes Steven to suffer a breakdown. However, when Mike and Nick join the game, they, as superior Americans, easily outwit and, Rambo-like, blow away their captors. They then escape, taking Steven with them, though the latter is seriously hurt in the process and ends up having to have both legs amputated. Back in Saigon, Nick recovers in a military hospital, and then goes into the streets, seeking out the city's savage underworld, which, among other things, features clubs in which Russian roulette is played as a sport.

In the third segment of the film, Mike, a decorated war hero, returns to Clairton to much fanfare, most of which he attempts to avoid. Nick has gone AWOL and remained in the Saigon underworld, while Steven is in a veterans' hospital, avoiding all of his old acquaintances, including Angela. Working-class morals being what they are, Mike becomes the lover of Nick's old girlfriend, Linda (Meryl Streep). But, with the American evacuation of Saigon underway in anticipation of the upcoming communist victory, Mike returns to Saigon to try to reclaim Nick, who has been sending money to Steven on a regular basis. The money, we discover, has been won in the Russian roulette game, in which he is a regular participant. Mike manages to locate him, only to watch him blow his brains out as his luck finally runs out in the gruesome game. The film then cuts to Nick's funeral back in Clairton, after which his friends gather to drink, toasting Nick and inanely singing "God Bless America," as the film finally, and mercifully, comes to a close in one final outburst of seeming patriotism.

There is, of course, some potential to read irony into this last scene, but most viewers have seen it as a genuine endorsement of the American way. Gilbert Adair sums up such responses in his book *Hollywood's Vietnam: From* The Green Berets *to* Apocalypse Now (Proteus Publishing, 1985) when he notes that *The Deer Hunter* is "a before-and-after advertisement for the USA" (p. 89). Meanwhile, the film's depiction of the Vietnamese as either savage killers or passive victims has been widely criticized as a racist fantasy designed to make Americans look and feel superior. In addition, the exaggerated emphasis on the fascination of the Vietnamese with Russian roulette attempts to tap into Cold War stereotypes about savage communists to reinforce its racist stereotypes about Orientals. The participants in the game even wear red headbands, as if the anticommunist suggestions were not clear enough. As Corrigan puts it in *A Cinema without Walls, The Deer Hunter* "captures the way the Vietnam War is often understood today only through the exaggerations, distortions, and incoherencies that impede any accurate historical representation of that war" (pp. 14–15). As such, it is not only an insult to the people of Vietnam but a sad comment on American society, which seems able, on the evidence of this film, to promote itself only through racist diatribes against others. It also probably says little for (but a lot about) the American film industry that *The Deer Hunter* was nominated for nine Academy Awards and won five, including those for best picture and best director.

The first major film entirely devoted to the postwar experiences of Vietnam veterans was Hal Ashby's *Coming Home* (1978), a critical and commercial success that was nominated for eight Academy Awards, winning three, including a best actor award to Jon Voight and best actress award to Jane Fonda, who was thus (at least in certain circles) forgiven for her political activities during the Vietnam War and invited back home to Hollywood. Although *Coming Home* lost the best picture Oscar to *The Deer Hunter*, it is a much finer film that at least attempts to establish a coherent political orientation, namely, one that is antiwar, profeminist, and suspicious of the motivations of the U.S. government.

Unfortunately, however, *Coming Home* still fails to explore the real historical background of the American involvement in Vietnam, settling for a couple of vague suggestions of admiration for the courage and determination of the Vietnamese communists (without any mention of their political ideology) and for a demonstration of the high cost of the pointless war in terms of its impact on the minds and bodies of the American soldiers who served there. Although still the definitive movie of returning from Vietnam, *Coming Home* is limited by the fact that the returning veterans it follows are in unusual situations and have little or no chance of resuming their former lives. As a result, the film says little about the difficulties suffered by the hundreds of thousands of veterans who returned home physically and psychological whole enough that they could at least attempt to rejoin American society—but often found it difficult to do so.

As the film begins, Marine Captain Bob Hyde (Bruce Dern) is being sent for a tour of duty in Vietnam, where he is anxious to go in order to fight for his country. He leaves behind his devoted and subservient wife, Sally (Jane Fonda), who struggles to cope with his absence by becoming a volunteer worker in a veterans' hospital. She is joined by her friend, Viola Munson (Penelope Mitford), whose brother, Bill (Robert Carradine), is a patient in the hospital's psychiatric ward, having suffered a breakdown as a result of his experiences in Vietnam. Among other patients, Sally meets Luke Martin (Jon Voight), a Marine sergeant paralyzed from the waist down as a result of wounds suffered in Vietnam.

Consumed by horrible memories of atrocities committed by American forces in Vietnam and by the feeling that his loss was for nothing, Luke is an angry and bitter young man who gradually gets back in touch with his humanity through his growing friendship with Sally. Sally, living on her own for the first time in her life and experiencing great personal growth, especially within the political context of the late 1960s, returns his feelings of friendship. In the meantime, Bill Munson commits suicide, driving Luke to an expression of protest against the war and its effects by chaining himself and his wheelchair to the gates of a Marine recruitment center. Sally gets Luke out of jail, and the two return to his apartment, where they become lovers. The film is, by Hollywood standards, quite daring in its depiction of their lovemaking, which is fulfilling for both of them despite his paralysis. At the same time, Luke remains haunted throughout their ongoing relationship, knowing that Sally will eventually return to her husband when he comes home.

Eventually, Bob does return home, with a minor leg wound. His psychic wounds are, however, more serious. He remains distant and emotionally unable to relate to Sally, even before he discovers her previous affair with Luke. Then, in one of the film's central commentaries on the sinister activities of the U.S. government, Bob is informed of this affair by FBI agents, who have had Luke under surveillance since his arrest at the recruitment center. There are some tense moments during which Bob, clearly unstable, seems on the verge of murdering Luke, or Sally, or both. In the end, unable to cope with civilian life, he strips off his Marine dress uniform on the beach and then swims away into the ocean. This scene is intercut with shots of Luke making an impassioned antiwar speech to a group of high school students. Luke thus finds, through his political activity, the meaning Bob no longer has in his life. Sally, meanwhile, will presumably survive as well, having learned important lessons about her validity as a human being apart from her marriage to Bob.

Stone's *Born on the Fourth of July* also explores the post-Vietnam experience. Like *Platoon, Born on the Fourth of July* was a considerable critical and commercial success. Nominated for eight Academy Awards, the film won two Oscars, including Stone's second award for best director. The film is based on the autobiography of Ron Kovic, a disabled Vietnam War veteran who eventually became an important antiwar activist—and who helped write the screenplay. In fact, *Born on the Fourth of July* is very much Kovic's personal story, to the point that it actually has very little to do with the war in Vietnam, focusing instead on the personal crisis encountered by Kovic after his return from Vietnam, paralyzed from the mid-chest down due to a bullet wound. The film does refer back to *Platoon*, however, as in the use of actors such as Tom Berenger and Willem Dafoe as supporting performers, somewhat in the same way that Stone's casting of Charlie Sheen in *Platoon* evoked images of Martin Sheen in *Apocalypse Now.*

Born on the Fourth of July begins on July 4, 1956, which happens to be Kovic's tenth birthday. It shows him and his family and friends participating in an all-American July 4 celebration in their home town of Massapequa, Long Island. This scene helps to establish the background that would eventually lead Kovic to accept the rhetoric of Americanism to the hilt, and the film's most powerful political statement is its clear suggestion, through the narration of Kovic's subsequent experiences, that this rhetoric is misleading and dishonest. Indeed, the film makes some potentially very dark comments about the dishonest (and even murderous) nature of American culture and the contribution of that culture to the debacle in Vietnam.

Kovic (played by Tom Cruise) joins the Marines at the end of his high school years, apparently genuinely convinced that he is going away to defend the American way of life against a serious communist threat. The situation in Vietnam, however, is not nearly so clear-cut, as Kovic dramatically discovers during one confusing day of combat in which he and his squad accidentally kill a number of innocent Vietnamese women and children, followed by a hasty retreat in which Kovic shoots and kills one of his own men. Only months later, Kovic receives his own paralyzing wound, as a bullet severs his spinal cord.

When the paralyzed Kovic finds himself being treated in a squalid, rat-infested veterans' hospital that is short of both doctors and equipment, he begins to suspect that the government for which he so proudly fought has sold him a bill of goods. Nevertheless, he remains a dedicated patriot and proponent of the war, disgusted by the antiwar protestors he sees on television and indeed finds all around him when he returns home to Massapequa. Eventually, betrayed by the government he served and unappreciated by the people he thought he was defending, Kovic sinks into self-pity and becomes a drunk, a descent powerfully captured in Cruise's performance as Kovic. He then winds up in a bizarre Mexican seaside resort staffed by hookers who cater to the sexual needs of crippled Vietnam veterans. There, he finally hits bottom. However, he begins to work his way back when he returns to America and pays a call on the parents of the American soldier he accidentally shot in Vietnam.

Then, without any real explanation, Kovic suddenly becomes an antiwar activist, leading a group of disabled veterans at the 1972 Republican National Conventional, where Richard Nixon is being nominated for his second term. Kovic and the other demonstrators are treated rudely, harangued by crazed Republicans and beaten by brutal police, in total disregard of the sacrifice made by these veterans in their military service. Then, there is a sudden cut to the 1976 Democratic National Convention, where Kovic, now a famous activist, is an honored invited speaker on the conventional platform. Unfortunately, the film does nothing to explain the developments that led to this turn in Kovic's fortunes, and the film closes with a conventional Hollywood happy ending (though one that potentially comments on the fickleness of the American public), with Kovic, now redeemed as an American hero, approaching the speaker's podium in his wheelchair, with the strains of "It's a Grand Old Flag" sounding in the background.

The final installment of Stone's Vietnam trilogy, *Heaven and Earth*, failed to gain the attention and acclaim of its two predecessors, perhaps because its major focus is on the war-related experiences of a Vietnamese woman, rather than an American. However, *Heaven and Earth* is in many ways the best of Stone's three Vietnam War films. If nothing else, based on the autobiographical writings of former Vietnamese villager Le Ly Hayslip, it is one of the few American films about the Vietnam War that makes a legitimate attempt to represent the war from a Vietnamese point of view. The film is particularly powerful in its contrast between the traditional values of Vietnamese peasant society and the lack of values in modern American consumer capitalism.

The film begins with Le Ly as a small child growing up in the South Vietnamese village of Ky La, where life has remained virtually unchanged for a thousand years. This idyllic existence is then suddenly interrupted in the summer of 1953, when French troops invade and destroy the village in an attempt to suppress an anticolonial rebellion. The brave and patient villagers endure this attack and gradually begin to rebuild their traditional lives. In 1963, however, this traditional way of life comes to an end once and for all as the village becomes a site of contestation between the Viet Cong and South Vietnamese government, with their American backers. The Americans and their allies attempt to impose their will and point of view on the village, but most of the villagers remain sympathetic to the Viet Cong, who better understand their way of life and who, they believe, are fighting for the liberation of this and other villages from neocolonial domination by the United States via the puppet government in Saigon. The film is relatively sympathetic to the Viet Cong and the North Vietnamese communists, making clear, among other things, the great respect and admiration with which Ho Chi Minh was viewed by the Vietnamese, North and South, as a result of his heroic leadership in the anticolonial struggle against both the French and the Japanese.

In one horrifying sequence, Le Ly (played by Hiep Thi Le), suspected of complicity with the Viet Cong (which her two brothers have joined), is taken for questioning by the South Vietnamese Army. She is then brutally tortured, while American advisors smugly look on. Eventually, Le Ly's mother (played by Joan Chen), bribes the corrupt South Vietnamese and gains Le Ly's release, but this release immediately makes Le Ly an object of suspicion to the Viet Cong, who subsequently take her for questioning of their own. One of them then rapes her, though he threatens to kill her if she tells anyone, making it clear that the rape is not approved Viet Cong practice. This experience shatters Le Ly's sense of connection with the village once and for all. At the age of eighteen, she moves with her mother to Saigon to try to make a life in the city.

Le Ly manages to gain employment as a servant in the home of a wealthy family. Seduced by the husband of the house, Le Ly experiences sexual tenderness for the first time; unfortunately, she also becomes pregnant and is therefore exiled, along with her mother to Da Nang. There, she has the baby boy, and struggles to survive, selling on the black market and digging through the garbage on the American base. Eventually, she meets Marine Sergeant Steve Butler (Tommy Lee Jones), who pays court to the much younger Le Ly, explaining to her (in a racist comment that does not bode well for their future together) that his bad first marriage has taught him that "I need a good Oriental woman." Steve and Le Ly live together essentially as a family, and she soon has a second son. Then, when South Vietnam falls, Steve takes Le Ly and the boys home with him to San Diego, where they marry and later have a third son.

Le Ly meets Steve's quintessentially American family and otherwise attempts to adjust to the new world of America, where material commodities are abundant, but where the people seem spiritually empty, with no connection to tradition. The presentation of American consumer society, seen through Le Ly's eyes, is genuinely horrifying, even when contrasted to the poverty and destruction that reign in Vietnam. Steve, meanwhile, is financially strapped by alimony and child support payments arising from his first marriage, though he envisions a coming better future when he can leave the marines and become an international arms dealer. Le Ly, having experienced the destruction that weapons can cause, is horrified by this plan, which anyway falls through after Steve, sinking into anger and despair, turns to drink and is kicked out of the marines. As Steve grows violent and abusive, Le Ly files for divorce. Distraught and unbalanced, Steve kidnaps and threatens the children, then ends up killing himself.

Meanwhile, drawing on support provided by the local Vietnamese immigrant community, Le Ly becomes a successful restaurant owner. Then, in the film's moving final sequence, Le Ly returns for a visit to Vietnam with her three children. In Saigon, her eldest, Jimmy, meets his father for the first time. They then return to Ky La to visit Le Ly's ailing mother. Bon (Vinh Dang), Le Ly's surviving brother, rejects her for marrying an American, given the destruction wrought in Vietnam by Americans. But Le Ly's mother, nearing death, accepts her daughter with open arms. We are then informed by on-screen text that Le Ly and her boys returned to San Diego, where she continued to work for her homeland by helping to build a series of health clinics there through her support for the East Meets West Foundation.

Heaven and Earth is a moving and powerful film. Its presentation of the war in Vietnam as a confrontation between Vietnamese tradition and American modernity may simplify the reality of the war by underplaying the Cold War aspects of the conflict, but it also calls attention to an aspect of the war that has generally been underemphasized in American accounts of the war. In any case, the film, released in 1993, came at an important time when it helped to counter revisionist histories that were beginning to efface the gruesome reality of the American intervention in Vietnam. As Stone put it, as quoted in Norman Kagan's *The Cinema of Oliver Stone* (Continuum, 1995), he sought in the film to "respond to, in part, the blind militarism and mindless revisionism of the Vietnam War as typified by a certain odious brand of thinking that has snaked its way into our culture over the past decade or so, in which the conflict is refought in comic-book style with a brand new ending . . . we win!"

Indeed, films such as *Rambo* sequence have ignored the historical reality of the war in Vietnam. On the other hand, several recent films have looked back on the Vietnam War from a perspective of greater historical hindsight. John Frankenheimer's made-for-HBO film *Path to War* (2002) is a detailed and effective behind-the-scenes look at the way in which the escalating war in Vietnam wrecked the presidency of Lyndon Johnson (convincingly played here by distinguished British actor Michael Gambon), derailing his original plans to build a "Great Society" from America's burgeoning wealth. These plans, which including the elimination of poverty and racial injustice, seem to be off to a good start, but the Vietnam conflict gradually draws off more and more money and begins to occupy an increasing amount of the time and energy of Johnson and his staff. Key figures on the staff are Defense Secretary Robert McNamara (Alec Baldwin) and advisor Clark Clifford (Donald Sutherland), who serve as opposed voices throughout. Initially, Clifford urges Johnson to get out of the conflict immediately, while American losses are still small. McNamara, on the other hand, is initially a hawk who believes that the war can be won quickly, gaining prestige for America in the ongoing struggle for global influence.

As the war proceeds, American casualties mount, while their communist adversaries in Vietnam remain firm in their resolve, despite the devastation being wrought in their country by American bombs and the steadily increasing number of American troops being deployed in the small southeast Asian country. Eventually, McNamara becomes convinced that the war cannot be won without a destruction of Vietnam so complete that the United States would actually lose prestige—and possibly trigger a greater war with China, or the Soviet Union, or both. Clifford, on the other hand, remains skeptical about the war in general, but becomes convinced that the United States cannot withdraw without appearing weak and providing substantial encouragement to America's enemies around the world. The American military, including General William Westmoreland (Tom Skerritt), commander of the American forces in Vietnam, and General Earle Wheeler (Frederic Forrest), Chairman of the Joint Chiefs of Staff, comes off particularly badly in the film. It is, in fact, their continual urging for escalation (in what comes off as a bloodthirsty desire to win at all costs and a blind inability to face reality) that is the strongest single force driving the Johnson presidency to ruin.

The real focus of *Path to War*, however, is on Johnson himself and on the increasingly heavy burdens that the war in Vietnam (and domestic outcries against that war) places on him and his presidency. Johnson emerges in the film as a tragic figure, genuinely devoted to his Great Society agenda but somehow unable to extricate himself from the Asian conflict that gradually replaces that agenda at the center of his presidency. By the end of his first full term in office, he is a beaten man, humbled by his failure to achieve his original goals, while at the same time haunted by the sense that he will never be loved by the American people in the way that his predecessor, John Kennedy, had been—or the way Kennedy's brother Robert (whom Johnson regards as his likely successor) promises to be.

Johnson, however, is not a man without flaws, and there are hints that his Great Society program is driven at least partly by his own egotistical need to build a legacy that will make history remember him as a great president, more than just a placeholder between the two Kennedys. Meanwhile, Johnson's personal ego serves as a sort of stand-in for American hubris in general, and the film makes it clear that the incredible carnage of Vietnam (with nearly 60,000 Americans and more than 2 million Vietnamese killed, not to mention the large number of people who were physically or emotionally maimed by the war) was largely the result of a national arrogance that simply refused to believe that a mighty power like the United States could not easily dispatch a foe so seemingly inferior as North Vietnam and the Viet Cong. That this arrogance remained stubbornly in place, continuing to wreak death and destruction in Vietnam long after it was clear that the Americans could not win, should serve as a sobering lesson, though it is one that the U.S. government, in the era of the destructive occupation of Iraq and the unfocused global war against terror, does not seem to have learned.

Something of the same message is conveyed from a very different point of view in Terry George's made-for-HBO film *A Bright Shining Lie* (1998). This film relates the career in Vietnam of American soldier and, later, civilian advisor, John Paul Vann (Bill Paxton), based on Neil Sheehan's book of the same title. Vann is presented as well-meaning and idealistic, if a bit too caught up in his own perspectives, thus making him a sort of allegorical representative of the whole American effort in Vietnam.

A Bright Shining Lie begins with what seems to be a self-conscious echo of the haunting opening of *Apocalypse Now*: scenes of American planes bombing jungles and rice paddies in Vietnam, producing spectacular fireballs and fireworks-like explosions that rock the otherwise placid landscape, while Jefferson Airplane's "Somebody to Love" plays in the background. Indeed, the film makes many of the same points about the absurdity of the war in Vietnam as does *Apocalypse Now*. However, it is mostly a straightforward exposition of Vann's career that does not seek to recreate the surreal atmospheric effects of the earlier film.

Actually, the film begins with Vann's burial, after which one of his old friends, a journalist (played by Donal Logue), tells us that the United States went to Vietnam believing in freedom and democracy, but "lost our moral compass." The story then begins in flashback when Vann originally travels to Vietnam in 1962 as a military advisor to the South Vietnamese army, quickly discovering that the situation in Vietnam is far different from what he had been led to believe. After he observes a Buddhist monk immolating himself in a public square in Saigon, Vann sums up the situation perfectly: "We have no idea what is going on around here."

When Vann returns to the states after his tour of duty, he devotes himself to trying to convince the Pentagon that they have fundamentally misjudged the situation in Vietnam and that they need to concentrate on winning the loyalty of the South Vietnamese people instead of supporting the South

Vietnamese army. The Pentagon old guard quickly closes ranks, turning a deaf ear to Vann's warnings, which causes him to retire from the military. In 1965, however, he is hired to return to Vietnam as part of a civilian aid program designed to win over the Vietnamese people, just as he had earlier advised. Unfortunately, he has little success. For one thing, he discovers that the South Vietnamese army is so vicious and corrupt in its dealings with civilians that they are driving the people of Vietnam into the communist camp. For another, it is clear that General William Westmoreland (Kurtwood Smith), the commander of the U.S. forces in Vietnam, is a bumbling incompetent who is no match for North Vietnamese commander General Giap, portrayed in the film as an unmatched military genius.

Eventually, in the last years of the Nixon administration, an effort to decrease the level of American forces in Vietnam leads to an increased emphasis on building the strength of the South Vietnamese military. At this point, Vann's star is on the ascendant. He is essentially placed in command of a large portion of the South Vietnamese army, quickly becoming obsessed with trying to outmaneuver Giap. He is, of course, unable to do so, partly because of the corruption and incompetence of the South Vietnamese army and government. Meanwhile, Vann himself is killed in a helicopter crash in bad weather on June 9, 1972, which brings us back to the beginning of the film.

One of the most interesting recent films related to the war in Vietnam is Joel Schumacher's *Tigerland* (2000), which focuses on a group of young American soldiers who are undergoing advanced infantry training at Fort Polk, Louisiana, prior to shipping out for Vietnam. The final week of their training occurs in the Tigerland of the title, a Louisiana swamp meant to mimic conditions in Vietnam, and these conditions exacerbate what is already a brutal training regime. This regime is made even worse because it seems pointless. Set in late 1971, the film takes place at a time when many believe the war has already been lost and when the war effort has in any case lost popular support among Americans. Indeed, *Tigerland* is bitterly cynical about the entire American military machine, which is depicted as a vast, soulless enterprise that strips all who participate in it of their humanity. The training undergone by the soldiers in the film thus becomes an emblem of this larger problem. Meanwhile, the film employs a gritty documentary style, reminiscent of cinema verité that effectively enhances its portrayal of the grinding, dehumanizing nature of this training.

As such, the film marked a major departure for director Schumacher, whose recent films had been slick, Hollywood blockbusters such as *Batman Forever* (1995) and *Batman & Robin* (1997). The film also made an American film star of Irish actor Colin Farrell, who plays Bozz, a talented young soldier whose rebelliousness and intense individualism stand in opposition to the military's insistence on mindless conformism. Bozz also tries to help others avoid military routine, and even serves as a sort of barracks lawyer, helping other soldiers get discharges on technicalities. He even goes so far as to shoot one of the other soldiers, Private Paxton (Matthew Davis), so that his wound will keep him out of the war (but leave no permanent damage). Bozz himself, however, goes off to Vietnam as the war ends, and a final voiceover from Paxton informs us that Bozz's subsequent fate is unknown.

Tigerland is bitterly cynical about the American military establishment and about the war effort in Vietnam, at least by 1971, though *A Bright Shining Lie* suggests that the American involvement in Vietnam began as an earnest effort to help the Vietnamese people, then went badly wrong. It also suggests that the Americans might have won the war but for the mismanagement of Westmoreland and his handlers in the Pentagon. A closer look, however, shows that the American intervention in Vietnam was contaminated from its very beginnings in the sponsorship of the Viet Minh in World War II. In addition, an astute observer might have realized that the United States could not win in Vietnam as early as the mid-1950s, when the French colonial occupiers of Vietnam were driven from the country.

That judgment, in fact, is the crucial message of Graham Greene's 1955 novel, *The Quiet American*, which unequivocally condemns the early U.S. intervention in Vietnam as just another (inevitably doomed) stage in the colonial domination of Vietnam by Western powers. That novel, among others, caused Greene to be placed under surveillance by American intelligence operatives for decades on suspicion that he was a communist sympathizer. In 1958, however, *The Quiet American* was made into a Hollywood film of the same title (directed by Joseph Mankiewicz); this film, in typically bizarre Cold War fashion, turns the message of the book on its head and makes the Americans the good guys, saving Vietnam from evil communists. Greene himself excoriated the film as a piece of Cold War propaganda.

Phillip Noyce's recent (2002) film adaptation of the novel returns much more to Greene's original vision. Noyce's film may not make the impossibility of an American victory quite as clear as does the novel. It does, however, make it clear that the Americans were involved in clandestine operations in Vietnam as early as 1952 and that they were perfectly willing to commit dreadful atrocities in order to prevent a popularly supported communist government from coming to power in the wake of Vietnam's impending independence from French colonial rule.

Actually, much of Noyce's version of *The Quiet American* focuses on a romantic triangle that involves aging British journalist Thomas Fowler (Michael Caine); his beautiful live-in Vietnamese lover, Phuong (Do Thi Hai Yen); and the newly arrived quiet young American, Alden Pyle (Brendan Fraser). Pyle has supposedly come to Vietnam as part of a medical aid mission, though it gradually becomes clear that he is an agent of the CIA, assigned to work secretly in support of the thuggish Vietnamese general The (Quang Hai), who has raised a private army and whom the Americans see as a potential "Third Force" that would provide an alternative to either communism or French colonial rule. His work is complicated, however, by the fact that he instantly falls in love after meeting Phuong, who eventually shifts her attentions from Fowler to Pyle after it becomes clear that Fowler's Catholic wife back in England will not grant him a divorce so that he can marry Phuong and bring her back home with him.

Even the personal drama of this love triangle has political implications. Among other things, it invites allegorical readings in which Phuong becomes an emblem of the colonial world, exploited by Western powers; Fowler a representative of the crumbling British Empire, losing its grip on the colonies; and Pyle an image of the younger and stronger United States, stepping in to fill the global power vacuum caused by the fading of British imperial might. In either case, Phuong is a sort of colonized victim forced to endure the attentions of these men because conditions in Vietnam leave her no other way to survive except by turning to all-out prostitution. Each man, of course, sees himself as her savior, oblivious to the fact that she would probably prefer to live independently of either of them, if only she could.

Meanwhile, if it seems unscrupulous of Pyle, who is supposedly Fowler's friend, to take Phuong away, the American is involved in a much more explicitly political treachery as well. This treachery is hinted at early on when Fowler travels to the distant Vietnamese village of Phat Diem to cover the fighting there, and then finds that Pyle inexplicably shows up there as well. Meanwhile, Pyle's arrival coincides with a gruesome massacre of the local villagers that is quickly attributed to the communists, though it eventually appears that the massacre was perpetrated by The's forces precisely so that it could be blamed on the communists for propaganda purposes.

Later, in the film's crucial scene, Pyle conspires with The to set off a series of powerful bombs in a busy public square in Saigon, causing heavy civilian casualties. The CIA propaganda machine again shifts into high gear, blaming this terrorist act on the communist insurgents and using the resultant publicity to convince Congress to increase funding for American anticommunist activities in Vietnam. This historically accurate development makes it clear that the U.S. involvement in Vietnam was morally tainted from the very beginning. This reminder of the long legacy of American terrorism abroad is a matter of historical fact. However, the film, originally scheduled to be released in the fall of 2001, was shelved for more than a year after the 9/11 bombings in New York and Washington for fear that it would seem to be presenting a justification for those bombings, and then released only after the enthusiastic critical response it received from a test screening at the 2002 Toronto Film Festival.

In response to the bombing, the Vietnamese communists assassinate Pyle, whom they are able to separate from his ever-present bodyguards with the help of Fowler; horrified when he learns that Pyle was the principal force behind the bombing, Fowler presumably makes the difficult decision to help with the assassination out of a sense of righteousness, though we are left to wonder how much of his act is motivated by a desire to win back Phuong. This swift retribution vaguely suggests the ability of the Vietnamese to resist American intervention in their country, but it does nothing to prevent the Americans from increasing their involvement there. In the end, Fowler stays in Vietnam to be with Phuong rather than returning to England, as he had been scheduled to do. The film then ends with shots of a series of Fowler's newspaper articles reporting events from the French withdrawal from Vietnam in 1954, to the subsequent partition of the country (to prevent the communist leader Ho Chi Minh from taking power in a national election), to Ho's declaration of a military effort to reunite the country, to the gradual escalation in U.S. involvement in the 1960s to prevent this reunification. The message here is quite clear, the clandestine American efforts that began during the French colonial period set in motion a series of events that built into a greater and greater tragedy for the Vietnamese people—and eventually for the Americans as well. At the same time, the film's indication that there were no effective indigenous alternatives to Ho and the communists suggests the pointlessness of this tragedy that could have been prevented simply by allowing free national elections upon the French withdrawal, even if these elections would inevitably have swept Ho into power.

The Quiet American suggests that a failure to understand the true nature of the Vietnamese situation back in the 1950s led to disaster for both the Americans and the Vietnamese. A film such as Randall Wallace's *We Were Soldiers* (also released in 2002) illustrates the extent to which the lessons of Vietnam have not been learned. This film seems to stipulate that the American effort in Vietnam was pointless and led to a vast number of senseless deaths. It also, through its focus on horrifying graphic scenes of combat, reminds us (as so many war films have done) that war is hell. Yet, through it all, this film manages to celebrate the nobility of the combatants in Vietnam—especially on the American side, on which the film focuses almost entirely, leaving the Vietnamese as faceless enemies. However, as opposed to a film such as *The Green Berets*, in which America's Vietnamese foes are depicted as ruthless, crazed savages, the opposing troops in this film are depicted as honorable warriors. Indeed, in an opening gesture toward evenhandedness, the film is dedicated to both the American soldiers and the opposing Vietnamese soldiers who died in the actual

November 1965 battle depicted in the film—the first major battle between American and Vietnamese forces in the war.

In its graphic depiction of ultra-violent battle scenes, *We Were Soldiers* shows the clear influence of recent World War II films such as Steven Spielberg's *Saving Private Ryan* (1998) and Terrence Malick's *The Thin Red Line* (1998), though it also looks directly back to earlier Vietnam War films such as *Hamburger Hill.* Its battle scenes are indeed effective and horrifying. However, its attempt to portray the courage and nobility of the combatants, led by American colonel Hal Moore (Mel Gibson), comes dangerously close to treating warfare as a sort of chivalrous sporting event. Meanwhile, the camaraderie that arises among the soldiers makes them brothers-in-arms (despite race, class, religion, or other differences) who experience, in the battle, a kind of lovely, utopian sense of community that they could never have known in any other way. As a result, the American presence in Vietnam is presented as having a certain nobility, even though the film makes clear that the ultimate American victory (thanks to the extensive support they receive from helicopters and fighter planes) in this first battle will achieve nothing except perhaps prolong the war and extend the number of casualties that will be suffered on both sides before the final victory of the Vietnamese communist forces. Indeed, after the battle ends, the American forces leave and the area is immediately reoccupied by the Vietnamese communists, whose leader assures them that their victory is inevitable. The battle depicted in the film thus functions as a sort of allegory of the entire war: the Americans win the battle (though with great difficulty) thanks to their superior firepower, but they achieve nothing and lose the war.

We Were Soldiers drops the anticommunist rhetoric of *The Green Berets,* but in doing so it never provides any explanation of what the American forces are doing in Vietnam in the first place. In addition, it does not acknowledge that this presence might be controversial. The American GIs depicted in the film have no doubts about the rectitude of their mission or that they are performing a noble, divinely ordained task by being there. The first soldier who is shown dying on the battlefield sums up the sentimentality with which the film ultimately treats warfare, despite the gruesome horrors that are shown in the combat scenes. As he drifts into death, his last words express his pride that "I can die for my country." Meanwhile, these soldiers are all devoted family men who leave loyal wives behind, and the wives who one by one receive notices of the deaths of their husbands never question that their husbands might be dying for a bad cause.

We Were Soldiers ends with a cut to the Vietnam War memorial, noting that the names of the men killed in the battle depicted in the film are inscribed on the memorial, along with more than 58,000 others. Yet there is no discussion of the possibility that the deaths of these young men might be all the more tragic (and obscene) because of the nature of the cause for which they died. No doubt much of the tone of the film comes about because it is based on a book coauthored by the real Hal Moore and is therefore related very much from his perspective. More generally, the film can be taken as part of a general wave of American revisionism in the early twenty-first century in which the Vietnam War has suddenly become a noble effort rather than a misguided and murderous attempt to extend the long Western colonial domination of Vietnam, with the Americans merely following in the footsteps of the French who had been there before them. In short, the film participates in a conscious attempt at historical amnesia that threatens to negate the lessons that otherwise should have been learned from the Vietnam experience—lessons that might have helped to prevent some of the more recent American military misadventures around the world, especially the quagmire resulting from the invasion of Iraq in 2003. These particular misadventures are still underway as of this writing, and American film is only beginning to reflect some of the more recent American military encounters around the world. Such films are discussed in the next chapter.

CHAPTER 8

United States vs. the World: American Film and Warfare after the Cold War

T he United States emerged from the Vietnam conflict with a tremendous loss of international prestige: not only had the American military proved far less invincible than many had previously thought, but the vast American Cold War propaganda effort to present the United States as an anti-imperialist defender of the weak had been entirely undermined. Internally, America's sense of its own national identity as the righteous destroyer of savage and vicious foes was shaken as well, both because the war had been lost and because the righteousness of the American presence there was seriously in question. Indeed, as Thomas Engelhardt demonstrates in his book *The End of Victory Culture: Cold War America and the Disillusioning of a Generation* (Basic Books, 1995), Vietnam was the culmination of a sequence of Asian misadventures—including the morally questionable atomic bombing of Japan, the loss of China to a communist revolution, and the inconclusive Korean War—that effectively destroyed the national narrative of America as the defeater of savage foes.

By the time Vietnam had capped off this sequence, Americans were no longer confident of victory in any and all conflicts; nor were they confident that the United States was by definition on the side of right. It is little wonder, then, that the United States avoided engagement in any significant military actions for nearly a decade after the 1974 withdrawal/retreat from Vietnam. This situation would come to an end with the interventionist truculence of the Reagan administration, though even then the American military trod very carefully, openly engaging only in minor conflicts they were sure to win, while the government preferred clandestine actions such as the extensive (and illegal) effort to undermine the legitimately elected

Sandinista regime in Nicaragua by secretly supporting the Contra rebels with arms and other forms of under-the-table military aid.

Late in the 1980s, American cinema finally began genuinely to come to grips with the Vietnam experience with the release, in rapid sequence, of such films as *Platoon* (1986), *Full Metal Jacket* (1987), and *Casualties of War* (1989). By this time, Hollywood apparently felt that sufficient time had passed to enable the Vietnam War to be dealt in a manner that could be effective without causing too much controversy. In the midst of these Vietnam films came Clint Eastwood's almost bizarre *Heartbreak Ridge* (1986), one of the first films about the post-Vietnam American military. It features Eastwood himself as laconic tough-guy Marine Sergeant Tom Highway, a seasoned combat veteran who is gung ho for the basic mission of the Marines, but not so enthusiastic about the bureaucracy and red-tape that seem increasingly to be a part of military life in the post-Vietnam era. Highway, in fact, has had a troubled career since Vietnam, though he served two successful tours of duty there. He served even more honorably in Korea, where he won a Congressional Medal of Honor in a battle to take a hill that the Marines themselves dubbed "Heartbreak Ridge," giving the film its title.

Not just Highway, but the entire American military seems haunted in this film by the legacies of Korea and Vietnam that leave them, as is pointed out in the film, with a 0–1–1 record in recent conflicts. Much of the film has to do with Highway's attempts to adjust to the fact that he is nearing mandatory retirement from the military and will soon have to find some other meaning in his life. In the meantime, he is given one last unit of recruits to train—a group of misfits that has been dismissed as hopeless by his Annapolis-educated commanding officer, Major Malcolm Powers (Everett McGill), a former college football star with no combat experience. Highway, predictably, succeeds in making his unit into an efficient military force, much to the aggravation of Powers, who disapproves of Highway's unconventional methods. In the meantime, Highway gets one last opportunity actually to win a war when word suddenly comes that Powers' battalion is being shipped to the Caribbean island of Grenada to participate in a U.S. invasion there to rescue some American civilians.

Doing for Grenada what *The Green Berets* did for Vietnam, *Heartbreak Ridge* essentially celebrates the American invasion; it certainly does nothing to question the politics or legality of that act. In this invasion (the first significant American military action since Vietnam), Highway and his men perform heroically as they become involved in significant combat with unidentified enemy soldiers, though there are numerous hints that these soldiers are Cuban. In any case, the enemy soldiers are the typical nameless, faceless foes of American war films, and the film is absolutely uninterested in exploring the actual reasons behind the American invasion or in explaining why Cuban soldiers might be in Grenada in the first place. And with good reason. The illegal American intervention in Grenada that caused considerable international controversy, was one of the most questionable military actions in U.S. history at the time, though it would eventually be eclipsed by the 2003 invasion and occupation of Iraq. Any interrogation of the Grenada invasion would completely undermine the film's effort to present the combat there as a victory that will allow Highway to retire with a record of 1–1–1 in wars, as if they were some sort of sporting event.

In fact, there were a number of Cuban advisors in Grenada at the time of the U.S. invasion, though most of them were not soldiers but civilian construction workers involved in building a new airport. In any case, the Cubans were there at the request of the legally constituted Grenadan government and were certainly not occupying the island, as *Heartbreak Ridge* seems to suggest. The official reason for the U.S. invasion was indeed to rescue Americans (mostly college students at St. George's University) who were on the island, where political violence had recently erupted, though order had largely been restored before the invasion occurred. The real reason for the invasion (other than providing a diversion from other problems being experienced by the Reagan administration) was to depose the left-leaning government there. This government had instituted major social reforms and instituted important development programs, making Grenada a close ally of the Castro-led socialist government in Cuba, which supplied substantial foreign aid to the new government in Grenada. However, factional disputes within this government led to violence in 1983, culminating in the U.S. invasion.

American troops, having deposed the legal government of Grenada, occupied Grenada until the end of 1984, when U.S.-sponsored elections returned the aging Herbert Blaize, a relic from the 1960s, to power as prime minister. U.S. troops finally left the island in the summer of 1985. Blaize was displaced in the subsequent 1990 elections, but his successors have kept Grenada within the orbit of U.S. aid and influence. In the meantime, numerous members of the original Grenadan government were arrested by the U.S. military and sentenced to death, though these sentences were commuted to life imprisonment after widespread international protests. At this writing, they remain incarcerated as political prisoners, though an investigation by Amnesty International has found their arrest and imprisonment to be a miscarriage of justice and a violation of international law.

Heartbreak Ridge shows no interest in portraying the Grenadan invasion as anything other than an opportunity for American soldiers to demonstrate their prowess and heroism in battle against evil Cubans, though in fact there were 7,000 American soldiers sent to the island, as opposed to forty-three Cuban soldiers and 636 Cuban construction workers who were there, so defeating them was hardly an impressive triumph. (A force of 1200 Grenadan soldiers also resisted the American invasion, though with little success.) Unfortunately, the film's lack of interest in the political background of the war would become fairly typical of American films dealing with post-Vietnam American military actions, which suggests not so much gung ho patriotism as a cynical assumption that the motivations for such actions are best not looked into.

The Grenada invasion was simply the most public of a number of American military interventions in Latin America during the Reagan administration. Several films dealing with U.S. efforts at political manipulation had been made even before *Heartbreak Ridge*; together, these films represent some of the last to openly and strongly critique American interventionism. Perhaps the best known of these films is *Salvador* (1986), the first in a string of remarkable political films directed by Oliver Stone, including his trilogy of Vietnam War films and extending through such classic political films as *JFK* (1991) and *Nixon* (1995). *Salvador* is based on the firsthand experiences of journalist Richard Boyle, who cowrote the screenplay with director Stone. It attempts to capture the atmosphere of terror and repression that reigned in El Salvador in 1980 and 1981, as right-wing military officers terrorized the people of the country with active support from the United States. The film begins in Los Angeles, where Boyle (played by James Woods) is down on his luck, looking for a chance to make a comeback as a journalist. The unrest in El Salvador seems to offer an opportunity, especially as Boyle already has extensive connections in the country. He thus decides to drive south to El Salvador in his beat-up convertible, hoping to get freelance work covering events there. He is accompanied (reluctantly) by his friend, Dr. Rock (James Belushi), an over-the-hill disc jockey.

The two Americans arrive in El Salvador amid a nightmare landscape of terror, violence, and confusion. Immediately arrested by the local authorities on their arrival, they are released because of Boyle's acquaintance with army colonel Figueroa (Jorge Luke), who hopes the journalist Boyle will make him famous. Boyle also renews his relationship with his former girlfriend, Maria (Elpidia Carrillo), as he and Dr. Rock try to get their bearings in the new country, where it is initially difficult to tell the good guys from the bad guys. At first, Boyle does not care which is which. He just wants a job and is willing to work with whichever side will give him a scoop. Finally, he begins to lean to the left when he manages to negotiate a deal to visit the leftist rebels hiding in the hills.

In the meantime, the murderous activities of the right-wing government, with official support from the United States, gradually increase Boyle's sympathy with the rebels. Indeed, one of the film's central stories is the gradual awakening of Boyle's consciousness as a result of his experiences in

Central America. In the midst of all this, Ronald Reagan is elected president of the United States, with concomitant promises of increased American support for the right-wing elements in El Salvador. Convinced that they can now act with impunity, these elements, under the leadership of the sinister Major Max (Tony Plana), step up their campaign of terror, and the country erupts in all-out civil war.

Boyle and another journalist, John Cassady (John Savage), cover the fighting, in which Cassady is killed. Boyle decides to flee the country with Maria and her children, at the same time taking the film shot by Cassady and himself back to America so that people there can get a better picture of what is really going on (and what the American government is supporting) in El Salvador. They are stopped at the border, and Boyle is nearly killed, though he is saved at the last moment through the intervention of the departing U.S. ambassador, Thomas Kelly (Michael Murphy), with hints that the incoming ambassador, appointed by Reagan, would not have made such a move. Soon afterward, Boyle and his new family reach California, land of freedom, but also of capitalism. Here, he tells Maria, "you can be what you want. Do what you want. As long as you have the money." The film then ends with an ominous commentary on American freedom as Maria and her children are dragged off a bus by immigration agents to be deported back to El Salvador. Boyle, who protests the move, is arrested, never to see Maria again.

This ending is powerful, and the film makes clear the extent to which right-wing terror in El Salvador was promoted by the policies of the United States, especially under the Reagan administration. At the same time, a central motif in its presentation of conditions in El Salvador is confusion, and the film sometimes seems to blur the rather stark political differences between the two sides. The film's greatest weakness, however, is its focus on Boyle and other Americans, which diminishes the power of the film in portraying the tragic suffering of the people of El Salvador.

Roger Spottiswoode's *Under Fire* (1983) focuses on the revolutionary victory of the Sandinista National Liberation Front in Nicaragua, a country whose political life had been dominated by the Somoza dictatorship for more than forty years. Meanwhile, the very name of the Sandinistas (adopted in 1963) points to the fact that American intervention in the internal affairs of Nicaragua had been a fact of life for most of the twentieth century. The name refers to Augusto César Sandino, who had led a nation-alist peasant rebellion in the 1920 and 1930s against a U.S. military occupa-tion of Nicaragua that had begun in 1912. U.S. forces were finally withdrawn in 1933, but Sandino was assassinated a year later by the U.S.-backed Nicaraguan National Guard in 1934.

Under Fire supplies relatively little of this historical background, while focusing on a group of American journalists who cover the last days of the

Somoza dictatorship in Nicaragua in 1979. The central character is world-renowned photojournalist Russell Price (Nick Nolte), who is first shown covering a civil war in the African country of Chad. He then moves on to Nicaragua, where the rebellion against Somoza is thus shown to be part of a larger global pattern of insurrections against repressive Third World governments, with the United States routinely intervening on the side of the governments in return for their pledge to oppose communism. Also moving from Chad to Nicaragua are Claire (Joanna Cassidy), a radio reporter, and Alex Grazier (Gene Hackman), a television reporter. Alex and Claire have been lovers for some time, but break up on the eve of their departure for Nicaragua. Alex soon departs for New York to become a network news anchor, while Claire becomes romantically involved with Price, a longtime friend.

Nicaragua, meanwhile, is in the midst of an all-out revolution, and the greatest weakness of the film is its tendency to focus more on the private problems of its American characters than on the revolution. Nevertheless, the film makes it clear that Somoza (René Enriquez) is a dictator and a murderer and that he maintains his power largely through U.S. support. But this support seems to be flagging in the face of the growing likelihood that the revolution is now unstoppable. At a crucial moment, however, the important rebel leader, Rafael, is killed in battle, a fact that might extend the conflict considerably, by both discouraging the rebels and encouraging the Americans to step up support for Somoza. The rebels thus try to convince Price, whose observations in Nicaragua have led him to sympathize with their cause, to fake a photograph that supposedly proves that Rafael is still alive. Price, whose motto is, "I don't take sides. I take pictures," hesitates but finally agrees.

The photograph causes such a sensation that Alex returns to Nicaragua, hoping Price can get him an interview with Rafael. When he learns of the faked photograph, he is furious but agrees to continue the deception. Soon afterward, Alex is killed in cold blood by Somoza's soldiers, an act Price captures on film. The photographs of the murder trigger a wave of anti-Somoza outrage in the United States, causing one of the Nicaraguans to complain that the Americans have been oblivious to the deaths of 50,000 Nicaraguans in the fighting but are now up in arms over the death of a single American. "Maybe we should have killed an American journalist fifty years ago," she complains.

In any case, the film ends as the Sandinistas sweep into power, an event that is greeted with considerable celebration by the Nicaraguan people. Despite its lack of historical details, the film makes it clear that the Sandinista victory in 1979 was the culmination of a long and heroic struggle by the Nicaraguan people to resist the forces of oppression in their country, forces that were consistently propped up by support from the United States.

In 1936, Anastasio Somoza seized power in the country. He ruled until his assassination in 1956, despite considerable resistance to his regime in Nicaragua. He was succeeded by first one son, then another, the Somoza of the film. The brutal Somoza regime, because of its opposition to communism, had long received support from the United States. When it fell in 1979, it was largely because President Jimmy Carter withdrew U.S. support for the regime due to its oppressive practices. Unfortunately, the Reagan-Bush administration resumed the U.S. intervention in Nicaragua after the Sandinista victory, sabotaging the nation's economy through a trade embargo, the illegal mining of the nation's principal harbors, and clandestine support for the right-wing Contra armies that repeatedly invaded Nicaragua from neighboring Honduras.

Haskell Wexler's *Latino* (1985) is a film that deals directly with the U.S.-Contra assault on Nicaragua and thus explores American military intervention in Central America thoroughly. Set in the 1980s, during the period of Sandinista rule in Nicaragua, *Latino* focuses on the illegal clandestine support provided by the Reagan administration to the right-wing Contra guerrillas who repeatedly invaded Nicaragua from Honduras during that decade. The central figure is Green Beret Lieutenant Eddie Guerrero (Robert Beltran), who is sent with a detachment of American forces to provide training and support to the Contras. Guerrero, a Vietnam vet, is devoted to performing his duty, but, in Central America, he develops the gradual suspicion that, in this case, he may be fighting on the wrong side. For one thing, the Contras with whom he works seem to be engaged in a campaign of murder, rape, terror, and torture against innocent civilians in Nicaragua. For another, Guerrero is uncomfortable with the fact that the activities in which he is engaged are being kept a secret from the American people.

The film begins with scenes of celebration in Nicaragua in 1979 as the Sandinista rebels, after years of struggle in which they have finally liberated the nation from the iron grip of the Somoza family, which had (with substantial U.S. support) dominated Nicaragua for more than forty years. Unfortunately, the joy of liberation is short-lived, and the film immediately proceeds to the subsequent attacks on Nicaragua by the Honduran-based Contra rebels. The focus, however, is on the clandestine support provided the Contras by Guerrero and his fellow soldiers—in direct violation of both U.S. and international law.

In Honduras, Guerrero becomes romantically involved with Marlena (Annette Cardona), a Nicaraguan agronomist working in Honduras. Marlena already sympathizes with her fellow Nicaraguans in the fight against the Contras, and these sympathies expand when her father is killed by the Contras in one of their raids. She helps Guerrero to see that the Sandinistas are attempting to build a genuinely democratic society in

Nicaragua but then decides to move back to Nicaragua with her small son, leaving Guerrero behind in Honduras.

The plot of the film culminates in a major Contra assault on the town of El Porvenir, where Marlena is now living and working with the local farmers. Guerrero is among the Americans who secretly participate in the raid, under orders not to carry with them their dog tags or other documents that would identify them as Americans, in the event they are killed or captured. The town and its surrounding fields go up in flames as a result of the attack, but the townspeople manage to defend themselves and beat back the attackers. Guerrero, disgusted with the whole situation, removes his uniform and surrenders, naked, to the Nicaraguans; but he carries with him the dog tags that will provide evidence of the participation of the U.S. military in the raid. Presumably, this evidence (and this film) will help inform the American people of the activities of their government in Nicaragua. Unfortunately, these activities were actually stepped up in 1985, when the Reagan administration, in violation of U.S. and international law, continued its secret support for the Sandinistas, while also declaring a trade embargo against Nicaragua. This intervention, combined with the illegal mining of Nicaragua's harbors in 1984, wrecked the Nicaraguan economy and thus played a major role in the eventual defeat of the Sandinistas in a popular election in 1990, after which many of their important reforms in education, health care, and land redistribution were immediately curtailed. Of course, the effectiveness of the film in preventing this eventuality was limited by the fact that, due to its politics, it received only limited distribution in the U.S.

The most recent American political film about the political situation in Central America, John Sayles's *Men with Guns* (1998), does not deal extensively with American intervention, though it does deal with certain baleful conditions that were the result of this intervention. It is also a particularly fine film that deserves to be singled out among American political films about Central America. Set in an unnamed Central American country (though partly based on Francisco Goldman's 1992 novel, *The Long Night of White Chickens*, which is set in Guatemala), *Men with Guns* explores the destructive impact of modernity on the lives of Central American Indians. Most specifically, it deals with the violence inflicted upon the Indians by the country's U.S.-backed military and, to a lesser extent, by guerrillas who are fighting against that military. However, the film also explores larger issues, noting the army's claim that its violence is necessary to suppress the guerrillas but suggesting that the real reason for the army violence is to drive the Indians off their traditional land so that, in order to live, they will be forced to hire themselves out as cheap labor for large coffee plantations or other capitalist enterprises. Meanwhile, the Indians who remain independent of such employment are generally forced to devote themselves to the production of specialized crops for consumption by North Americans and wealthy citizens of their own country, thus rendering themselves unable to produce enough food for their own sustenance.

The plot of the film revolves around a vacation trip by the aging Dr. Humberto Fuentes (Federico Luppi), who decides to venture out of the insulation provided by the modern city in which he lives in order to drive into the mountainous interior of the country to visit some of his former students, who went to work among the Indians two years earlier but have not been heard from since. On the trip, Fuentes experiences one revelation after another, gradually coming to realize that he has lived his life in a cocoon of privilege that has blinded him to the harsh realities of life for the poorer people of his country. He also discovers that all his former students have apparently been killed, mostly by the army, though one may have been killed by the guerrillas.

Early in his trip, Fuentes acquires a guide, young Conejo (Dan Rivera Gonzalez), a boy who has been orphaned by the killings of his parents by soldiers. The boy helps Fuentes find his way through the alien landscape of the mountains and also serves as his interpreter, as most of the Indians they meet do not speak Spanish. Fuentes gradually acquires a collection of other passengers, including Domingo (Damian Delgado) a soldier who has deserted and become a thief; Padre Portillo (Damian Alcazar), a priest whose cowardice has apparently caused many in his Indian congregation to be killed by soldiers; and Graciela (Tania Cruz), a young woman who has become mute after the trauma of being raped by soldiers. Together, they travel into the remote mountains of the country, having several frightening encounters with menacing soldiers on the way. At a roadblock, Portillo is arrested and taken away. The others continue, eventually seeking a village, Cerca de Cielo, which is rumored to be a sort of paradise and where Fuentes still hopes to find one of his former students.

As the journey gradually shifts to a search for Cerca de Cielo, it takes on increasingly allegorical resonances, reminiscent not only of the Spanish conquistadors' search for El Dorado but of a number of literary precedents. *The Pilgrim's Progress* (in which the protagonist flees the City of Destruction, then picks up various companions on his way to seek the Celestial City) seems an especially important predecessor. The travelers, minus Portillo, continue their search for Cerca de Cielo, going on foot when it becomes impossible to proceed further in Fuentes's Jeep. Climbing up the densely forested mountain, which they think is far from any contact with civilization, they come upon two American tourists (Mandy Patinkin and Kathyrn Grody) examining some ancient Indian ruins. These tourists mean well, and actually seem to know more about the history and culture of the Indians than does Fuentes, but, at the same time, their treatment of Central

America as a vacation spot is emblematic of the tendency of the United States to see Latin America as its own domain. As director Sayles put it in an interview about the film, they symbolize the American attitude that "Anything that goes on in this hemisphere, we want to control."

High on a mountain, the travelers encounter a band of guerrillas, who treat them with respect and camp with them for the night. But the guerrillas, like the army, have never been able to find Cerca de Cielo. Finally, near the peak of the mountain, the travelers find a small hidden village of impoverished Indians, who eke out a meager existence under the cover of the forest. These Indians, almost totally free from contact with the modern world, are able to continue to pursue their traditional way of life, but at a high cost. For one thing, they are unable to grow crops because clearing land would make it possible for the army to find them. For another, they are not totally free of intrusions from the modern world. When the travelers arrive, a woman of the village has been seriously hurt after stepping on a mine dropped into the area by an army helicopter.

Soon after the travelers arrive, Fuentes sits down at the base of a tree and quietly drifts off into death. Domingo, who had been a medic in the army, is convinced by Graciela, despite his initial reluctance to get involved, to take up Fuentes's bag and treat the woman who was injured by the mine. Graciela then walks into a clearing at the peak of the mountain and observes the astonishing natural beauty of the area. This is indeed Cerca de Cielo, and it is indeed a different world. But it is far from a paradise, and modernity—not to mention the U.S.-backed army—still lurks very near. Actually, *Men with Guns* fails to indicate this U.S. backing, which may be a shortcoming of the film as a political commentary. On the other hand, this failure can be seen as part of the film's overall focus on Latin American, rather than North American characters, a welcome and refreshing departure from more mainstream Hollywood films about Latin America that seem to feel that attracting a large audience in the United States requires a focus on North American characters.

Of course, the various attempts of the Reagan administration to intervene in Latin American politics are all part of a larger arc of anticommunist interventions around the world. The invasion of Guatemala, the clandestine support for the Nicaraguan Contras, and the support given to various right-wing Latin American dictatorships through the 1980s were thus clearly a part of the Cold War, even if the notion that all of the Western hemisphere somehow falls within the sphere of U.S. power goes back all the way to the Monroe Doctrine of the early nineteenth century. With the collapse of the Soviet Union at the beginning of the 1990s, the global political situation dramatically changed, though U.S. interventionism in the Third World continued unabated, if now for different reasons.

In addition, a film such as Michael Moore's *Canadian Bacon* (1995) suggests the way in which events like the first Gulf War of 1991 extend the mentality of the Cold War as the United States looks for enemies against which to define itself. This film also looks forward to films such as *Wag the Dog* (1997) and to the invasion of Iraq in 2003, which Moore brilliantly critiques in his documentary *Fahrenheit 9/11* (2004). In addition, *Canadian Bacon* suggests that American politicians (and arms manufacturers) cynically play upon (and help to create) the perception of foreign threats in order to boost their own power and profits.

The scenario of *Canadian Bacon* is simple: the U.S. President (played by Alan Alda) is on the verge of a difficult reelection campaign. He and his staff, including National Security Advisor Stuart Smiley (Kevin Pollak) conclude that his chances will be significantly boosted by an international crisis, but are unable to identify such a crisis. Then Smiley sees a television news report of a fight that breaks out between Canadians and Americans at a hockey game and decides that Canada would be the perfect antagonist. The American propaganda machine then goes into high gear in an attempt to drum up anti-Canadian sentiments and to convince the American people that the Canadians represent a serious threat that can best be met by keeping the current president in office.

Unfortunately, this campaign is all too successful, stirring a group of Americans, led by Sheriff Bud Boomer (John Candy) and his deputy Honey (Rhea Perlman), into such an anti-Canadian fury that they decide to cross the border from their home in Niagara Falls, New York, to launch a guerrilla assault against Canada. This assault leads mainly to comic confusion, both because the Americans are bumbling idiots and because the Canadians are so laid-back and nonviolent that it is almost impossible to provoke a battle. Things turn ugly, however, when it is revealed that sinister arms magnate R. J. Hacker (G. D. Spradlin) has planted the "Hacker Hellstorm," a doomsday device, in the Canadian National Tower in Toronto in retaliation to the fact that the U.S. government has refused to fund the development of the device, which is designed to trigger a massive launch of American nuclear missiles against the former Soviet Union. Knowing that this attack will prompt a response from the still-existing Soviet nuclear arsenal, the president and his staff (in a sequence reminiscent of Cold War thrillers such as *Dr. Strangelove* or *Fail-Safe*) scramble to prevent the device from activating and provoking a nuclear holocaust. Hacker then demands a trillion dollars ransom in return for deactivating the device. The President refuses to pay, but all is well when Deputy Honey destroys the device in the nick of time, thinking it a Canadian weapon.

Canadian Bacon may be a bit too amusing for its own good, making its critique of American politics seem comically trite. However, if satire as a genre thrives on exaggeration, subsequent events have made the film seem less exaggerated than it appears at first. In particular, the demonization of Canada in the film has a great deal in common with the media blitz that preceded the invasion of Iraq, which was designed to demonize Iraq and make the Middle Eastern nation appear to be a serious threat to American national security. Meanwhile, the obvious harmlessness of Canada foreshadows the fact that Iraq turned out not to be in possession of weapons of mass destruction that could be turned on the U.S. and its allies. However, while the president in *Canadian Bacon* does not succeed in winning reelection (he loses to none other than Oliver North), the real-life reelection campaign of George W. Bush, centered specifically on the argument that it was dangerous to change leaders while the United States was in the midst of a dangerous confrontation with sinister enemies, was in fact successful—despite Moore's best efforts.

Moore's extension of Cold War motifs into the era of tensions between the United States and Iraq is also central to Rod Lurie's *Deterrence* (1999), which similarly builds upon the Gulf War of 1991, though it obviously does not anticipate the U.S. invasion and occupation of Iraq in 2003. Set in 2008, Lurie's film imagines an Iraq now ruled by Saddam's son Ude Hussein (who was actually killed in the 2003 invasion); the president of the United States is Walter Emerson (Kevin Pollak, having apparently been promoted from his role in *Canadian Bacon*), an appointed vice president who has assumed the presidency after the death of his predecessor in office. Emerson (who also happens to be the first Jewish president, further complicating his relations with the Arab world) is in the process of running for election in his own right when Iraq once again invades and occupies Kuwait, as it had done in 1990, triggering the first Gulf War. To make matters worse (and even more unlikely), Emerson and his entourage are campaigning in Colorado when a snowstorm forces them to take refuge in a remote mountain diner, where they are snowed-in for the duration of the crisis.

With most of the U.S. military already tied up in crisis elsewhere (especially Korea), Emerson decides (rather bizarrely, some might say) to issue an ultimatum: unless Iraq immediately withdraws from Kuwait and Hussein turns himself in for arrest, the United States will drop a 100 megaton bomb on Baghdad, completely destroying the Iraqi capital. Iraq responds by threatening to launch a series of nuclear missiles that it has secretly stashed around the world at targets in the United States and Israel. When Emerson, who seems oddly undisturbed by the threat, refuses to call off the American strike against Baghdad, the Iraqi missiles (which turn out to be American-made, obtained by the Iraqis from France) are indeed launched. In what would be one of the most shocking tragedies in human history, Baghdad is indeed destroyed. However, the film seems completely unconcerned with the ramifications of that destruction. Instead, it concludes with the all's-well-that-ends-well device of revealing that the Iraqi warheads are all duds, intentionally sent by the United States to the Iraqis via the French (who were in on the scam) to give the Iraqis a false sense of power and thus prevent them from developing other weapons of mass destruction. Emerson, of course, knew it all along—though he does not seem to have realized that the false sense of security given the Iraqis by the defective missiles would lead to the assured destruction of Baghdad.

That the film seems to have a happy ending despite the destruction of Baghdad and its millions of inhabitants might be taken as a chilling commentary on Americans' lack of concern for Iraqi lives. Similarly, the ploy of selling nonfunctioning nukes to the Iraqis might potentially be taken as a criticism of the manipulative, dishonest, and potentially irresponsible nature of American foreign policy. Yet there is no real evidence that such criticisms were intended in the film. All in all, *Deterrence* has its effective moments of suspense, but Pollak's Emerson is not a very believable president and the entire scenario is a bit too implausible. On the other hand, the film does contain some thoughtful dialog on important issues, while it takes on a great deal of additional irony in the light of the 2003 invasion. In particular, the mistaken Iraqi belief in the film that they have mighty weapons of mass destruction ironically echoes (but gives a twist to) the real-world erroneous claims on the part of the U.S. government in 2003 (justifying the invasion) that the Iraqis had such weapons.

If *Deterrence* represents a clear attempt to transfer the energies of the Cold War thriller to the contemporary tensions between the United States and Iraq, Jonathan Demme's *The Manchurian Candidate* (2004)—a remake of John Frankenheimer's 1962 Cold War classic—is an even more direct attempt to move from the Cold War to the Gulf War as cinematic material. In Demme's film, an American patrol is again captured and brainwashed, this time in the Gulf War rather than the Korean War. Once again, the unit's commander, Ben Marco (now played by Denzel Washington), is conditioned to spearhead an effort to get a Congressional Medal of Honor for Sergeant Raymond Shaw (here played by Liev Schreiber), though this time the choice of Shaw actually makes sense: it is he who is tabbed by the conspiratorial brainwashers to return home and eventually run for president after Marco assassinates the presidential frontrunner. The character of Rosie (now played by Kimberly Elise) once again becomes romantically involved with Marco, though this time around her role in the plot becomes clear: she is an FBI agent assigned to keep tabs on Marco. The film ends in a fashion that is somewhat similar to that of the original: Marco overcomes his programming and, instead of the target he was conditioned to kill, he shoots both Shaw and Shaw's sinister mother (Meryl Streep), now updated to be a U.S. senator in her own right. In a final twist, though, Rosie and the

FBI cover Marco's tracks so that he gets away with the killings, having actually done a service for America by preventing Shaw, a drone of America's enemies, from taking power.

Many elements of this new version of *The Manchurian Candidate* hit close to home, making the film more believable than its predecessor, even if it is dramatically less effective. For one thing, the technology has been updated with the addition of science fictional electronic implants that serve to make the conditioning of Marco and Shaw seem more feasible than in Frankenheimer's original. What is really believable about Demme's film, however, is that the conspirators who brainwash the American patrol and plot to gain control of the presidency are not, as one might expect, the Iraqis. Instead, they are representatives of the powerful Manchurian Global Corporation, a giant multinational conglomerate with its fingers in all manners of pies around the world, who merely use the Gulf War as a convenient opportunity for their mind control scheme. This twist makes the film more credible both because a conglomerate like Manchurian Global might well have the resources (and the will) to carry out such a scheme and because it simply literalizes the fact that corporations already exert an alarming amount of control over American politicians up the very highest levels.

Demme's *Manchurian Candidate* effectively uses the Gulf War as a pretext, but does not really tell us anything about the war itself. In fact, the 1991 Gulf War has inspired relatively few films, despite (or perhaps because of) the extensive media hype that accompanied that event when it was underway. While a couple of low-budget films were released soon after the war in an attempt to cash in on it, it was not until Edward Zwick's *Courage Under Fire* (1996), that a major Hollywood film based on the first Gulf War was released. And even this film avoids any extensive commentary on the political ramifications of the war, concentrating instead on scenes of intense combat that are quite independent of the issues being fought over. At that, the film presents only the American point of view, while the Iraqi combatants are faceless and anonymous, seemingly dedicated (quite maliciously, in fact) to killing Americans for no apparent reason.

Actually, *Courage Under Fire* focuses not on the combat itself, but on its aftermath. Most of the film consists of an investigation being conducted by Lieutenant Colonel Nathaniel Serling (Denzel Washington) to determine whether an army helicopter pilot, Captain Karen Emma Walden (Meg Ryan), should be awarded a posthumous Medal of Honor after her death in combat in Iraq. Walden would thus become the first woman to have earned this medal. However, as Serling interviews the surviving members of Walden's helicopter crew, he gets conflicting stories of what happened in Iraq, depicting Walden as anything from a sniveling coward to the ultimate military hero. For this reason, *Courage Under Fire* has frequently been compared with Akira Kurosawa's Japanese classic *Rashomon* (1950), in which a series of witnesses give differing accounts of a crime. However, while the witnesses in Kurosawa's film all truthfully relate their memory of the events being accounted (thus making fundamental comments on human perception and memory), the differing accounts in *Courage Under Fire* result from the fact that some survivors, especially Staff Sergeant John Monfriez (Lou Diamond Phillips) are lying to cover their own improper conduct during the incident in which Walden was killed. Indeed, Monfriez, who ultimately commits suicide (whether out of guilt or simply out of a desire not to face charges is not clear), may have been directly responsible for Walden's death, which may have come about by friendly fire.

All of this is complicated by the fact that Serling's own life is coming unraveled due to his own feelings of guilt from the fact that a friend and fellow soldier was killed by friendly fire on his own mistaken orders while in Iraq. Further, Serling experiences considerable political pressure because the White House wants Walden approved for the medal, feeling that granting the medal to a woman will be good public relations at a time when the pro-administration fervor that peaked during the war is beginning to fade. Serling, however, refuses to bow to this pressure and insists on conducting a full investigation, even after he is officially removed from the case. Luckily, the investigation ends well: it ultimately becomes clear that Walden does indeed deserve the medal, while Serling achieves a certain amount of peace when he is not only cleared by the military of wrongdoing in his own friendly fire incident, but also forgiven by the parents of the soldier killed due to his orders. However, in the film's most trenchant moment of political commentary, the film does end on a somewhat sardonic note, as President Bush (senior) is shown presenting the medal to Walden's young daughter in a ceremony cynically designed to cash in on the public-relations value of this classic sentimental moment.

The made-for-HBO film *Live from Baghdad* (2002) dramatizes the real-world experiences of a CNN news crew sent to Baghdad to cover the situation there as tensions build toward war in the wake of the Iraqi invasion of Kuwait in August 1990. The crew is headed by executive producer Robert Wiener (Michael Keaton) and producer Ingrid Formanek (Helena Bonham Carter). Their attempts to get stories sometimes lead to negative consequences, as when an interview with Bob Vinton (Murphy Dunne), an American in Baghdad, calls attention to the man's presence and leads to his arrest by the Iraqi authorities for potential use as a hostage. All in all, however, television news is for once treated positively in this film—perhaps because it was cowritten by Wiener based on his own book about the events described in the film. Wiener, Formanek, and their crew are depicted as honest and courageous in their pursuit of information about the crisis. Further, it is clear that Wiener, in particular, hopes that the information he obtains can further understanding between Iraq and the United States and perhaps prevent a war. Unfortunately, this quest is unsuccessful, and American bombs and missiles eventually strike Baghdad—while the CNN crew continues to broadcast, even with bombs bursting around their hotel.

Initially, Wiener's principal goal is to get an exclusive interview with Iraqi president Saddam Hussein. Scooped on that story by CBS and Dan Rather, Wiener manages to use the contact he has established with Naji Al-Hadithi (David Suchet), a high official in the Iraqi Ministry of Information, to get exclusive entry into occupied Kuwait. However, when they arrive in Kuwait, they find that the information to which they have access is being carefully manipulated by the occupying Iraqi forces; moreover, they find that they are simply being used as part of an Iraqi propaganda ploy to counter reports of atrocities being perpetrated against Kuwaiti civilians.

In the wake of this debacle, Wiener finally manages to arrange an interview between Saddam and CNN news anchor Bernard Shaw (Robert Wisdom), though the interview at this point seems anticlimactic. Soon afterward, all foreign nationals in Iraq are allowed to go home, including Vinton, who assures a relieved Wiener that he is fine and has not been mistreated. Wiener's genuine relief shows a compassion and concern of the kind seldom associated with television news people on film. Soon afterward, it becomes clear that CNN is becoming a central player in the crisis (despite the journalist's credo of never becoming the story), providing a conduit through which each side can air messages meant for the other. Unfortunately, neither side is listening to the other and the situation spirals inevitably toward war.

On the eve of the American-issued deadline for bombing to begin, Shaw returns to Baghdad for another interview with Saddam, hoping the Iraqi president will accede to U.S. demands during the interview. However, the interview never takes place, and Shaw is recalled to Atlanta to anchor the coverage of the upcoming war. Wiener and most of the rest of his crew elect to stay, despite being offered the opportunity to leave with Shaw. Then the bombing begins earlier than expected, leaving Shaw and the entire crew trapped in their Baghdad hotel as the bombing begins. By that time, the CNN crew has been supplied equipment by the Iraqis that allows them to become the only news organization able to report live on the air (and virtually the only Western news organization still in Baghdad at all—despite pressure from the U.S. government to leave). Shaw and much of Wiener's crew (including Formanek) are able to return to the United States the day after the bombing begins, and Wiener returns a week later. The film ends here, though CNN reporter Peter Arnett (Bruce McGill) remained behind to become the official voice and face of the war, sometimes angering U.S. authorities with his reports of civilian casualties and collateral damage in Iraq, reports that, while apparently accurate, conflicted with the official U.S. picture of precise surgical bombing with minimal collateral effects. Nevertheless, CNN became the source of record for information about the war, establishing its reputation as a major player in global news reporting.

Sam Mendes's *Jarhead* (2005) has the distinction of being the first major film about the first Gulf War that was made after the beginning of the second. It also features a big budget and an A-list cast and director, which initially triggered some speculation that it might be the definitive film about the 1991 Gulf War. The fact is that it is not. The film is a compelling account of life in the Marine Corps ("jarhead" is slang for marine) just before and during the war; it is, in fact, based on a memoir by ex-marine Anthony Swofford, who is the protagonist of the film (played by Jake Gyllenhaal). However, the film is about the small details of the experiences of individuals. It is not about the bigger picture, and it carefully avoids any real engagement with the numerous political issues surrounding the war, opting instead to comment on those issues only peripherally or in passing. Indeed, the film's political philosophy seems in many ways to be summed up by an exchange that occurs soon after the marines arrive in Saudi Arabia. When one marine complains that they are only there to defend the interests of oil companies, Swofford's buddy Alan Troy (Peter Sarsgaard) responds, "Fuck politics! We're here. All the rest is bullshit." Consequently, while the film indicates that the American troops have been sent to the Middle East in response to the August 1990 Iraqi invasion of Kuwait, there is no exploration of the history of Kuwait or that Kuwait is regarded by most Iraqis as a part of their own country, carved off and established as a separate state by the British Empire in order to ensure their own access to Kuwait's rich oil resources.

For that matter, (in a motif that perhaps explains the paucity of films about the Gulf War) the marine unit that we follow through the film, though deployed to the front lines in the war, sees virtually no actual combat; as they advance toward Iraq, they encounter only dead Iraqi soldiers, already killed (and generally charred beyond recognition) by American bombing attacks. These scenes actually provide the film's most trenchant political commentary, because the dead Iraqis (referred to by one cynical marine as "crispy critters") seem more like innocent victims of the vastly superior American firepower than like sinister villains. In one scene, the marines realize that an entire convoy of Iraqi soldiers had been wiped out unnecessarily while trying to flee from Kuwait back to Iraq. Though no details are provided in the film, such scenes call attention to the contro-versial attacks that in fact occurred against retreating Iraqi forces on the so-called "highway of death" from Kuwait City back to Basra in Iraq on the night of February 26–27, 1991. Estimates of Iraqi deaths in this slaughter have run as high as 10,000, though the attacks were so destructive that no reliable estimates are available.

The marines in the film suffer more from boredom than from battle, more from discomfort than from danger. After the marines wait for six months in the Saudi desert , the actual war lasts only four days. Swofford, a sniper, never fires his rifle. Swofford, Troy, and the other members of their unit, including their leader, the gung ho Staff Sergeant Sykes (Jamie Foxx), encounter absolutely hellish conditions as they grind through the desert toward Iraq, especially after the Kuwaiti oilfields are set afire, sending oil and acrid smoke spewing into the air. In one final bit of social commentary, the marines return home after the war to find that they are greeted with little appreciation for their efforts. Swofford finds that his girlfriend has left him for another man, while Troy is drummed out of the marines because of a previous criminal record that he had not revealed when he joined up. In one of the final scenes, Swofford attends Troy's funeral, with the implication that Troy's discharge has led to suicide. Swofford then returns home, lonely, and thinks to himself that, whatever he does with the rest of his life, he will always be a jarhead.

Looking back to such films as *Full Metal Jacket*, *Jarhead* begins with extended coverage of the training undergone by the marines before going into combat—though in this case the training occurs before the recruits realize that they are going to be in a war. The rock music soundtrack is reminiscent of Vietnam War films such as *Full Metal Jacket* and *Apocalypse Now* as well—so much so that Swofford complains at one point while the Doors' "Break on Through" is playing in the background: "That's Vietnam music. Can't we get our own music?" Indeed, *Jarhead* is consistently aware of its status as a post–Vietnam War film, and films about the Vietnam War hover over *Jarhead* throughout. In one early scene, for example, the trainees watch *Apocalypse Now*, cheering riotously at the horrifying scene in which American helicopters execute a devastating attack on a virtually defenseless Vietnamese village (to the blaring sound of Wagner's "Ride of the Valkyrie"), encapsulating not only the horrors of that war but the sometimes gruesome impact of Western modernity throughout the Third World. This scene is then interrupted by an announcement that the trainees are heading for the Middle East, which directly links Vietnam with the Gulf War, especially linking the helicopter attack on the Vietnamese village to the later carnage on Iraq's highway of death.

In another scene set while the bored jarheads wait in the Saudi desert, one marine, Dettman (Marty Papazian) receives from home what appears to be a videotape of *The Deer Hunter*. However, it turns out that the tape actually contains a video that the Dettman's wife made of herself having sex with a neighbor—then sent to the marine in apparent retribution for his own earlier infidelities. Taping this scene over a recording of *The Deer*

Hunter is, of course, entirely appropriate, given that both videos dramatize in their different ways the disjunction between military life in war and civilian life back home. This disjunction is one of the many phenomena indicated by Swofford in his voiceover late in the film when he notes that, "Every war is different. Every war is the same."

Jarhead makes clear that the Gulf War was vastly different from Vietnam (if only because it lasted but four days and the Americans won). But it also suggests the way in which any American war is at this point inevitably viewed through the optic of Vietnam, at the same time potentially providing a subtle reminder of the much more extensive parallels between the Vietnam War debacle and the later American invasion of Iraq in 2003. The shadow of Vietnam also lurks over David O. Russell's *Three Kings* (1999), a hip, stylish effort that nevertheless provides some of the most telling and trenchant commentary on the American involvement in Iraq. The film also indicates the way memories of Vietnam have haunted the American military since the 1970s. Thus, television news reporter Adriana Cruz (Nora Dunn), interviewing a group of celebrating American soldiers after the victorious conclusion of the Gulf War, asks for their comments on the notion that they have "exorcised the ghost of Vietnam with a clear moral imperative." Their only comment is the official government line: "We liberated Kuwait." *Three Kings* even foreshadows the difficulties that arose after the 2003 invasion in an early scene in which Army Special Forces Major Archie Gates (George Clooney) expresses doubt that Operation Desert Storm has really accomplished anything. His superior officer, Colonel Ron Horn, sardonically asks, "What do you want to do? Occupy Iraq and do Vietnam all over again?"

Mostly, however, *Three Kings*, which actually begins just after the 1991 war has ended and a peace agreement has been signed, deals with the political and moral ramifications of that war. In particular, it questions the morality of U.S. president George Bush's call for the Iraqi people to rise up against Saddam Hussein after the war, a call many heeded, expecting support from the recently victorious U.S. military. That support came, and many of the Iraqi insurgents were consequently slaughtered. In this sense, the tone of the film is set in the very first scene, when Sergeant First Class Troy Barlow (Mark Wahlberg) wanders through the Kuwaiti desert with his unit and spots an Iraqi on a distant sand dune. Confused about the recently signed peace accord, he asks, "Are we shooting people, or what?" When he sees that the Iraqi seems to be carrying a gun, he shoots him down, only later to discover that the man was actually waving a white flag, attempting to surrender. The message of this scene is clear: however well-meaning the American soldiers involved in Operation Desert Storm might have been, they did a great deal of damage to innocent Iraqis.

Three Kings also comments on the role of the media in the Gulf War, especially in the early scenes in which the military is encouraged by their commanders to cooperate with the numerous media reporters who are covering the event—but to try to steer these reporters in directions that are favorable to the official American line. As Horn explains early on, "This is a media war!" The influential telejournalist Cruz is thus a particularly important presence in postwar Iraq, though she has trouble getting the cooperation of Gates, who is too busy having sex with a rival reporter, Cathy Daitch (Judy Greer).

The film also comments on the racist underpinnings of the American presence. We learn in an early scene that Private First Class Conrad Vig (Spike Jonze), something of a stereotypical ignorant redneck, tends to refer to Iraqis as "dune coons" or "sand niggers." When the black Staff Sergeant Chief Elgin (Ice Cube) objects to this language, it is clearly only because it tends to include African Americans in the racist slur against Iraqis. He and Barlow thus convince Vig to try to start calling Iraqis "towelheads" and "camel jockeys," so that his racist language will be aimed strictly at Arabs, without implicating African Americans. However, in the course of the film, Gates, Barlow, Elgin, and even Vig emerge as heroes and prove willing to risk their lives to help Iraqis who have been placed in danger by the American call for them to revolt against Saddam.

The four essentially constitute a gang of lovable rogues, a standard category of American film hero, somewhat along the lines of the gang of casino robbers in the remake of *Ocean's Eleven* (2001) or even the escape convicts of *Oh Brother, Where Art Thou?* (2000), both of which also starred Clooney. The main plot of the film is triggered when Barlow discovers a map secreted in the rectum of a captured Iraqi soldier. This map, he and Elgin conclude, shows the location of bunkers near the Iraqi city of Karbala where the Iraqis may have hidden loot taken from Kuwait during their recent occupation. When Gates suggests (repeating post-coital information he received from Daitch) that the bunkers probably contain Kuwaiti gold bullion, the possibilities suggested by the map appear even more lucrative. Gates, Elgin, Barlow, and Vig thus commandeer a Humvee and head into Iraq to try to recover the gold. In this sense, they are merely opportunistic raiders; as originally intended, their mission in entirely selfish (not to mention illegal). Meanwhile, they find the gold fairly easily—and even find that Iraqi soldiers in the area are willing to help them load it on a truck. However, they encounter significant obstacles when they discover that these same soldiers are slaughtering civilians in the area to suppress the uprising against Saddam's regime that has arisen at the urging of the United States.

As they are about to leave with the gold, the four Americans see an Iraqi woman summarily shot, execution style, by an Iraqi soldier in the street while the woman's husband and daughter look on. The Iraqis are about to execute the father as well when the Americans intervene, leading to a brief firefight in which the Iraqis are subdued. The Americans load the remaining Iraqi civilians into the Humvee and prepare to leave the area, but they hit a minefield, which, combined with a subsequent attack by the Iraqi military, destroys both of these vehicles and leaves the Americans in disarray. Most of them are forced to take refuge with the Iraqi civilians, though Barlow is captured and subsequently interrogated and tortured by an Iraqi soldier whose family was killed in the recent American bombing of Baghdad. This scene is thus one of the few in American film in which an Iraqi soldier becomes a specific individual with a name, a face, and a life outside of the war. The Americans and Iraqi civilians mount a rescue effort (using a fleet of luxury vehicles that the Iraqis had stolen from Kuwait as transportation) in which Barlow is freed, though seriously wounded. Vig, however, is shot and killed by an Iraqi sniper during the rescue.

The remaining Americans distribute some of the gold among the Iraqi civilians, then stash most of it before making their way with the Iraqi civilians to the Iranian border so that the Iraqis can seek sanctuary in Iran. However, in one of the film's most powerful political moments, they are stopped at the border by an American military force (led by Horn) that has been sent there to enforce the American policy of not intervening in the domestic affairs of Iraq. The three remaining American adventurers are arrested and placed in handcuffs, while the Iraqi refugees are rounded up and locked in a stockade, presumably awaiting slaughter by the Iraqi military. Gates, however, is able to convince Horn to release the refugees and let them cross the border; in return, he promises to reveal the location of the hidden gold. In short, the official American military does the right thing out of a desire to recover gold, not out of concern for Iraqi civilians, a motif that rather clearly reinforces the notion that the American forces are in the Middle East to defend the massive oil reserves there, not to help the Saudi, Kuwaiti, or Iraqi people.

As Horn releases the refugees, he promises to see to it that Gates, Elgin, and Barlow are all court-martialed. However, the film closes with a brief coda that takes place after Gates, Elgin, and Barlow have been honorably discharged from the military, rather than court-martialed. We also learn that Gates and Elgin are now working together as military advisors in Hollywood, while Barlow has his own carpet business—with a hint that their post-military businesses might have been funded by their ability to get away with some of the Kuwaiti gold, despite everything. Apparently, the positive media coverage of their rescue of the Iraqi civilians (spearheaded by Cruz) has made it untenable for the military to prosecute them. Thus, for once, the American media come off well in a political film. In addition, individual American soldiers also come off very well, while the American government comes off very poorly indeed.

Three Kings is almost like a movie-watcher's tool kit: not only does it include a panoply of filmmaking techniques, but it can be interpreted in a number of different ways and as a number of different kinds of movie depending on the inclination of the viewer. On one level, it is a slightly wacky, very amusing, and highly entertaining buddy film. On another, it is a thoughtful political drama that asks (but does not answer) a number of questions about the propriety of American interventionism around the world. It includes a great deal of self-consciously artistic flourishes, including numerous forays into MTV-style postmodern quick-cut editing, but its artistry and humor never prevent it from dealing with serious issues in an appropriately serious way.

The quest-rescue plot of *Three Kings* gives it an almost mythic structure (reinforced by the Biblical allusion in the title), even if its protagonists are far from being classic mythical heroes. A similar structure is used (much less successfully) in the 2003 film *Tears of the Sun* (directed by Antoine Fuqua). This film lacks both the zany energy and the weighty political ramifications of *Three Kings,* settling instead for a much more formulaic action plot in which virtuous American commandos (led by Bruce Willis's Lieutenant A. K. Waters) rescue a group of helpless African Christians from a ruthless and murderous group of African Muslims. Indeed, this film is rife with objectionable stereotypes about the savagery of Africans and of Muslims, and does little to challenge any of those stereotypes. Otherwise, there is little by the way of political commentary, and the situation in which the action takes place (a civil war in Nigeria) is entirely fictional, though Nigeria has certainly had more than its share of such strife. However, most of the ethnic violence in Nigeria has been visited by Christians upon other Christians, and the film's decision to lay the blame for such violence on the Muslim Hausa population of Nigeria merely reinforces fears about the bloodthirstiness of Muslims that have inhabited the popular American imagination at least since the taking of American hostages in Iran in the 1970s and that received a particular boost from the destruction of the World Trade Center Towers on September 11, 2001.

Of course, *Tears of the Sun* is potentially critical of the American tendency not to intervene in the various debacles that have swept postcolonial Africa. These tragic events, such as the genocidal conflicts that swept Rwanda in the mid-1990s, have themselves been the subject of a number of films, including the Haitian director Raoul Peck's made-for-HBO *Sometimes in April* (2005), Michael Caton-Jones's *Shooting Dogs* (2005), and (most notably) Terry George's *Hotel Rwanda* (2004). The family of films that details the horrors of apartheid in South Africa until the collapse of that system in 1994—including such films as *Cry Freedom* (1987), *A Dry White*

Season (1989), *The Power of One* (1992)—also suggests (sometimes directly, sometimes by implication) U.S. complicity in one of the worst human rights abuses in modern history. However, these films can primarily be taken as a rare attempt on the part of Hollywood to make a genuine contribution to political change by promoting opposition to apartheid among their American (and other) viewers.

Of course, the lack of U.S. action in the face of such tragedies as apartheid and the Rwanda massacres (and now the ongoing devastation of the Sudan) becomes even more problematic when compared to the extensive interventions that have been undertaken elsewhere—including a substantial number of (most clandestine) actions in Africa itself. Such interventions were especially common in the years just before and after independence, when the CIA and other American agencies quite routinely acted in an attempt to prevent African leaders with leftist tendencies from rising to power in the new nations. Little is known of these top-secret actions, though they apparently included a number of CIA-sponsored assassinations of such leaders, possibly including the killing of the Congo's Patrice Lumumba in 1961. It is certainly the case that Lumumba had been marked for death by the CIA (on order of President Dwight Eisenhower) soon after his rise to prominence in the late 1950s. Lumumba's life (and death) is the subject of Peck's very effective Argentine film *Lumumba* (2000), though Hollywood has generally shied away from interrogating this aspect of American (and African) history.

Even in *Tears of the Sun*, Waters and his men have actually been sent in only to rescue an American doctor (who becomes, partly thanks to Monica Bellucci's intelligent performance, the film's most interesting character). Their decision also to try to rescue as many Africans as possible (triggered by the doctor's insistence that they do so) requires that they go directly against their official orders. Ultimately, though, the American military authorities come through in the clench and provide the firepower needed to save the Africans in a last minute intervention that descends into cinematic cliché (and destroys any possible political punch that the film might have had). As the film closes, Waters and the doctor fly away on an American helicopter, clasped in a Hollywood-ending embrace.

Tears of the Sun is an entirely fictional film that presents a fantasy version of an American intervention in African postcolonial violence. Things do not work out so well in Ridley Scott's *Black Hawk Down* (2001), a film that deals with the first major American military experience after the first Gulf War, the near-disastrous intervention in Somalia in the fall of 1993. Among other things, *Black Hawk Down* points to the complexity of postcolonial African politics, suggesting that, even were the United States willing to intervene in Africa, such intervention would not be a simple matter. Meanwhile, *Black Hawk Down* also portrays contemporary military action in a mode that anticipates *Jarhead*'s portrayal of combat as a form of male bonding that has little or nothing to do with the political reasons for the combat. This attitude is in fact quite typical of early twenty-first-century films dealing with recent American wars, including the Vietnam War film *We Were Soldiers* (2002).

In fact, an American force was sent to Somalia in the summer of 1993 in an attempt to bring an end to the violence that had erupted there after warlord Mohamed Farrah Aidid had risen to prominence amid the power vacuum caused by the fall of dictator Mohamed Siad Barre, leading to an all-out civil war and turning life in Somalia into a hellish nightmare of violence. Seeing Aidid as the primary instigator of the violence, the Americans hoped to capture him and force an end to the fighting fairly quickly.

The film begins after the Americans have been in Somalia for six weeks and have still been unable to catch Aidid. It deals with a mission in early October that was designed to capture two of Aidid's top lieutenants, who are rumored to be attending a high-level meeting near the Bakara Market, an Aidid stronghold in the capital of Mogadishu. The mission is envisioned as a quick in-and-out move that will take no more than thirty minutes. Unfortunately, the Americans have sadly underestimated the strength and determination of Aidid's heavily armed supporters. Moreover, the mission begins to go wrong when an army ranger, the newcomer Blackburn (Orlando Bloom), is badly hurt when he falls while descending by rope from a helicopter to the street below. The effort to rescue the injured man puts the American forces into disarray, and the situation quickly deteriorates as they come under heavy fire from the unexpectedly strong Somali opposition, leading to the downing of first one then another American helicopter.

Most of the rest of the film presents the ensuing urban battle, capturing well the extreme level of violence and the atmosphere of complete confusion and chaos. As an action film focusing on these battle sequences, *Black Hawk Down* is superb. As a political film, however, it is quite weak, and it does absolutely nothing to explore the terms of the conflict or to explain why American troops are in the streets of Mogadishu or why the inhabitants of the city meet them with such concentrated violence. The film's philosophy in this regard is summed up early on, when one of the American soldiers, Sergeant First Class Norm "Hoot" Hooten (Eric Bana), dismisses the idealistic notions of another sergeant, Matt Eversmann (Josh Hartnett), that the American forces are in Mogadishu to help the Somali people. Instead, Hooten simply declares that "once the first bullet goes past your head, politics and all that shit just goes right out the window." Hooten follows this statement with another declaration near the end of the film, after the surviving Americans finally make their way back to safety. Noting that people back home will probably wonder why soldiers such as him do what they do, Hooten suggests that "it's about the man next to you. That's it."

Of course, Hooten's response, however understandable its emphasis on camaraderie among the American soldiers, does not really answer the question of why the soldiers are in Somalia with bullets flying past their heads in the first place. To an extent, this lack of political engagement can be attributed to the hand of director Scott, who has quite frequently been criticized for being more interested in style than substance, more concerned with the ways his films look than what they say. But the lack of concern with politics that informs *Black Hawk Down* is obviously part of a much broader phenomenon in American film of the early years of the twenty-first century. However, given the tendency of American forces to get involved in quagmires around the world because their government appears to be ignorant of the actual political situations into which they are going, this lack of interest on the part of American film is a serious shortcoming.

The Somali situation is a particular case in point. The commander of the American forces, General William F. Garrison (Sam Shepard), indicates early in the film that complex political concerns might be at stake in the Somali conflict when he notes, "This isn't Iraq, you know. It's more complicated than that." Of course, after the invasion and subsequent occupation of Iraq in 2003, we now know that Iraq is complicated as well. Meanwhile, few lessons were learned from the Somali experience because very little has been done in the media to explain what went wrong there. Part of what went wrong in Somalia (as, later, in Iraq) was simply due to bad intelligence, leading to a serious underestimation of the strength of Aidid's forces. But, in this case, the inexperienced Clinton administration (in office for only a few months at the time the intervention in Somalia was ordered) seemed completely unaware of the historical background to the political collapse of Somalia, knowledge of which should have alerted them to the high level of animosity toward the United States among Somalis.

In particular, the chaos in Somalia came about in the wake of the downfall of long-term dictator Siad Barre, who for more than a decade prior to his downfall (especially during the entire term of the Reagan administration) had brutally terrorized the Somali population with the support of the U.S. government. (Indeed, Aidid's heavily armed supporters were largely using weapons that had been sent to Somalia by the American government.) Despite this background, in a classic bit of American hubris, the American forces arrived in Somalia expecting to be greeted as saviors, an expectation that greatly contributed to the fiasco that subsequently occurred there. The American news media did little or nothing to explain this background either before or after the American experience there, instead portraying the Somalis who fought against the American forces as gangs of savage thugs. *Black Hawk Down* is only slightly more sympathetic to the Somalis. It notes that the battle portrayed in the film led to the deaths of more than 1,000 Somalis, as opposed to the media coverage that empha- sized only the nineteen American deaths, but it does nothing to explain the high level of animosity encountered by the Americans.

The same might be said for John Moore's unremarkable *Behind Enemy Lines* (2001), one of the few films to deal with the U.S./NATO interven- tions in the former Yugoslavia in the late 1990s. Here, an American pilot and navigator, flying a reconnaissance mission over Bosnia, spot mass graves in which Serbian troops have buried their Bosnian Muslim victims. Realizing this, the Serbs shoot down the plane. They also capture and murder the pilot, though the navigator Lieutenant Chris Burnett (Owen Wilson) manages to escape, with the Serbs in hot pursuit. The rest of the film then details his harrowing flight to safety, punctuated by the battles of American Admiral Leslie McMahon Reigart (Gene Hackman), with the NATO bureaucracy, which fears that efforts to rescue Burnett might disrupt a recent NATO-brokered cease-fire in Bosnia.

If this battle of tough, American individuals against heartless, dim-witted European bureaucrats is a bit stereotypical, then the depiction of the Serbs as crazed, bloodthirsty murderers is even more so. The film does absolutely nothing to explore the terms of the conflict, other than to suggest that it might have been caused by Serbian murderousness. To top it all, the film ends with one of the most ludicrous action-battle sequences in all of American film, as U.S. helicopters (without NATO permission) charge into Bosnia, blow away the Serbia troops, and rescue Burnett—but only after he has to leap off of a cliff to be barely caught, trapeze-style, by a U.S. marine dangling from one of the helicopters.

This film thus illustrates once again that, if the American war film reached a peak of political engagement with the Vietnam War films of the late 1980s, subsequent films about American military endeavors after Vietnam have tended to retreat from that engagement and to attempt to restore the national identity of the United States as a virtuous opponent of savage foes. Meanwhile, the latter films have tended to focus on the experiences of individual soldiers rather than on the political background of the various conflicts. Even worse, they have sometimes used real-world wars as a pretext for the making of action films that have little connection with the political reality of war and that convert the death and destruction associated with these wars into mere entertainment. In an era when the instant media coverage of wars has been widely criticized for turning war into a video game, this recent tendency in American war films is troubling indeed.

Conclusion:
Political Film in the Twenty-First Century

I f anything, American political film seems to have taken a decided step backward in critical power in the early years of the twenty-first century, even as the political problems facing America have grown more and more pressing. The first six years of the new century have seen virtually no genuine interrogation, within fictional films, of recent events such as the 2003 invasion of Iraq and other contemporary policies of the Bush administration. Similarly, there has been relatively little exploration of the increasingly overt criminal conduct of major multinational corporations such as Enron and WorldCom. Meanwhile, the growing global environmental crisis has received essentially no serious treatment in fictional film. Indeed, an exception such as Roland Emmerich's global-warming disaster flick *The Day after Tomorrow* (2004) only sensationalize such issues, serving to prove the difficulty of producing compelling fictional films about the environment without exaggeration and distortion for dramatic effect.

There are a number of reasons for the relative paucity of American political film in the past few years. For one thing, around-the-clock cable news channels such as CNN, FoxNews, and MSNBC provide so much coverage of and commentary on political events (however biased and superficial) that the market for such coverage and commentary may already be saturated. Of course, the best political films—such as *Dr. Strangelove* and *JFK*—are able to approach political issues in thought-provoking ways that are not available to viewers of television news. However, these provocative approaches can also be highly controversial; and movie studios, with

215

films becoming increasingly expensive to produce and distribute, have tended more and more to shy away from controversy. Further, many of America's most important (and controversial) directors of genuinely political films are no longer making such films. John Sayles continues to labor away (in increasing obscurity), but Stanley Kubrick and Martin Ritt are dead. Haskell Wexler now directs only documentaries, though occasionally working as a cinematographer for Sayles, as in *Silver City* (2004), one of the few effective cinematic critiques of the values and tactics of the Bush administration and its corporate backers. Even Oliver Stone (perhaps growing old?) has retreated from the remarkable political punch of films such as *JFK* and his Vietnam trilogy to concentrate (not very successfully) on more commercial projects, though one can certainly see some critique of American violence and greed in *Any Given Sunday* (1999), while some have even seen (or tried to see) oblique shots at the policies of the Bush administration in *Alexander* (2004).

Then again, *Alexander* could just as easily be seen as an endorsement of Bushite expansionism and interventionism (for the right cause). Even Stone's latest film, *World Trade Center* (2006), shies away from an exploration of the political background of the September 11, 2001, terrorist bombings of the World Trade Center and the Pentagon. Instead, Stone— like Paul Greenglass in *United 93* (2006)—concentrates on the (admittedly compelling) personal dramas of the victims of that attack, thus avoiding any real probing of what is still America's sorest political spot. The only genuine potential for political controversy to be found in Stone's recent work can be found in his two-part made-for-HBO documentaries *Comandante* (2003) and *Looking for Fidel* (2004), which contain some criticism of Cuban leader Fidel Castro and avoid any large-scale investigation of the role of the United States in Latin America, but nevertheless undermine the demonization of Castro in U.S. propaganda.

These latter films highlight two of the more positive developments in American political film in recent years. For one thing, the HBO pay-cable network, widely acknowledged as the home of the most innovative and sophisticated original programming available on American television, has also emerged as a venue for some of the most important political films in contemporary American culture. With a solid base of subscribers who are not likely to be turned away by the implications of an individual film, HBO can afford to risk more controversy than the producer of a major theatrical film (with more eggs in a single basket) might be willing to do. In addition, Stone's Castro documentaries (like the documentaries of Wexler) participate in what James McEnteer in his book *Shooting the Truth: The Rise of American Political Documentaries* (Praeger, 2006) has characterized as a genuine Golden Age of American political documentaries in the past few years.

Indeed, one reason for the recent weakness of fictional political films might simply be that the energies that had once gone into fiction film are now going into documentaries, which have often explored issues too controversial (or too noncommercial) for fictional films. For example, Davis Guggenheim's *An Inconvenient Truth* (2006) documents the efforts of vice president and presidential candidate Al Gore to draw much-needed attention to the global-warming crisis. Documentaries have even dared to challenge capitalism itself, as in Mark Achbar and Jennifer Abbott's *The Corporation* (2003), a serious exploration of the capitalist corporation as an entity in which the filmmakers conclude that the typical behavior of capitalist corporations closely resembles that of pathological killers. Eugene Jarecki's *Why We Fight* (2004) reaches somewhat the same conclusion in a different way, arguing that American militarism is largely motivated by the fact that war is good business—good, at least, for the military-industrial complex. Meanwhile, Alex Gibney's *Enron: The Smartest Guys in the Room* (2005) also looks at the sinister side of capitalism, focusing specifically on the combination of hubris, greed, and corruption that led to the downfall of the once-mighty Enron Corporation.

Granted, it is hardly news that American corporations are greedy and heartless, though such documentaries at least attempt to make the case that this greed and heartlessness are out of control and that there is an urgent need to reign corporations in. In this sense, the recent critiques of capitalism in documentary film build upon a tradition established in such documentaries as Barbara Kopple's *Harlan County, U.S.A.* (1976) and *American Dream* (1992) and Michael Moore's *Roger & Me* (1989) and *The Big One* (1997). Meanwhile, Moore himself has emerged as the biggest star in the twenty-first-century documentary boom. His Oscar-winning *Bowling for Columbine* (2002), an examination of America's fascination with guns and violence, drew considerable attention to that issue. Meanwhile, his *Fahrenheit 9/11* (2004), which treads on tremendously dangerous territory with its bitter (though entertaining) critique of the Bush administration's handling of the 9/11 bombings and their aftermath, became, in its theatrical release, the most commercially successful documentary in American film history by a wide margin. Moore's revelations of the ineptitude and dirty dealings of the Bush administration are damning, yet the film failed to prevent Bush's reelection. However enlightening (and even inspirational) the film might have been to those who suspected Bush of incompetence and corruption all along, it obviously failed to convince any significant number of Bush supporters to shift their political allegiance. Moore's follow-up film, *Fahrenheit 9/11½* (scheduled for release in 2007), is currently in production as of this writing. Meanwhile, Moore's campaign against Bush has triggered a series of conservative rebuttals, but is supported by the work of important documentary filmmaker Robert Greenwald, including such films as *Unprecedented: The 2000 Presidential Election* (2002) and *Uncovered: The Whole Truth about the Iraq War* (2003).

The recent documentary boom, as McEnteer notes, suggests that Americans, however cynical they have become, are still hungry for information about important issues. Of course, the recent strength of political documentaries relative to fictional political films might also be attributed to the fact that we have reached the point in our contemporary world at which truth really is stranger than fiction, making the subject matter available to documentaries, more interesting than that available to fiction films. Then again, the territory available to fiction films is broad indeed, and the most promising and powerful fictional political films of recent years have explored real issues in satirical modes that go well beyond realism. George Romero's zombie-film *Land of the Dead* (2005), with its skewering of the class inequalities of American consumer society, is a case in point.

Particularly interesting in this regard is James McTeigue's *V for Vendetta* (2005), a dystopian fantasy that moves in genuinely new directions and even dares (despite the demonization of terrorism in post-9/11 America) to suggest terrorist violence as a legitimate political response to oppression. *V for Vendetta* was scripted by the Wachowski brothers (creators of the *Matrix* trilogy of science fiction films), adapted from a graphic novel of the same title by Alan Moore (illustrated by David Lloyd). It projects a dark, near-future world in which a deadly contagion has contributed to the collapse of the United States into civil war, while Britain finds itself in the iron grip of a dystopian dictatorship that seems modeled largely on the Oceania of George Orwell's *Nineteen Eighty-Four*. The link to Orwell is reinforced by the casting of John Hurt (who had starred in the film version of Orwell's novel) as Chancellor Adam Sutler, the Big Brother-like ruler of the dystopian state in *V for Vendetta*. However, Orwell's grim, gray dystopian regime is given an update through the inclusion of a dash of religious fundamentalism and through the use of the power of modern media to help hold the population in thrall to the dictatorship. In short, the regime of *V for Vendetta* has essentially been updated to make it an obvious stand-in for the contemporary U.S. Bush administration—so much so that Moore had his name removed from the credits to the film because he thought his original vision of a fascist Britain had been excessively modified in order to make it more of a comment on American politics. The film's dystopian regime, like the American Bush administration, is informed by a powerful self-righteous religiosity, while it defines itself through its hatred of "immigrants, Muslims, homosexuals, terrorists, and disease-ridden degenerates." Meanwhile, the eponymous anarchist protagonist of Moore's novel has been transformed essentially into an agent of bourgeois liberalism in the film, fighting for a restoration of old-style civil liberties rather than struggling against government altogether.

That said, while the politics of the graphic novel may be distorted in the film, it is also the case that the film represents a powerful and even daring critique of the Bush administration. For example, the film's very transformation of Moore's fascist state into a version of Bush-era America is itself a powerful statement about the affinities between fascism and the current political situation in the United States. The film version of *V for Vendetta* is particularly courageous, given the climate of Patriot Act America, in its exploration of the centrality of the war on terrorism to the agenda of the Sutler (i.e., Bush) administration. For one thing, Sutler's government directly echoes the political strategies of the Bush administration in its use of the fear of terrorism as its most important tool of power. The film is also critical of America's "war on terrorism" in its suggestion (looking back from 2020) that this war actually stimulated terrorism—to the point that Britain was increasingly subject to terrorist attacks, helping Sutler to rise to power. However, the film even goes so far as to suggest that the most important terrorist attack on England (the release of a deadly virus in London fourteen years before the present setting of the film) was actually engineered by the government in order to generate fear of terrorists and support for increased government power.

This motif potentially suggests a conspiracy theory in which the Bush administration was actually responsible for the 9/11 bombings. However, it is probably more appropriate to read this aspect of the film merely as a comment on the way in which that administration has capitalized on those bombings to generate a climate of fear that has enabled it to pursue its own agenda essentially unimpeded by making any critics of the administration appear to be unpatriotic or even sympathetic to terrorism. Meanwhile, the film's most controversial engagement with the issue of terrorism resides in its clear endorsement of the use of terrorist tactics by its protagonist in his attempt to bring down the Sutler government, an attempt that is ultimately successful as he blows up Parliament (on Guy Fawkes Day, of course) while thousands of Londoners march through the streets, showing their support for V by wearing the Guy Fawkes masks of the kind V himself wears throughout the film.

V for Vendetta has its flaws, including the lack of a coherent political philosophy to put forth as an alternative to Sutlerism. Nevertheless, its pointed attacks on the policies of the Bush administration suggest that it is still possible to make controversial political statements in American films. After all, the film was commercially successful, though modestly so (especially relative to the *Matrix* films), and it also garnered a great deal of positive critical response. Meanwhile, the film drew surprisingly little criticism either for its critique of the Bush administration or for its seeming endorsement of terrorism, no doubt partly because the film's statements about American politics were cloaked by its pop generic form and British setting. Then again, that such indirection and "disguise" may be necessary in order to allow potentially controversial political statements to be made on film is not exactly promising. The case of *V for Vendetta* thus suggests both positive and negative potential for the future of American political film. Indeed, American political film in the early twenty-first century may be at an important crossroads that could lead either to a genuine renaissance in political filmmaking or to the disappearance of real political commentary from American film altogether. Only history will tell, but men make their own history, and the film-going audience is certainly in a position to encourage the rebirth, rather than the final death, of American political film.

Films Cited

Abraham Lincoln. Dir. D. W. Griffith (1930).
Abraham Lincoln in Illinois. John Cromwell (1940).
Absolute Power. Dir. Clint Eastwood (1997).
The Abyss. Dir. James Cameron (1989).
Advise and Consent. Dir. Otto Preminger (1962).
Air Force One. Dir. Wolfgang Petersen (1997).
Alexander. Dir. Oliver Stone (2004).
All the King's Men. Dir. Robert Rossen (1949).
All the President's Men. Dir. Alan J. Pakula (1976).
All Quiet on the Western Front. Dir. Lewis Milestone (1930).
American Beauty. Dir. Sam Mendes (1999).
American Dream. Dir. Barbara Kopple (1992).
The American President. Dir. Rob Reiner (1995).
The Americanization of Emily. Dir. Arthur Hiller (1964).
An Inconvenient Truth. Dir. Davis Guggenheim (2006).
Any Given Sunday. Dir. Oliver Stone (1999).
Apocalypse Now. Dir. Francis Ford Coppola (1979).
Apocalypse Now Redux. Dir. Francis Ford Coppola (2001).
The Assassination of Richard Nixon. Dir. Niels Mueller (2004).
The Bad and the Beautiful. Dir. Vincente Minnelli (1952).
Badlands. Dir. Terrence Malick (1973).
Batman Forever. Dir. Joel Schumacher (1995).
Batman and Robin. Dir. Joel Schumacher (1997).
Behind Enemy Lines. Dir. John Moore (2001).
Being There. Dir. Hal Ashby (1979).
Ben-Hur. Dir. William Wyler (1959).
The Best Man. Dir. Franklin Shaffner (1964).

Big Jim McLain. Dir. Edward Ludwig (1952).
The Big One. Dir. Michael Moore (1997).
The Birth of a Nation. Dir. D. W. Griffith (1915).
Black Hawk Down. Dir. Ridley Scott (2001).
Blue Collar. Dir. Paul Schrader (1978).
Bob Roberts. Dir. Tim Robbins (1992).
Body and Soul. Dir. Robert Rossen (1947).
Bonnie and Clyde. Dir. Arthur Penn (1967).
Born on the Fourth of July. Dir. Oliver Stone (1989).
Born Yesterday. Dir. George Cukor (1950).
Born Yesterday. Dir. Luis Mandocki (1993).
Bound for Glory. Dir. Hal Ashby (1976).
Bowling for Columbine. Dir. Michael Moore (2002).
The Boys in Company C. Dir. Sidney J. Furie (1978).
A Bright Shining Lie. Dir. Terry George (1998).
Buffalo Bill and the Indians. Dir. Robert Altman (1976).
Bulworth. Dir. Warren Beatty (1998).
Canadian Bacon. Dir. Michael Moore (1995).
The Candidate. Dir. Michael Ritchie (1972).
Casualties of War. Dir. Brian De Palma (1989).
Champion. Dir. Mark Robson (1949).
Chasing Liberty. Dir. Andy Cadiff (2004).
The China Syndrome. Dir. James Bridges (1979).
Citizen Kane. Dir. Orson Welles (1941).
City Hall. Dir. Harold Becker (1996).
Comandante. Dir. Oliver Stone (2003).
Coming Home. Dir. Hal Ashby (1978).
The Constant Gardener. Dir. Fernando Meirelles (2005).
The Contender. Dir. Rod Lurie (2000).
The Contrast. Dir. Guy Hedlund (1921).
The Conversation. Dir. Francis Ford Coppola (1974).
The Corporation. Dir. Mark Achbar and Jennifer Abbott (2003).
Cornered. Dir. Edward Dmytryk (1945).
Courage under Fire. Dir. Edward Zwick (1996).
Cry Freedom. Dir. Richard Attenborough (1987).
Dave. Dir. Ivan Reitman (1993).
The Day After. Dir. Nicholas Meyer (1983).
The Day after Tomorrow. Dir. Roland Emmerich (2004).
The Day of the Locust. Dir. John Schlesinger (1975).
The Day the Earth Stood Still. Dir. Robert Wise (1951).
The Day the World Ended. Dir. Roger Corman (1955).
The Deer Hunter. Dir. Michael Cimino (1978).
The Defiant Ones. Dir. Stanley Kramer (1958).

Deterrence. Dir. Rod Lurie (1999).

Dick. Dir. Andrew Fleming (1999).

The Distinguished Gentleman. Dir. Jonathan Lynn (1992).

Dr. No. Dir. Terence Young (1962).

Dr. Strangelove; or, How I Learned to Stop Worrying and Love the Bomb. Dir. Stanley Kubrick (1964).

The Doom Generation. Dir. Greg Araki (1995).

A Dry White Season. Dir. Euzhan Palcy (1989).

Easy Rider. Dir. Dennis Hopper (1969).

Eight Men Out. Dir. John Sayles (1988).

Enron: The Smartest Guys in the Room. Dir. Alex Gibney (2005).

Erin Brockovich. Dir. Steven Soderbergh (2000).

Exodus. Dir. Otto Preminger (1960).

A Face in the Crowd. Dir. Elia Kazan (1957).

Fahrenheit 9/11. Dir. Michael Moore (2004).

Fail-Safe. Dir. Sidney Lumet (1964).

Fellow Traveler. Dir. Philip Saville (1989).

Fight Club. Dir. David Fincher (1999).

First Blood (Rambo). Dir. Ted Kotcheff (1982).

First Daughter. Dir. Forest Whitaker (2004).

Franklin and Eleanor. Dir. Daniel Petrie (1976).

Franklin and Eleanor: The White House Years. Dir. Daniel Petrie (1977).

From Dusk to Dawn. Dir. Frank E. Wolfe (1913).

The Front. Dir. Martin Ritt (1976).

The Front Page. Dir. Lewis Milestone (1931).

Full Metal Jacket. Dir. Stanley Kubrick (1987).

Fury. Dir. Fritz Lang (1936).

Gabriel over the White House. Dir. Gregory La Cava (1933).

Go Tell the Spartans. Dir. Ted Post (1978).

The Golden Boy. Dir. Rouben Mamoulian (1939).

Good Night, and Good Luck. Dir. George Clooney (2005).

The Graduate. Dir. Mike Nichols (1967).

The Grapes of Wrath. Dir. John Ford (1940).

The Great McGinty. Dir. Preston Sturges (1940).

The Green Berets. Dir. Ray Kellogg and John Wayne (1968).

Grumpy Old Men. Dir. Donald Petrie (1993).

Guarding Tess. Dir. High Wilson (1994).

Guilty by Suspicion. Dir. Irwin Winkler (1991).

Hamburger Hill. Dir. John Irvin (1987).

Harlan County, U.S.A. Dir. Barbara Kopple (1976).

Head of State. Dir. Chris Rock (2003).

Heartbreak Ridge. Dir. Clint Eastwood (1986).

Hearts of Darkness. Dir. Fax Bahr and George Hickenlooper (1991).

Heaven and Earth. Dir. Oliver Stone (1993).

High Noon. Dir. Fred Zinnemann (1952).

His Girl Friday. Dir. Howard Hawks (1940).

Hollywood on Trial. Dir. David Helpern, Jr. (1976).

Home of the Brave. Dir. Mark Robson (1949).

Hotel Rwanda. Dir. Terry George (2004).

The House on 92nd Street. Dir. Henry Hathaway (1945).

How Green Was My Valley. Dir. John Ford (1941).

I Was a Communist for the FBI. Dir. Gordon Douglas (1951).

In the Line of Fire. Dir. Wolfgang Petersen (1993).

Independence Day. Dir. Roland Emmerich (1996).

The Insider. Dir. Michael Mann (1999).

Invaders from Mars. Dir. William Cameron Menzies (1953).

Invasion of the Body Snatchers. Dir. Don Siegel (1956).

Invasion U.S.A. Dir. Alfred E. Green (1952).

Jarhead. Dir. Sam Mendes (2005).

Jefferson in Paris. Dir. James Ivory (1995).

JFK. Dir. Oliver Stone (1991).

The Jungle. Dir. Augustus Thomas (1914).

Kalifornia. Dir. Dominic Sena (1993).

A King in New York. Dir. Charlie Chaplin (1957).

Kingfish: A Story of Huey P. Long. Dir. Thomas Schlamme (1995).

Kiss of Death. Dir. Henry Hathaway (1947).

Labor's Reward. American Federation of Labor (1925).

Land of the Dead. Dir. George A. Romero (2005).

The Last Hurrah. Dir. John Ford (1958).

Latino. Dir. Haskell Wexler (1985).

The Life and Assassination of the Kingfish. Dir. Robert E. Collins (1977).

Little Big Man. Dir. Arthur Penn (1970).

Live from Baghdad. Dir. Mick Jackson (2002).

The Long Goodbye. Dir. Robert Altman (1973).

Looking for Fidel. Dir. Oliver Stone (2004).

Lumumba. Dir. Raoul Peck (2000).

Mad City. Dir. Constantin Costa-Gavras (1997).

The Manchurian Candidate. Dir. John Frankenheimer (1962).

The Matrix. Dir. Andy Wachowski and Larry Wachowski (1999).

The Matrix Reloaded. Dir. Andy Wachowski and Larry Wachowski (2003).

The Matrix Revolutions. Dir. Andy Wachowski and Larry Wachowski (2003).

A Martyr to His Cause. Seely (1911).

M*A*S*H. Dir. Robert Altman (1970).

Matewan. Dir. John Sayles (1987).

Medium Cool. Dir. Haskell Wexler (1969).

Meet John Doe. Dir. Frank Capra (1941).

Men with Guns. Dir. John Sayles (1998).

Metropolis. Dir. Fritz Lang (1926).

The Milagro Beanfield War. Dir. Robert Redford (1988).

Mildred Pierce. Dir. Michael Curtiz (1945).

The Missiles of October. Dir. Anthony Page (1974).

Missing. Dir. Constantin Costa-Gavras (1982).

Mr. Smith Goes to Washington. Dir. Frank Capra (1939).

Modern Times. Dir. Charlie Chaplin (1936).

Murder at 1600. Dir. Dwight Little (1997).

My Fair Lady. Dir. George Cukor (1964).

My Fellow Americans. Dir. Peter Segal (1996).

The Naked Kiss. Dir. Samuel Fuller (1953).

Nashville. Dir. Robert Altman (1975).

Natural Born Killers. Dir. Oliver Stone (1994).

Network. Dir. Sidney Lumet (1976).

The New Disciple. Dir. Ollie Sellers (1921).

Night and the City. Dir. Jules Dassin (1950).

Nine to Five. Dir. Colin Higgins (1980).

Nineteen Eighty-Four. Dir. Michael Radford (1984).

Nixon. Dir. Oliver Stone (1995).

No Way Out. Dir. Joseph L. Mankiewicz (1950).

Norma Rae. Dir. Martin Ritt (1979).

North Country. Dir. Niki Caro (2005).

O Brother, Where Art Thou? Dir. Joel Cohen (2000).

Ocean's Eleven. Dir. Steven Soderbergh (2001).

On the Beach. Dir. Stanley Kramer (1959).

On the Waterfront. Dir. Elia Kazan (1954).

Panic in the Streets. Dir. Elia Kazan (1950).

Panic in Year Zero. Dir. Ray Milland (1962).

The Parallax View. Dir. Alan J. Pakula (1974).

The Passaic Textile Strike. Dir. Sam Russack (1926).

Path to War. Dir. John Frankenheimer (2002).

Paths of Glory. Dir. Stanley Kubrick (1957).

Pickup on South Street. Dir. Samuel Fuller (1953).

Platoon. Dir. Oliver Stone (1986).

The Player. Dir. Robert Altman (1992).

The Plow that Broke the Plains. Dir. Pare Lorentz (1936).

The Power of One. Dir. John G. Avildsen (1992).

Pretty Woman. Dir. Garry Marshall (1990).

Primary Colors. Dir. Mike Nichols (1998).

The Professionals. Dir. Richard Brooks (1966).

PT 109. Dir. Leslie H. Martinson (1963).

Purple Hearts. Dir. Sidney J. Furie (1984).
The Quiet American. Dir. Phillip Noyce (2002).
Quiz Show. Dir. Robert Redford (1994).
Rashomon. Dir. Akira Kurosawa (1950).
The Red Menace. Dir. R. G. Springsteen (1949).
Red Planet Mars. Dir. Harry Horner (1952).
The River. Dir. Pare Lorentz (1937).
Road House. Dir. Jean Negulesco (1948).
Roger & Me. Dir. Michael Moore (1989).
Rollerball. Dir. Norman Jewison (1975).
Salt of the Earth. Dir. Herbert Biberman (1954).
Salvador. Dir. Oliver Stone (1986).
Saving Private Ryan. Dir. Steven Spielberg (1998).
Secret Honor. Dir. Robert Altman (1984).
The Set-Up. Dir. Robert Wise (1949).
Seven Days in May. Dir. John Frankenheimer (1964).
Shock Corridor. Dir. Samuel Fuller (1963).
Shooting Dogs. Dir. Michael Caton-Jones (2005).
Silkwood. Dir. Mike Nichols (1983).
Silver City. Dir. John Sayles (2004).
Soldier Blue. Dir. Ralph Nelson (1970).
Sometimes in April. Dir. Raoul Peck (2005)
Space Cowboys. Dir. Clint Eastwood (2000).
Spartacus. Dir. Stanley Kubrick (1960).
Starship Troopers. Dir. Paul Verhoeven (1997).
State of the Union. Dir. Frank Capra (1948).
Storm Center. Dir. Daniel Taradash (1956).
The Stranger. Dir. Orson Welles (1946).
Sullivan's Travels. Dir. Preston Sturges (1942).
Sunrise at Campobello. Dir. Vincent J. Donehue (1960).
Sunset Boulevard. Dir. Billy Wilder (1950).
Syriana. Dir. Stephen Gaghan (2005).
Tanner '88. Dir. Robert Altman (1988).
Tanner on Tanner. Dir. Robert Altman (2004).
Taxi Driver. Dir. Martin Scorsese (1976).
Tears of the Sun. Dir. Antoine Fuqua (2003).
The Terminator. Dir. James Cameron (1984).
Terminator 2: Judgment Day. Dir. James Cameron (1991).
Terminator 3: Rise of the Machines. Dir. Jonathan Mostow (2003).
Testament. Dir. Lynne Littman (1983).
They Live by Night. Dir. Nicholas Ray (1948).
The Thin Red Line. Dir. Terrence Malick (1998).
The Thing from Another World. Dir. Christian Nyby (1951).

Thirteen Days. Dir. Roger Donaldson (2000).

Threads. Dir. Mick Jackson (1984).

Three Days of the Condor. Dir. Sydney Pollack (1975).

Three Kings. Dir. David O. Russell (1998).

Tigerland. Dir. Joel Schumacher (2000).

The Time Machine. Dir. George Pal (1960).

Tobacco Road. Dir. John Ford (1941).

Touch of Evil. Dir. Orson Welles (1958).

Traffic. Dir. Steven Soderbergh (2000).

True Colors. Dir. Herbert Ross (1991).

Truman. Dir. Frank Pierson (1995).

The 27th Day. Dir. William Asher (1957).

Two Mules for Sister Sara. Dir. Don Siegel (1969).

Ulzana's Raid. Dir. Robert Aldrich (1972).

Uncovered: The Whole Truth about the Iraq War. Dir. Robert Greenwald (2003).

Under Fire. Dir. Roger Spottiswoode (1983).

United 93. Dir. Paul Greenglass (2006).

Unprecedented: The 2000 Presidential Election. Dir. Robert Greenwald (2002).

V for Vendetta. Dir. James McTeigue (2005).

Wag the Dog. Dir. Barry Levinson (1997).

Wall Street. Dir. Oliver Stone (1987).

Warm Springs. Dir. Joseph Sargent (2005).

We Were Soldiers. Dir. Randall Wallace (2002).

Weekend. Dir. Jean-Luc Godard (1967).

What Is to be Done? Dir. Joseph Leon Weiss (1914).

Why? ÉÉclair (1913).

Why We Fight. Dir. Eugene Jarecki (2004).

The Wild Bunch. Dir. Sam Peckinpah (1969).

Will Success Spoil Rock Hunter? Dir. Frank Tashlin (1957).

Wilson. Dir. Henry King (1944).

Working Girl. Dir. Mike Nichols (1988).

World Trade Center. Dir. Oliver Stone (2006).

World without End. Dir. Edward Bernd (1956).

You Only Live Once. Dir. Fritz Lang (1937).

Young Mr. Lincoln. Dir. John Ford (1939).

Z. Dir. Constantin Costa-Gavras (1969).

Index

Unless otherwise indicated, italicized entries represent film titles.

About the Author

M. KEITH BOOKER is Professor and Director of Graduate Studies in the Department of English at the University of Arkansas. He is the author of many Greenwood and Praeger volumes, including most recently *Science Fiction Television* (2004), *Alternate Americas: Science Fiction Film and American Culture* (2006), and *Drawn to Television: Prime Time Animation from "The Flintstones" to "Family Guy"* (2006).